best hikes with dogs

SOUTHERN CALIFORNIA

best hikes with *dogs*

SOUTHERN CALIFORNIA

Allen Riedel

THE MOUNTAINEERS BOOKS

Dedication

*For my beautiful daughters, Sierra and Makaila, and my amazing wife,
Ta'Shara; without her support, none of this would have been possible.*

THE MOUNTAINEERS BOOKS
*is the nonprofit publishing arm of The Mountaineers Club, an organization
founded in 1906 and dedicated to the exploration, preservation, and
enjoyment of outdoor and wilderness areas.*

1001 SW Klickitat Way, Suite 201, Seattle, WA 98134

© 2006 by Allen Riedel

First edition, 2006

Published simultaneously in Great Britain by Cordee, 3a DeMontfort Street,
Leicester, England, LE1 7HD

Manufactured in the United States of America

Acquiring Editor: Laura Drury
Project Editor: Christine Hosler
Copy Editor: John Burbidge
Cover and Book Design: The Mountaineers Books
Layout: Mayumi Thompson
Cartographer: Moore Creative Design
All photographs by the author unless otherwise noted.

Cover photograph: *Socrates poses for the camera.*
Frontispiece: *Socrates cools off after a refreshing dip in Cedar Creek.*

Maps shown in this book were produced using National
Geographic's TOPO! software. For more information, go to
www.nationalgeographic.com/topo.

Library of Congress Cataloging-in-Publication Data
Riedel, Allen.
  Best hikes with dogs. Southern California / Allen Riedel.—1st ed.
    p. cm.
  ISBN 0-89886-691-X
  1. Hiking with dogs—California, Southern—Guidebooks. 2. Trails—California,
Southern—Guidebooks. 3. California, Southern—Guidebooks. I. Title.
  SF427.455.R55 2006
  796.5109794'9—dc22
                              2006012637

❖ Printed on recycled paper

CONTENTS

Angeles National Forest–San Gabriel Mountains

San Bernardino National Forest

San Gorgonio Wilderness

Lake Perris State Recreation Area

Huntington Dog Beach

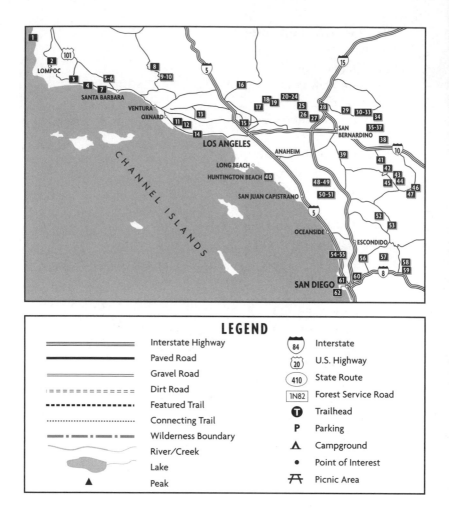

LEGEND

═══════════	Interstate Highway
───────────	Paved Road
───────────	Gravel Road
:==========:	Dirt Road
▬▬▬▬▬▬▬▬▬	Featured Trail
··················	Connecting Trail
▬ ▬·▬ ▬·▬ ▬	Wilderness Boundary
	River/Creek
	Lake
▲	Peak

(84)	Interstate
(20)	U.S. Highway
(410)	State Route
[1N82]	Forest Service Road
T	Trailhead
P	Parking
▲	Campground
•	Point of Interest
⛱	Picnic Area

HIKE SUMMARY TABLE

Hike	Less than 5 miles	About 5 miles	More than 5 miles	Water (S) = seasonal, (O) = ocean	Swimming	Shade	Minor rock scrambling	Backpacking	Good for senior dogs	Best for fit dogs	4WD/high clearance suggested	Off leash (Y = Yes, P = Partial)
1. Point Sal State Beach			•	O				•		•		
2. La Purísima Mission State Historic Park		•		S		•			•			
3. Nojoqui Falls County Park	•			S		•			•			
4. Refugio to El Capitan State Beach		•		O					•			
5. Aliso Trail	•			S								Y
6. Knapp's Castle	•								•			Y
7. Coal Oil Point	•			O	•				•			
8. Reyes Peak			•			•		•				Y
9. Piedra Blanca	•			S	•		•		•			Y
10. Rose Valley Falls	•			S	•	•			•			
11. Satwiwa Loop	•			S					•			
12. Mishe Mokwa to Mount Allen (Sandstone Peak)			•	S			•					
13. Simi Peak		•					•			•		
14. Zuma Canyon Loop	•			S		•			•			
15. Mount Hollywood	•					•			•			
16. Vasquez Rocks	•						•		•			
17. Strawberry Peak		•					•			•		Y
18. Mount Hillyer	•					•	•		•			Y
19. Waterman Mountain		•				•	•					Y
20. Devils Punchbowl	•			S			•		•			
21. Devils Chair		•		S	•		•			•		P
22. Mount Williamson		•								•		Y
23. Mount Islip			•				•		•			Y
24. Mount Baden-Powell			•			•				•		Y
25. Big Horn Mine	•		•						•			Y

Hike	Less than 5 miles	About 5 miles	More than 5 miles	Water (S) = seasonal, (O) = ocean	Swimming	Shade	Minor rock scrambling	Backpacking	Good for senior dogs	Best for fit dogs	4WD/high clearance suggested	Off leash (Y = Yes, P = Partial)
26. Mount Baldy–Manker Flats Loop			•	•			•			•		Y
27. Ontario Peak			•	•	•	•		•		•		
28. Cleghorn Mountain			•								•	Y
29. Little Bear Creek	•			S	•							Y
30. Grays Peak			•			•	•					Y
31. Cougar Crest–Bertha Peak			•			•						
32. Castle Rock	•			S		•	•					
33. Grand View Point			•	S		•						Y
34. Sugarloaf Mountain			•			•				•	•	Y
35. Shields Peak			•	•			•	•		•	•	
36. Dry Lake			•	S	•	•				•		
37. San Gorgonio			•	•	•		•			•		
38. Kitching Peak			•	S		•				•	•	
39. Terri Peak	•					•						
40. Huntington Dog Beach	•			O	•				•			Y
41. Black Mountain			•	S		•				•		Y
42. Tahquitz Peak			•			•				•	•	
43. Palm View Peak			•							•		Y
44. Pyramid Peak			•				•			•		Y
45. Thomas Mountain			•	•		•						Y
46. Sheep Mountain			•	S			•			•		
47. Toro Peak	•					•					•	Y
48. San Juan Loop	•			S	•	•			•			
49. Morgan Trail			•	S	•							P
50. Fishermans Camp			•	S	•	•		•				
51. Tenaja Falls	•			•	•				•			
52. Barker Valley			•	S			•	•			•	Y
53. PCT to Eagle Rock		•		•								Y
54. San Elijo Lagoon	•			O					•			
55. North Beach–Del Mar Dog Beach	•			O	•					•		Y

Hike	Less than 5 miles	About 5 miles	More than 5 miles	Water (S) = seasonal, (O) = ocean	Swimming	Shade	Minor rock scrambling	Backpacking	Good for senior dogs	Best for fit dogs	4WD/high clearance suggested	Off leash (Y = Yes, P = Partial)
56. Iron Mountain		•					•					
57. Cedar Creek Falls		•		•	•					•	•	Y
58. Pioneer Mail Trail	•								•			Y
59. Laguna Mountain–Sunset Trail	•			S	•	•			•			Y
60. Cowles Mountain		•		S					•			
61. Fiesta Island	•			O	•				•			Y
62. Cabrillo Tide Pools	•			O	•				•			

ACKNOWLEDGMENTS

I would like to thank all of my friends and family who have hiked and shared with me adventuring in the great outdoors. Thank you, Ta'Shara, for being supportive and understanding when I've left for weeks at a time to camp, hike, and otherwise explore. Special thanks go out to all the federal and state employees of the Forest Service, county parks, state parks, national parks, and recreation areas who cross-checked the information in this book to ensure the legality of transportation and trespassing issues, along with current trail information and accuracy. My family has always supported me in every venture I have ever undertaken, and I will forever appreciate that. Thank you to the wonderful people at The Mountaineers Books—especially Laura, Cassandra, Christine, Kathleen, John, and Jo—who have been cordial and understanding throughout this entire process. I would also like to thank the people who allowed me to randomly photograph their dogs for inclusion within this book. Lastly, I would like to send a heartfelt show of support to all the organizations that have fought and continue to fight for protection of our forest areas and wild places. These resources are constantly being encroached upon; nowhere can that be seen more plainly than in Southern California. I hope that everyone reading this can take up or continue the fight to ensure that these wild places exist for our children's children and beyond.

PART 1

Hiking with Your Dog

Getting Ready

Hiking is an activity that almost anyone can engage in. People at varying stages of fitness and ability can take pleasure in different trails and experience nature on an intrinsic level, sharing and exploring their own inner selves while enjoying the natural world. In fact, most people forget that hiking is also a great way to exercise; doing it consistently not only helps to keep you in shape but also conditions your body for longer and harder hikes, assuring you a life of health and fitness.

Exploring the trail with friends of a four-legged variety can ultimately be more rewarding than almost any other adventure in the wild. Walking and sniffing is what your dog loves to do most. There is no other activity he would rather take part in, except maybe having a bite of food fed directly from your hand into his mouth. Your pet loves the outdoors, and is guaranteed excitement every time you reach for the leash, hiking boots, backpack, and doggie supplies. A hiking dog is a healthy dog, a happy dog, and a well-cared-for pet.

Good Dogs Require Good Owners

Owning a pet is an incredible responsibility. Raising a puppy is obviously more difficult than adopting a full grown dog. Either way, your dog has needs that must be constantly taken care of. There are general health and training needs that must be addressed before ever attempting to get a dog on the trail. Dogs must also be socially ready to be around other people and other dogs. It is important that you train your dog with at least basic voice commands before you endeavor to take your pet off leash and into a forested area.

Basic health needs are pretty simple to meet by always ensuring your dog has ample amounts of water and the appropriate amount of food for his or her size and age. Active dogs are relatively well-suited for satisfying their basic dietary needs if you leave food out for them. Sedentary dogs, like humans, may tend to overeat, but a little activity will change that and make your dog happier, healthier and more responsive to everything you want him to do.

A rough guideline to follow is thirty minutes of activity a day. If you take dogs on a walk for that short amount of time, their stamina, and most importantly their paws, will be able to handle almost any hike you throw at them. Even small dogs can handle big-time hikes if they are conditioned for it. Dogs as light as twenty pounds can easily walk over 25 miles in a day. They may still have the energy to run and play at the trailhead before getting back into the car, but they have to be ready for something like that. Like humans, dogs cannot just leap into vigorous exercise without some consequences. Dogs get tired and can also suffer from sore muscles and tendons. Their pads can crack and bleed if you are not watchful and careful.

Training your dog need not be a chore; instead it should be a fun and rewarding experience for both of you. Other than walking, the main desire that registers with a dog is food. Dogs love food, treats especially. Spending a little time each day training with your dog and rewarding him with treats will lead to bonding. Ultimately your dog will understand what you want and expect. To blame a dog for running, jumping, and not returning to you when you call it is ridiculous if you have not properly trained the dog. It would be akin to blaming the full moon for shining too brightly while you are trying to sleep outdoors. There are things in a dog's nature that can only be changed by training. Some behaviors are harder to train out of than others. Jumping and licking can be well nigh impossible to get rid of. A dog that jumps needs to stay on a leash, period. Dogs that are vicious or mean should be left at home. With that said, dogs are not mean by nature; they have either been bred or trained that way.

Most pet stores in Southern California offer dog-training classes where you bring in your pet and do it yourself with the help of instructors. These can be very useful and informative. Once you have taken a few basic levels of training, you should be well versed enough to continue your dog's training on your own or perhaps with the help of books or videos. Of course, the affluence of Southern California also affords more prohibitive outlets for training your pet, and if you are monetarily so inclined, then by all means, feel free to partake in them.

Training your dog to respond to voice commands is not enough. Your dog must also be socialized to be around other people, dogs, and even children. Your dog must be used to being on a leash, being unleashed, and being told "no" when confronted with new or daunting situations. "Stay" is the most important command in your dog's vocabulary, and only when this one is mastered is your dog ready to go off leash. A dog that will not stay has the real danger of being hurt or killed by a wild animal should it choose to pursue and chase. More importantly, your dog should be able to stay when you are confronted by a surprise party of hikers. You will not always be ready for these encounters, but your pet must be.

A hollow pine tree sits just off the trail in the San Jacinto Mountains.

An important step to getting your pooch ready for other people and dogs is to take him to places where other people and dogs are. When training, there should be distractions all around, up to and including other people and even other dogs. A dog trained in silence and solitude will do fantastic things in silence and solitude, but once the real world is introduced, that world will be much more entertaining than the secluded and serene one. A seemingly educated and well-mannered dog can transform into a beast when introduced to such an environment. Please prepare accordingly.

While training and conditioning might work wonders for most dogs, some dogs are inherently ill-tempered around other dogs and people. It is best to keep vicious dogs away from public lands altogether. Remember, as a pet owner, you are liable for anything that your pet does, so use your judgment. A dog bite has lots of legality tied to it, and you are on the responsible end, so it is best to avoid such confrontations.

Trail Etiquette for Dogs and the People Who Hike with Them

Dogs can supply an unlimited source of enjoyment on the trail, and their indefatigable running, jumping, and basic playfulness can bring delight to the dourest of faces. However, there are people out there, for whatever reason, who are not particularly fond of dogs. Some even make it their own personal mission to tirelessly complain to local, state, and national officials about dogs in one form or another. Unfortunately, these people are often supplied reasons by careless, neglectful, and oblivious dog owners. When a dog acts up or is belligerent on a trail, it regrettably reflects upon all dog owners. An unleashed dog that jumps on people, or worse, growls or barks at them can be a traumatizing experience for someone afraid of dogs.

Uncovered doggie droppings are not only disgusting, ugly, and a threat to shoes everywhere, but also a form of pollution. Most people who venture into the outdoors would never even dream of throwing an empty water bottle or energy-bar wrapper on the ground; it is just unthinkable. However, many dog owners in the city and elsewhere let their dogs go wherever the need arises. These people then saunter off as if nothing happened. This is one of the biggest complaints non-dog owners lodge against those of us with pets. While sometimes the offending perpetrators are humans, it is not often that a dog leaves a waving flag of toilet paper (see the upcoming Leave No Trace section) tangled in its scat; dogs are sure to be blamed for almost anything left on or alongside the trail. It is imperative that you clean up after your dogs. If you cannot pack it out in baggies, you should always bury it as you would your own in a "cat hole" six to eight inches deep. The best solution is to carry it out with you by putting it in your dog's pack.

As a pet owner, it is your responsibility to keep control of the actions of your dog at all times. Not only do you have to be omnipresent and in command, you also act as an ambassador for the entire dog-owning population whether you like it or not. Any careless act will further ingrain stereotypes that all pet owners are irresponsible. Here are some tips that will reflect your responsibility and further champion the cause of dogs in the forest and wild places.

1. Always carry a leash, even if you are hiking in areas where leashes are not required. If you come upon other hikers with or without dogs, always leash your pet. This is common courtesy.
2. Always pick up after your dog, either by bagging it and carrying it out or by burying it six to eight inches deep, at least 200 feet away from water and 50 feet off the trail.

3. Apologize if your dog barks or acts vicious, and in the event that it gets away from you, always make immediate attempts to gain control. An apology can go a long way. When people do complain, one of the things they complain about is that dog owners do not even seem to care that their wilderness experience has been made less enjoyable by an unruly pet.
4. Always remember to be considerate and polite. Some people feel very strongly that dogs have no place in national forests or wilderness areas. Even if someone says something rude to you, you do not have to return the emotion. It is best to politely go about your way.
5. Remember that dogs are visitors; they should follow guidelines that humans follow, such as staying on trails and not harming flora or fauna. In some areas, such as national and state parks, dogs are not allowed off main roads, and even then only on a leash. In other areas people are considering taking away the privilege of hiking with dogs. This is all due to destructive and inconsiderate practices by irresponsible dog owners. You must act as a steward when taking your dog into public lands.
6. Make sure you follow the letter of the law. Have your dogs vaccinated, tagged, licensed, and responsibly spayed or neutered before venturing out onto public lands.

Permits and Regulations

California has more national forest land, wilderness, and parks than any other state besides Alaska, which means there is ample room to stretch your legs and wander. However, it is important to understand the rules and regulations of the area you plan to hike in before you set out on your adventures. Wilderness areas have their own guidelines, districts under the Bureau of Land Management have different rules than do national forests, etc., so make sure you comprehend the laws and necessary permits before undertaking any outdoor hiking with your dog.

Many of the hikes in this book are located in Southern California's national forests. In 2002, the Recreation Fee Program made it mandatory to purchase an Adventure Pass. Passes are required for parking your vehicle in most areas in the forest, and cost $5 daily, or $30 for an annual pass. A second vehicle pass can be purchased along with the annual pass for $5. The fees have been used for clean-up, maintenance, improvements, and building new facilities within the forest. Some people oppose the passes based upon our right as citizens and taxpayers to free use of public lands. There are positive arguments on both sides of the issue, but regardless of how you feel about it, you will be cited if you do not display the pass from your rearview mirror when you park at a trailhead.

United States Forest Service (USFS)

The USFS manages the Los Padres, Angeles, San Bernardino, and Cleveland National Forests, which covers over 70 percent of the hikes in this book. It has jurisdiction over all wilderness and recreation areas within forest lands, and these areas have stricter regulations that must be heeded as well.

Hiking

Always stay on the trail, and train your pets to stay on the trail as well. In national forests, it is normally not required that your dog be leashed; however, wilderness areas and many recreation areas prohibit dogs off leash. Some high use areas may also have signs requesting that you leash up your trusty companion. Please follow specific guidelines for each trail.

Adam rests and checks for blisters atop Mount Baden-Powell.

If there is an informational kiosk at the trailhead, make certain that you read all of the data on it. Pack out all trash and more if you see it on the trail. You will be sharing the trail with other hikers, equestrians, and in some areas mountain bikes. Large animals and bikers have the right of way, so step aside and let them pass. Purify all water with a filter, iodine, or by boiling before drinking.

Camping

Pack out what you pack in. Pay fees before using any campsite. Wilderness camping is fine in many areas as long as Leave No Trace practices are used and camping takes place at least a mile from roads, other campgrounds, and 200 feet from streams and water sources.

Wilderness Areas

The Wilderness Act of 1964 defined wilderness as "an area where the earth and its community of life are untrammeled by man, where man himself is a visitor who does not remain." This principle governs the regulations that surround wilderness, and the general guidelines are as follows.

Visitors must have a wilderness permit to enter wilderness. This goes for the majority of wilderness areas in Southern California, except for Santa Rosa and San Mateo Canyon. Normally, the permits are easy to get and all you have to do is stop by the visitor center and talk to a ranger or self-register at a kiosk. The San Gorgonio area in Southern California is the only area that has quotas on hiking trails. Campsites can be more difficult to secure as they are in limited supply. If you get your permit in advance or very early in the morning, you shouldn't have any trouble, unless you plan to visit on crowded weekends. Campfires are prohibited entirely in many wilderness areas, except in specifically designated yellow-post campsites. Check before you go.

Groups should be no larger than 12 persons and possess no more than 8 stock animals. Camping is only permitted in designated areas. Stock animals cannot be camped within 200 feet of meadows, streams, or trails. It is illegal to dispose of garbage, debris, and other waste materials. Using substances that may pollute bodies of water is also illegal.

Visitors to the wilderness need to carry a hand trowel or shovel for the disposal of human waste in a "cat hole" at least six inches deep 50 feet away from both trails and water. It is illegal to operate machinery of any kind including any type of bicycle or wheeled cart. Wheelchair use is permitted, however, under the Americans with Disabilities Act. Small battery-powered devices such as flashlights, Global Positioning Satellite (GPS) units, cell phones, and cameras are exempted. Smoking is only permitted in a seated area that has been cleared of all flammable material at least 3 feet in diameter.

Lastly, all dogs are required to be on a leash or otherwise confined.

National Park Service (NPS) and National Recreation Areas (NRA)

The Santa Monica Mountains National Recreation Area and Cabrillo National Monument are two areas managed by the NPS. Normally, dogs are restricted to specific areas, roads, and campsites and are not allowed on trails in any park governed by the NPS. The two parks mentioned above are the exception to the rule. Cabrillo National Monument has a small tide pool walk where leashed dogs are permitted. However, dogs are not permitted in the main visitor area or on the Bayside Trail. The Santa Monica Mountains are a conglomerate of local, state, and federal divisions that fall under the umbrella of the NPS. Dogs are allowed in many of the park units that are not under the jurisdiction of California State Parks. A few of the areas are outlined in this hiking guide, and there are more that are not covered in this book.

In the park regions where dogs are allowed, they must be leashed, and it is imperative that all park regulations and guidelines be followed. Federal regulation states the leash should not be longer than six feet. Pets must remain on designated trails, and are not allowed off-trail. Hopefully, in time, other national parks will open up trails to pet owners, but as of now, it is the duty of responsible pet owners to protect the two NPS units in Southern California that are open to dogs. Please obey all rules and check trailhead kiosks for current information.

California State Parks (SP), State Historic Parks (SHP), State Beaches (SB), and State Recreation Areas (SRA)

Most state parks do not allow dogs to set foot on the grounds. When they are allowed, they are usually confined to a small area or campgrounds, always on a leash, and never on the trails that run through them. There are some exceptions to that rule, however, and those few are covered here in this book. La Purísima Mission SHP has an excellent system of trails and all are open to dogs on leash. Refugio and El Capitan State Beaches do not allow dogs on the beaches, but they are allowed on a bluff trail that connects the two. Point Sal SB is reachable only by hiking; dogs are okay on the road, but not allowed on the beach. Perris Lake SRA is another area where leashed dogs are allowed on the trails, but not in or near the lake. All rules and regulations should be obeyed. Check the trailhead kiosks for further updated information. Remember that rules regarding leashes state that all tethers must be six feet or less in length.

Bureau of Land Management (BLM)

The BLM is a federal agency that operates under the Federal Land Policy and Management Act of 1976 (FLPMA), which declared "public lands be retained in Federal ownership and utilized in the combination that will best meet the present and future needs of the American people." These lands offer recreation through hiking, hunting, fishing, camping, horseback riding, and other outdoor activities. This agency also oversees mining rights and has the right to sell land when the sale is within the guidelines of the FLPMA. Many of these lands do not require dogs to be leashed, while others do. Some of the areas are very seldom traveled, which makes them ideal for hiking with dogs. There are no hikes in this book covered under BLM guidelines, although some skirt the periphery of lands controlled by this agency.

Lulu prances and plays on the beach.

County, City and Regional Parks

Usually county and regional parks have only two restrictions on dogs. One is that they must remain on a leash. The second restriction is that the owner must clean up after them. Other than that, dogs are generally free to hike and explore. The only exception to this is coastal areas. Dogs are not allowed on many beaches between San Diego and San Luis Obispo. It is just a sad reality.

California Department of Fish and Game (DFG)

San Elijo Lagoon is the only hike in this book under the jurisdiction of the DFG. The regulations covering dogs require owners to keep them on a leash and in control, prevent them from harassing wildlife, and completely clean up their waste.

Leave No Trace

Leave No Trace is a national (and now international) movement designed to protect the outdoors and our wild heritage. From 1965 to 1984, the number of backcountry visits went from four million a year to over fifteen million. That number has easily doubled or even quadrupled with the coming of age of Generations X and Y. Urbanization and suburban sprawl is impinging upon the wilderness and forest areas more than ever. This impact and the constant influx of more and more visitors are seriously threatening the integrity of our forests and wild places. Leave No Trace is more of an ethical paradigm or mantra than strict enforcement of rules or harsh guidelines. It should be encouraged and taught to anyone who uses the outdoors, especially the young and those new to hiking and other outdoor activities. Everyone has to pitch in if we wish to keep these lands intact for shared future use. It is up to all of us to keep our wild places unspoiled.

Even people who love the outdoors are prone to neglectful mistakes. Take, for instance, sunflower seeds. They are wonderful to eat, make for great trail food due to the sodium involved, but they become unsightly husks when covering a trail. Many people do not understand that in an arid environment, it may take over ten years for the shell of a sunflower seed to decompose. One person eating sunflower seeds and spitting out the shell might not pose a huge problem, but when you disaggregate the reality and allow for even one per hundred engaging in the same activity, it won't be long before all the nation's trails are covered in semi-biodegradable refuse. One irresponsible campfire might not pose a significant

A solitary coyote stops for a respite in the middle of the roadway.

risk, but if all fifteen million visitors irresponsibly built campfires in the backcountry, there wouldn't be much of a backcountry left. Please, encourage the use of Leave No Trace ethics by everyone you know.

There are seven guiding principles behind the Leave No Trace movement:

1. **Plan ahead and prepare**
   - Learn the rules and special conditions of the places you plan to visit.
   - Be prepared for exceptional circumstances, such as hazards, drastic changes in weather, and emergencies.
   - Go during off-times; schedule your trips for when areas are less crowded.
   - Go with small groups of people. For larger outings, split into groups of four to six.
   - Cut down on waste by taking only the food and packaging you will need.
   - Use a GPS, or map and compass. Do not build cairns or mark a trail with paint or flags.

2. **Travel and camp on durable surfaces**
   - Durable surfaces are previously established trails and camp-sites, rock, gravel, dry grasses, snow, and dirt.
   - Keep wetland and riparian areas protected by camping at least 200 feet away from water sources.
   - Campsites are found, not made. Do not alter campsites.

   If you travel in heavy-use areas:
   - Stay on the trail and camp only in designated campsites.
   - Always stay in the middle of the trail, single file, even if the trail is muddy or wet.
   - Make your campsites as compact as possible. Stay in areas where there is no vegetation.

   In pristine or wilderness areas:
   - Spread out to avoid the creation of new campsites and trails.
   - Do not camp or walk in places that are showing signs of impact.

3. **Dispose of Waste Properly**
   - Whatever you pack in, pack out. Always try to carry out more refuse than you took in. Always check your campsite and carry out all trash, leftover food, and litter.
   - Keep all solid human waste in a "cat hole." These should be dug six to eight inches in the ground, and always at least 200 feet from water, campgrounds, and trails. Always cover and disguise the cat hole.
   - Do not bury toilet paper. It does not degrade, and animals will dig it up. Pack it out in locking plastic bags.
   - If you must wash dishes, carry all water at least 200 feet away from the water source. Only use small amounts of biodegradable soap. Spread strained dishwater around.

4. **Leave What You Find**
   - Protect and preserve history. You may look, but don't touch cultural or historic structures, artifacts, or other objects.
   - Do not disturb rocks, plants, or anything else you might find on the trail. Leave things the way you found them.
   - Do not transport or introduce non-native species.
   - Do not create structures, dig trenches, or otherwise disturb the natural surroundings.

5. **Minimize Campfire Impacts**
   - Do not build campfires if you can avoid them. Campfires

can create lasting impacts in a wild setting. In desert environments, it may take thousands of years for ashes and campsites to degrade. Instead, use a stove for cooking and natural or battery operated sources for light.

- If you do build a fire, use only established fire rings, and only in areas where campfires are permitted.
- Build small fires. Do not break off branches, or collect large pieces of fallen wood; instead use only small sticks that can be broken by hand. This not only keeps the fire more maintainable, but also reduces smoke.
- Let fires burn all of their fuel and coals to ash. Make certain that they are entirely extinguished before leaving camp.

6. **Respect Wildlife**
   - Never approach wildlife, be observant from a distance. Do not try to follow or let your dogs give chase.
   - Never give food to wild animals. Animals have sensitive stomachs and diets. Feeding animals can upset the natural balance and change their behavior, which not only endangers the animals, but possibly humans as well. Feeding wildlife can be detrimental to their health, and expose them to predators.
   - Store your food and trash securely. In bear areas, use bear canisters, and try to keep food scents off of you, your clothing, and out of your tent.
   - Make certain to control all pets at all times, either on voice command or on leash.
   - Do not make contact with wildlife during critical and sensitive times such as rutting, mating, nesting, nursing or raising young, hibernation, or during winter.

7. **Be Considerate of Other Visitors**
   - Think about other visitors. Do not do anything that would hinder or mar their experience.
   - Be thoughtful and courteous. People hiking uphill have the right-of-way because it is harder to get started again, but they may be happy to allow you to pass. When hiking with dogs, it is always courteous to leash your pets and step aside, allowing all other visitors to pass.
   - Horses and other pack animals always have the right-of-way. Step off the trail to the downhill side to allow them room to

pass. Always leash your pets when encountering large pack animals. Take breaks and camp away from trails and other visitors.

- Do not yell, scream, or sing loudly. Let wild sounds ring out, so that others may enjoy the silence and solitude that an outdoor experience should bring.

The Essentials
Ten Essentials: A Systems Approach

1. **Navigation (map and compass).** While compass skills are not essential on most trails, having a detailed topographic map is a necessity, unless you are already familiar with the trails and landmarks in the area. A portable GPS unit is a good idea for off-trail and cross-country navigation.

2. **Sun protection (sunglasses and sunscreen).** At higher elevations the sun's rays are more damaging. There is more ultraviolet radiation and the risk of burning is exponentially greater the higher you go. Spend a summer day at the beach without sunblock and you'll get a bad sunburn. Spend all day in the mountains and you could end up in the hospital with third degree burns. Sun protection is a must for all complexions.

3. **Insulation (extra clothing).** Clothing should be layered when hiking, so that you can take layers off or add them as needed. Avoid cotton if at all possible. Cotton does not retain its warmth when wet, and clothing should be your foremost protection against hypothermia and heat exhaustion. Neoprene, wool, or polyester shirts retain their insulation even when wet. There are many types of underapparel that work wonders for keeping you cool or warm depending on the need. Fleece is a wonderful second layer. Fleece also retains its ability to insulate when wet. Hikers in the know understand that vigorously swinging a fleece sweater above your head will force the water molecules from the fabric, giving you a dry fleece in seconds. Rain protection is not a necessity on most hikes, though it is advisable for backpacking trips. A little water never hurt anyone, but the first time you hike in torrential rain without rain gear, you'll gain a better understanding of its value. Luckily most

days in Southern California are sunny, even in wintertime. The mountains do harbor their own climate, however, and storms can appear rapidly, so it is a good idea to carry at least some sort of rudimentary rain protection. Gloves and thermal head protection are also a good bet. Peaks can be chilly and windswept even in summer.

4. **Illumination (headlamp or flashlight).** Besides water and fire, light is the next most important thing on this list. It can mean the difference between having to spend the night unprepared on a cold mountain trail, or stumbling out after dark and hopping in your car and driving home. Of course, you should always set turn-around times and never push the time factor, but there are reasons why this list is called essential.

5. **First-aid supplies.** You should always carry some type of crude first-aid kit, with a minimum such as bandages (both adhesive and cloth), antibiotic ointment, alcohol wipes, a multi-tool pocketknife, and first-aid tape (duct tape works as a fine substitute for repairing all sorts of things, not just body parts).

6. **Fire (fire starter and matches/lighter).** Being able to keep warm in a life-threatening emergency is the most important factor in staying alive. If you hike avidly for enough years, chances are that you will eventually spend a night under the stars that you hadn't planned on. It happens at least once even to the best of us; however, fire is never to be taken lightly. In recent years, several boneheads have accidentally destroyed many of Southern California's forests without using the proper precautions necessary that one would use to start a barbeque. Please understand that Southern California is an arid region that has used fire suppression as a forest management tool for over a century. Thoughtless fires can be deadly to you and others, not to mention devastating to our recreation areas. Starting a fire should be your last resort, and even then, proper precautions should be taken. Clear the area in a 10-foot radius and build an enclosure so that your fire will not escape its bounds. The smaller the better for both fire and enclosure. Before you leave, make sure that your fire is completely extinguished. And again, fire should only be used in the direst of life-and-death emergencies.

7. **Repair kit and tools (including knife).** A multi-tool pocketknife and duct tape can serve both as part of your first-aid kit and a basic repair kit. For long trips fishing line and a needle are a good idea, and super-strong glue can work miracles for many items, including boots.

8. **Nutrition (extra food).** Always take enough food so that if you have to spend an unexpected night outdoors, you can at least do so with a full belly and enough to last you on the hike out the next day.

9. **Hydration (extra water).** A quick rule of thumb is for every hour spent hiking, you should drink between sixteen and twenty ounces of water. More liquid should be ingested as temperatures rise, and sipping along the way is a good way to stay hydrated with occasional stops for longer drinks. Make certain to take more water than you will need. It is also advisable to carry a water filter or iodine tablets for water purification should the need arise.

10. **Emergency shelter.** Most day hikers do not carry tents to the top of local mountains, although the cautious may want to do just that. It is a bit of overkill, but a lightweight tarp tent is an option for those who desire to be prudent. A space blanket is a much more modest and adequate substitute for a heavy tent. While it may not provide the most effective cover, it will supply sufficient warmth and protection to keep you alive should disaster strike.

Canine First Aid

If you are not a veterinarian, you should not try to treat serious injuries to a dog. However, there are many things that you can do to prevent injuries in the first place. You are also able to treat some of the more common injuries your pet will most likely face if you plan to hike with him often. Carrying a first-aid kit that suits not only yourself but also your dog is the best idea. Simple procedures can help protect cracked pads, or facilitate removing a tick or thorn.

Southern California has a semi-arid climate, and dehydration and heat exhaustion are real issues that face not only you but your dog as well. The best way to avoid these issues is to always bring plenty of water for your pet, and avoid hiking in extreme temperatures. Dogs vent heat from their bodies through panting, they do not sweat; therefore, hiking

Canine Ten Essentials

You should also carry these "Ten Essentials" for your dog:

1. **Obedience training.** Before you set foot on a trail, make sure your dog is trained and can be trusted to behave when faced with other hikers, other dogs, wildlife, and an assortment of strange scents and sights in the backcountry.

2. **Doggy backpack.** This lets your dog carry his own gear.

3. **Basic first-aid kit (details listed below).**

4. **Dog food and trail treats.** You should bring more food than your dog normally consumes since it will be burning more calories than normal. If you do end up having to spend an extra night out there, you need to keep the pup fed, too. Trail treats serve the same purpose for the dog as they do for you—quick energy and a pick-me-up during a strenuous day of hiking.

5. **Water and water bowl.** Don't count on there being water along the trail for the dog. Pack enough extra water to meet all of your dog's drinking needs.

6. **Leash and collar, or harness.** Even if your dog is absolutely trained to voice command and stays at heel without a leash, sometimes leashes are required by law or just by common courtesy, so you should have one handy at all times.

7. **Insect repellent.** Be aware that some animals, and some people, have strong negative reactions to DEET-based repellents. So, before leaving home, dab a little DEET-based repellent on a patch of your dog's fur to see if he reacts to it. Look for signs of drowsiness, lethargy, and/or nausea. Restrict repellent applications to those places the dog can't lick—the back of the neck and around the ears (staying well clear of the ears and inner ears) are the most logical places mosquitoes will look for exposed skin to bite.

8. **ID tags and picture identification.** Your dog should always wear ID tags, and micro-chipping is heartily recommended as well. To do this, a vet injects a tiny encoded microchip under the skin between a dog's shoulders. If your dog ever gets lost and is picked up

Water please!

by animal control, or is taken to a vet's office, a quick pass over the dog's back with a hand scanner will reveal the chip, and allow the staff at that shelter or hospital to identify your dog and notify you. Micro-chipping is so prevalent that virtually every veterinarian and animal shelter automatically scans every unknown dog they come in contact with to check for chips. Picture identification should go in your pack. If your dog gets lost, you can use the picture to make flyers and handbills to post in the surrounding communities.

9. **Dog booties.** These can be used to protect the dog's feet from rough ground or harsh vegetation. They are also great at keeping bandages secure if the dog damages its pads.
10. **Compact roll of plastic bags and trowel.** You'll need the bags to clean up after your dog on popular trails. When conditions warrant, you can use the trowel to take care of your dog's waste. Just pretend you are a cat—dig a small hole six inches deep in the forest dirt, deposit the dog waste, and fill in the hole.

in temperatures above 101 degrees is inadvisable. It should be stated that such temperatures are not safe for humans either.

A variety of plant communities exist in Southern California, from lowland desert, riparian woodland, coastal chaparral, yellow pine forest, to alpine. Many of these plants can scrape and cut your dogs. Their vantage point is much lower than your own. Dogs are susceptible to spines from cacti and parasitic ticks that fall and leap from low-lying plant life.

The first thing to do is to make certain your dog is healthy by having regular checkups with a veterinarian, getting proper vaccinations, and regular exercise. Spending thirty minutes a day walking with your pet on pavement is enough to get him in shape for long days of hiking. If properly conditioned, your dog is just naturally better suited for long distance travel than you are.

Paw issues. Footpad ailments are the most common medical problem for hiking dogs. It is virtually guaranteed that from time to time, your dog will crack and injure his pads. Your dog will most likely continue to troop on and quite possibly continue to run even with severely cracked pads. It is imperative that you repeatedly monitor the state of your pet's pads. Rocks and rough sand can wear down pads, even when they have proven to be tough in the past. A cracked pad can take days to heal; and the less severe, the quicker the healing. Pads can also tear and bleed, which is more serious. If your dog's pads are bleeding, you will notice a limp. Usually after cracking occurs, a limp will start to become more noticeable. It is best to clean the affected area with iodine or water and put on dog booties, which can be purchased at most hiking stores and many online sites. Baking soda will stop the bleeding before you apply the dog booties. Bandages and tape work effectively too. If a serious pad issue develops, it is a good idea to turn around. It is better to have your pet walk out than to carry him out on a long hike. Nails should be kept trimmed but not too short. If you hike and exercise regularly with your dog on hard surfaces, your pet's nails will probably take care of themselves.

Barrel cacti are common in Southern California deserts.

California fan palms line a desert oasis.

Scrapes, spines, and cuts. These things happen. If your dog is bleeding, it is always best to clean the wound and stop the bleeding. Apply a gauze bandage, and seek further treatment if necessary. If you hike in arid environments, your dog will get stuck by cacti. Remove the spines with tweezers and it will normally do the trick to get your dog back to his normal self.

Sore muscles and joints. Dogs, like humans, get sore muscles when they are tired. If you blast your dog with a killer workout, chances are that he may lie around the house and limp around for a few days. If there is no injury and you suspect sore muscles, tendons, or joints, they can be treated with buffered aspirin. (In general, it is best to avoid giving human medicines to dogs. Some medicines, such as ibuprofen, are toxic to dogs). Your dog will generally be back to normal in a couple of days as the soreness wears off. You may feel bad about it, but you can always remember the old adage of "no pain, no gain." Just make certain to offer lots of attention, love, and kindness. Even with the soreness, your pet will literally leap at the next chance to explore the wilderness.

More serious ailments. There are many types of ailments and injuries that can affect your pooch while hiking. Hypothermia, heat stroke, snake bites, and stomach turning are just a few. All of these illnesses can be fatal or at least life threatening. Hypothermia can be caused when the temperatures are too cold for the dog to sustain heat. Shorter-coat dogs are more susceptible to losing heat in cold temperatures. Hypothermia can lead to shivering and disorientation. If you suspect your dog has hypothermia, wrap him in a blanket to warm him.

Heat stroke is caused by exerting too much energy in hot environments. Excessive panting and salivation are symptoms of overheating in dogs. The best way to keep a dog cool is to keep him properly hydrated, which means stopping about every twenty minutes to give the dog water. If your pet shows signs of hyperthermia (overheating), put water on his pads to cool him down quickly.

Snake bites can occur anywhere but are very rare. Snakes do not want to get into altercations with dogs as they will most likely lose. If a dog is bitten by a rattlesnake, wrap the wound tightly but do not cut off the flow of blood. Get your pet to a vet as soon as you leave the trail. Rattlesnake bites are not as serious for dogs as they are for humans. Dogs are more resistant to the venom, but it is still something that needs to be treated right away.

Stomach turning is a serious and deadly condition that can occur in large dogs that drink too much water too quickly. Do not allow your dog to drink too much water all at once. Usually your pet is pretty good at self-monitoring. If you keep your dog hydrated throughout the hike, this situation will have no chance of occurring. Simple rest stops to keep you and your dog hydrated are the best way to prevent the most serious conditions.

If you do encounter a serious situation for you or your dog, do not panic. Take control of the situation and figure out the best way to calmly deal with it. Becoming frantic will only exacerbate the situation. Should your dog become seriously ill, you will need to calm it as you leave the area and seek medical attention.

Gear for You and Your Dog

Shoes are the most important thing you bring with you on the trail. The difference between a solid well-fitted pair and a poorly fitting pair is enough to make a trip enjoyable or miserable. Any good specialized hiking store can properly fit you for hiking boots. You should be able to test them on an angled surface that resembles a boulder. Depending on your hiking needs, it is best to have different pairs for different types of hikes. Long distance backpacks spent carrying heavy loads on your back are usually better suited to heavier boots that offer good ankle support. Day hikes and summit pushes might necessitate medium-weight boots

Doggy First-aid Kit

Having a first-aid kit for your furry friend is necessary, even if it has only the bare-bones essentials. For a complete, comprehensive canine first-aid kit though, anyone heading into the wild with a canine companion should carry the following essentials:

Instruments
Scissors/bandage scissors/toenail clippers/tweezers
Rectal thermometer (a healthy dog should show a temperature of 101 degrees when taken rectally)

Cleansers and Disinfectants
Hydrogen peroxide, 3 percent
Betadine
Canine eyewash (available at any large pet supply store)

Topical Antibiotics and Ointments (nonprescription)
Calamine lotion
Triple antibiotic ointment (Bacitracin, Neomycin, or Polymyxin)
Baking soda (for bee stings)
Petroleum jelly
Stop-bleeding powder

Medications
Enteric-coated aspirin or Bufferin
Imodium-AD
Pepto-Bismol

Dressings and Bandages
Gauze pads (4 inches square) or gauze roll
Non-stick pads
Adhesive tape (one- and two-inch rolls)

Miscellaneous
Muzzle
Dog boots
Any prescription medication your dog needs

For Extended Trips
Consult your vet about any other prescription medications that may be needed in emergency situations, including:
Oral antibiotics
Eye/ear medications
Emetics (to induce vomiting)
Pain and anti-inflammatory medications
Suturing materials for large open wounds

made of leather or waterproof Gore-Tex. Medium boots are best suited for rocky surfaces and scrambling. If you can only afford one pair of boots, it is a good idea to go with something in the medium range, unless you know you will only be hiking short distances. For shorter hikes or fast-packing, lightweight trail-running shoes are the best bet.

Many hikers are permanently making the switch to summer style hiking shoes that offer less support but are so lightweight as to hardly be felt. If speed and comfort are your goals, and you stick to shorter and flatter dirt- and duff-filled trails, then you can't go wrong with a pair of ultralight hikers. These shoes are not recommended for snow or brutally rocky conditions. Your feet and ankles will pay dearly under such circumstances.

Your dog may need booties too. These can be purchased at most outdoor stores and will protect your dog against punctures and cracked pads. They also work well in the snow or in rocky conditions. Sandstone can be murder on your dog's pads. The grittiness is exactly the same consistency as sandpaper. Other types of rocks are sharp and can damage your pet's pads in a short amount of time. Booties are best kept in case of emergencies and cracked pads. You'll be happy if you have them when you need them.

Packs are also crucial, not just for you but your dog as well. Back-packs have significantly advanced over the past ten years. They are more lightweight, have their own built in hydration systems or are at least compatible with one, and offer a variety of configurations. Look at a good assortment before deciding on a pack that is suitable for your needs. Talk to a salesperson. You do not need a pack that can carry fifty pounds if you are only planning on day hiking. Again, a variety of packs are available for different uses, and if you can afford it, you might want one for each type of outing you plan to regularly take part in. For day hiking, a medium-size pack that can hold around twenty pounds is optimal. The more pouches the better, as you will need to be able to access your dog's water and bowl without taking off your pack every twenty minutes.

If your pets are small, chances are they won't be able to carry much. The rule of thumb is twenty percent of body weight. If your pet weighs twenty pounds he won't be able to carry much more than four pounds; in cases like this, it might be best if you just carry it in your pack. A solid hundred-pound dog, however, can carry its own food, water, and waste that you pick up and put back into his pack. Your dog will probably balk at having to wear the pack at first, so test it out and let him get used to it.

Some packs fit better than others, so it might be a good idea to take your dog with you when making the purchase. There are many options available. For the fashion conscious there are even multiple colors. After a while, Fido will get excited when the pack comes out. It will be like another leash.

Water Bottles. The arid nature of Southern California makes it necessary to always bring your own water. To use an old cliché, it is better to be safe rather than sorry. It is just not possible to rely on water sources. Packs today have optional hydration systems, which are optimal for humans. For your pet, it is best to carry containers that screw closed and can be easily accessed. Pack extra water for your pets at all times.

Dangerous Wildlife
Mammals
Many species of mammals live in Southern California. Most are rarely seen, unless you spend an inordinate amount of time in the wilderness and have infrared goggles to watch many that are nocturnal during their nightly work. Raccoon, skunk, black bear, coyote, deer, feral pig, bobcat, bighorn sheep, mountain lion, and bobcat all prowl the local mountains. Smaller mammals such as squirrels, rodents, and chipmunks abound, but the larger creatures are seldom seen—even mule deer are a rare sight, unless you know when and where to look.

All wild animals can be dangerous, so never let your dog chase them. If your dog is unable to contain himself when he sees another animal, you may want to consider further training, keeping him on a leash at all times, or simply leaving him at home. Although wild animals are not seen very often, you will have unexpected encounters, and your pet can cause problems for the both of you should he attempt to give chase.

Most animals, even large mammals, are afraid of humans and flee at the first sign of encounter. In fact, animals probably watch you a lot more than you watch them. Recently, highly publicized attacks by **mountain lions** in Southern California have dominated the news media. The reality is that these attacks are incredibly rare, even though the frequency has been more common due to encroachment upon the animals' domain and territory. Your dogs have more of a chance of being a victim of a large mammal like a mountain lion due to their smaller size, but chances are that you will never come into contact with these majestic beasts.

If you should encounter a mountain lion, make noises and try to make yourself appear larger by raising your arms. Never crouch—that just makes you look smaller. Keep small children nearby at all times. Slowly

Endangered desert bighorn sheep are reclusive and terribly afraid of dogs. Be sure to keep your dogs leashed when entering sheep country; being chased by dogs can lead to dehydration and death for the sheep.

stop and move away. Do not run, as this will trigger a flight response in the creature and make it think you are game. If you are attacked, fight back with all means at your disposal.

Bears will most likely flee when they notice you, especially your dog, which can cause a bear distress. It is a good idea to make noises as you hike so that you will never surprise a wild animal. This is when they are the most dangerous. A publicized attack in the Angeles National Forest happened a few years ago when a careless camper left his full pack out and unattended. The bear was later destroyed for having contact with humans. Never leave food items out in the open; always secure them in a bear canister or hang properly from a tree.

Bighorn sheep are becoming increasingly rare in the southern part of the state. They are nearing extinction due to encroachment upon their territory and increased predation by mountain lions. Never take your dog into sensitive areas for bighorn sheep. The scent of a dog registers as a predator in the minds of the sheep, and they will stay away from water for days if a dog's smell is nearby. This can result in their eventual death by dehydration. Bighorn sheep also have a limited amount of energy reserves due to the heat and extreme environment. Undue stress can make it difficult for them to survive when drought conditions have undermined their food and water supplies. It is imperative that your dog never chase a bighorn sheep.

Coyotes are common in lower elevations. Packs of coyotes may try to lure a dog away from its owner. Do not allow your pet to succumb to this trickery. Usually a single coyote will attempt to draw your pet away in order to be attacked by the rest of the pack. Coyotes do kill dogs, so it is critical that your dog understands and always obeys the commands "stay" and "come here." If not, you may want to always keep your pet on a leash.

Reptiles

A variety of reptiles live in Southern California, the most common being the bluebelly lizard. Snakes are also common though rarely seen. **Rattlesnakes** are the only danger to you and your pets, but encounters can be greatly reduced if you monitor where you sit and place your hands. The telltale rattle is also a dead giveaway and a sign to back away from the slithering creature. Bites are venomous, but not immediately life-threatening. If you or your dog is bitten, wrap the affected area tightly and seek medical attention immediately.

Birds

There are a number of birds and migratory patterns that cover Southern California. Opportunities abound for bird watchers in national forests and public areas. Hawks, owls, turkey vultures, and other birds of prey are brilliant to watch. Many other species are fun to notice due to their striking color or appearance. Woodpeckers can be heard rattling trees in many for-

Though scary, rattlesnakes are an uncommon sight. Avoid them by staying out of striking range, which is half their body size. Rattlesnakes can be found anywhere that is hot.

Tarantulas are misunderstood arachnids. They are big but not deadly to humans. Look for them in the evening from fall to spring at elevations below 4000 feet.

est areas, and roadrunners make the chase look exciting especially when they flee from the wily coyote.

Insects and Spiders

Ticks are the biggest concern when hiking in low-lying regions and coastal areas of Southern California. Higher elevations do not harbor ticks, but they are abundant in lower regions especially after prominent rainfall. Use tweezers to get the bloodsuckers out of your dog's skin. Make certain to remove all of the head and body parts as infection can set in if not removed properly. Lyme disease is a threat in Southern California, though not nearly as prevalent as in other regions of America. Ticks also carry other diseases, so check your pet daily after hikes and remove ticks promptly. Watch for a change in your dog's behavior that may signal an infection. There are a variety of good topical preventative measures out there for ticks. Make sure to protect your dog before hiking in tick-infested regions.

Mosquitoes have carried the West Nile virus to Southern California, and both you and your dog are susceptible to it. DEET-based solutions can effectively keep mosquitoes away if you apply some to you and to your dog in an area on the back of the neck where it cannot be licked off.

Black widows are dangerous and potentially deadly to humans, but they rarely bite, and they usually stay hidden. They should not even be a concern for you and your pet. **Tarantulas** look imposing and their bites can hurt, but their venom is not a serious threat to humans. The chances of a bite are slim even when handling the creature, though the bite can produce swelling and stinging.

Other Hazards
Weather

Southern California weather is usually warm and mild. However, mountain weather is entirely different and can change on a moment's notice. A pleasant day in the flatland can be windy, chilly, and wintry at 10,000 feet. Conversely, a wet day can create cloud cover below 6000 feet and the higher elevations can allow you to look down on the storm from sun-filled heights.

It is very important to be prepared for all sorts of weather and layer your clothing. It is always better to have items you may not need, than to need them and not have them. Summer rainstorms can occur at any time in the higher elevations, and a winter excursion can turn deadly when you are not properly prepared. On the opposite end, the summer sun can cause blistering sunburn if you hike without sun protection, and high and dry temperatures can lead to heat ailments.

Every year, hikers are lured to the high mountains of Southern California in the wintertime. This can be a rewarding experience if you are properly prepared, outfitted, and have knowledge of how to use the right equipment. However, the quick and easy access gives some a fool's hope of achieving things beyond their ability level. Roads lead all the way up to the base of Baldy, Gorgonio, and San Jacinto. The mountains are unforgiving, and the mild coastal winters do not translate well into alpine climates. Every year, people die in the local mountains because of tragic

Cumulonimbus clouds form and prepare to drop precipitation high in the San Bernardinos.

mistakes and hubris. Never overestimate your ability, and turn around if you cannot handle something, or the situation is beyond your control.

Poison Oak

This noxious plant is ubiquitous in elevations below 5000 feet in coastal canyons and along streams. It can grow anywhere, though it prefers shady areas along waterways. The oil from the plant enters your pores and spreads to everything you touch until it is washed off. Some soap can further spread the oil instead of dissipating it. Dogs are immune to the effects of the plant, but the oil can cling to their fur and spread to everything their fur touches. The plant is harmful even in winter when the leftover twigs still secrete the oil. If you or your dog is exposed, wash vigorously in cold water with oil-dispersing agents that can be bought at local drug stores.

Natural Disasters

Flash floods, mudslides, and avalanches are uncommon occurrences that can affect you if you are in the wrong place at the wrong time. Avoid hiking in canyons during or directly after heavy rainfall. Also avoid hiking in avalanche paths. Keep an eye on your surroundings and always be aware of what is going on around you. Keep abreast of changes in the weather and always err on the side of caution.

Using This Book

This book is an introduction to many areas. Further exploration will lead you to find your own favorites, but the trails covered here are meant to give you a good sampling of what is out there. Seasonal variations may close some of the trails at times or make them impassable. At other times, entire forests can shut down due to fire season. Trails can be washed out or compromised during winter storms. It is best to contact the agency that manages the area you want to hike in before you leave. You can get up-to-date information and be informed of any hazards to watch out for.

Phone numbers and website addresses are given for each hike. Distances are measured in miles by GPS units. GPS provides remarkable accuracy, but sometimes the measurements will differ slightly than that from maps or trail signs. It is not an exact measurement and a little variation should be expected when hiking. Elevation and steepness of trail can impact how long a trail seems, so it is not an exact science anyway. Hike difficulty is given as a figure that represents a hiker of average ability and fitness. Paw comfort is listed to provide you with information that will allow you to choose the best hikes your dog is suited for. Hiking time is based upon a mile for every thirty minutes of hiking. This is a rough estimate and some people will walk slower, others faster. The Hike Summary Table can also help you quickly locate suitable hikes for your fitness level and desired trip length. The overview map can quickly help you locate hikes in your area.

Difficulty of hike is not an exact science; many factors come into play in deciding the rigor of a hike. The baseline guide is as follows. Easy hikes are always less than 5 miles and do not gain more than 1000 feet of elevation. Moderate hikes are usually from 5 to 8 miles and climb 1000-2000 feet in overall elevation gain. Difficult hikes are usually longer than 5 miles and can ascend anywhere between 2000 and 3000 feet. Very difficult hikes are all above 5 miles in length and rise between 3000 and 4000 feet in altitude from start to finish. Extremely difficult hikes gain severe amounts of elevation and travel distances of 10 miles or more. Any trip that gains more than 4000 feet of elevation and 10 miles distance requires you and your pet to be in good health. These trips should not be attempted until you have several easier hikes under your collective hip belts. Other factors that influence the severity rating of a hike can include steep gains and losses, scrambling over loose rock, or traveling off-trail. Additional considerations may also apply. Make sure the hikes you take are within your ability range and that of your pet before you set out on an epic voyage. The smartest way to avoid mistakes in the wilderness is to avoid them in the planning stages.

How the Trails Were Selected

The trails in this book were carefully selected to provide the most hiking enjoyment for you and your dog. Most are very scenic but less frequented than many of the more popular hikes. Some of those are included too, but this book attempts to give details on how to avoid crowds, and when popular hikes are documented, it provides what times to go to avoid the crunch. Hikes were also selected to meet varying levels of fitness and activity, as well as ease of use and difficulty for those so inclined. A nearly equal number of hikes under and over 5 miles are represented with a good portion of hikes right at 5 miles that both beginner and advanced hikers and their dogs can enjoy.

Most of Southern California is incredibly arid, even in the mountains, but hikes with water available were chosen specifically for this book. Off-leash hiking was a motivating factor in many of the trail choices, even though many places do not allow for your pet to roam freely. Leashes are always recommended and encouraged, even when specific regulations do not require them. Hikes on-leash were chosen for their premium destinations, such as those in wilderness areas. Hikes were also chosen to provide a variety of experiences in different locales. Some areas are little more than strolls, while others are full-on adventures that can be turned into multi-day backpacking trips.

Head for the Trails: Get Involved

The noblest reason for writing this book is to get people involved. Increasingly, America's wild and public lands are at risk to encroachment by developers, mining interests, overpopulation, poor planning, pollution and a host of other detrimental factors. Southern California's forests need your voice, and there are a number of ways to become active. Voting, word of mouth, volunteering, joining a hiking group of like-minded individuals, or donating money to groups whose ideals you support are all methods of support. There are a number of good nonprofit organizations that vigorously defend America's last remaining wild spaces. Use your voice, and let your views be heard.

A Note About Safety

Safety is an important concern in all outdoor activities. No guidebook can alert you to every hazard or anticipate the limitations of every reader. Therefore, the descriptions of roads, trails, routes, and natural features in this book are not representations that a particular place or excursion will be safe for your party. When you follow any of the routes described in this book, you assume responsibility for your own safety. Under normal conditions, such excursions require the usual attention to traffic, road and trail conditions, weather, terrain, the capabilities of your party, and other factors. Because many of the lands in this book are subject to development and/or change of ownership, conditions may have changed since this book was written that make your use of some of these routes unwise. Always check for current conditions, obey posted private property signs, and avoid confrontations with property owners or managers. Keeping informed on current conditions and exercising common sense are the keys to a safe, enjoyable outing.

The Mountaineers Books

PART 2

The Trails

CALIFORNIA CENTRAL COAST

1. Point Sal State Beach

Round trip: 10.3 miles
Hiking time: 5 hours
High point: 1300 feet
Elevation gain: 2000 feet
Best season: Year-round
Difficulty: Difficult, lots of elevation gain and loss
Paw comfort: Pavement and dirt
Water: Bring your own (springs drip onto the beach but must be filtered)
Map: USGS Point Sal
Contact: Point Sal State Beach (805) 733-3713, *www.parks.ca.gov*

Getting there: From Buellton, follow U.S. Highway 101 north about 25 miles to the town of Orcutt, just south of Santa Maria. Exit onto Clark Avenue, turn left and follow it for several miles to its conclusion. Turn right onto Casmalia Road, which is also Highway 1. Stay on Highway 1 for 7 miles until it intersects with Brown Road. Make a left and follow it 4 miles through the valley to the right turn and locked gate just before Corralitos Ranch. Some parking near the gate may be on private property; be sure to obey all posted warnings and no trespassing signs.

Point Sal State Beach has been closed to vehicular traffic since 1993, and it appears that it will not be reopened any time soon. The road to

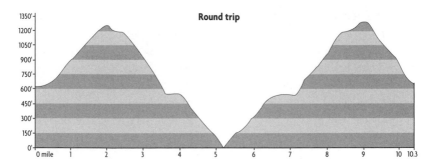

Point Sal once accommodated vehicle traffic and access to the beach. The area never swarmed with people; mostly it brought out adventurers like mountain bikers and hikers. Occasionally, access is restricted due to missile launches and other military dealings.

The water is cold, the riptides and undertow in the surf can be deadly, and the primitive beach is just too far out of the way for many people who prefer convenience stores and soda machines. On one hand, it is a shame that there is no easy entrance, but on the other, the lack of access has gotten rid of the partiers, the people who litter, and other undesirables, and left the place to hikers, dogs, and mountain bikers, which makes for a pretty positive environment all around. It's about the nearest thing there is to beachside wilderness anywhere in Southern California. The lack of vehicle traffic actually makes the entire experience rather idyllic. This pristine area is now left to those who will work to get there.

The hike in is a kicker. It is a tough piece of work to get in and out of the beach. The path in follows eroded Point Sal Road 800 feet up the mountainside, and you gain most of that elevation in a little over a mile's distance. The road is in pretty decent shape on the far side of the ocean. It is mostly dirt, but some areas are paved. Once you reach the top of the bluffs, and cross over onto Vandenberg Air Force Base (VAFB) property, the road really begins to suffer. The El Niño years in the 1990s did quite a bit of extensive damage to the road and blocked off all vehicular travel. As of printing, VAFB has no plan to rebuild or restore the road. The extent of damage is too severe to justify the funding to repair the road. From the top, you look down onto impressive viewpoints that extend far out into the Pacific. The bluffs slide away from you nearly straight down 1300 feet to the ocean. On clear days the beach view stretches all the way to San Simeon in the north and Point Conception in the south. The sensory overload is tangible, and the view itself is well worth the hike up. Some people may prefer to hike in just for the view alone. If so, this is a perfectly acceptable alternative and turn around point for a moderate 4-mile hike.

Hiking down to the beach is easy. Just remember every step you take downward is a step upward you must take back out. This is a day hike; make sure to keep your energy in reserve. Inverse hikes can be tough, especially over long distances. Having the coastal moisture helps out a lot. If the fog rolls in, which it does quite a lot in the afternoon, the temperature can feel pretty low. This can make all the difference between a hot sweaty hike and an enjoyable cool one.

Since this is Santa Barbara County and a state park, regulations prohibit

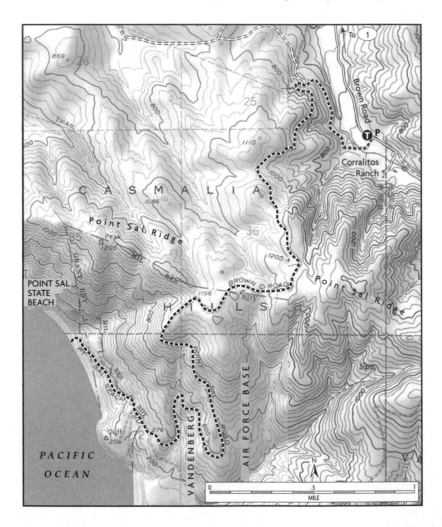

Cameron walks toward a California sea lion that prepares to enter the Pacific Ocean surf.

dogs from setting foot anywhere on the beach. There is no easy beach access, as a decent trail was never built. There are still a lot of scrambles that you can clamber down and then back up; it is up to you to find the best path to take. Return the way you came, and treasure the special memories of this magical beach. No camping is allowed.

2. La Purísima Mission State Historic Park

Round trip: 5 miles
Hiking time: 2 hours
High point: 400 feet
Elevation gain: 300 feet
Best season: Year-round, hot in summer
Difficulty: Easy
Paw comfort: Dirt and pavement
Water: Cisterns and mission irrigation aqueduct ditches may have water year-round
Fees and permits: $4 entrance fee
Map: USGS Lompoc
Contact: La Purísima Mission State Historic Park (805)733-3713, *www.parks.ca.gov*

Getting there: From U.S. Highway 101 in Buellton, take Highway 246 west toward the town of Lompoc for 14 miles. Veer right onto Purísima

Road. Follow it exactly 1 mile to the entrance to the mission parking lot. Turn right into the parking lot and pay the $4 entrance fee.

Trail maps are available for $1 at the kiosk and the visitor center. There are over 25 miles of trail to explore on the mission grounds, and an almost infinite number of combinations can be put together to design your own hike and cover any amount of distance. The trails are made up of pavement, sand, and dirt. They are well signed and correspond with the names on the map, so you can find your way around quite easily. Watch out for poison oak. The trails are relatively free of this obnoxious plant, but it grows ubiquitously everywhere else. Ticks are also prevalent at certain times, so protect yourself and your pets. A mountain lion was spotted recently on the south loop, and these animals are common in coastal hills. Rattlesnakes are another thing to be mindful of, but are rarely spotted.

Misión la Purísima Concepción de Maria Santísima (Mission of the Immaculate Conception of Most Holy Mary) is the most immersing of the twenty-one missions of Alta California. Unlike most missions that had large pueblos and cities spring up around them, La Purísima failed to achieve its political and religious goal of bringing Spain to the Native Americans. That "failure" is California's gain; La Purísima Mission exists almost in a time warp of sorts, where the conditions of the past are nearly tangible. You can truly get a sense of what life might have been like two centuries ago while strolling around the nearly one thousand square acres of the state park. La Purísima is one of the rare state parks in California to allow dogs. Dogs must be on a leash, but are allowed on all trails and around the mission grounds. Please be sure to clean up after your pet and follow all guidelines. When dogs are allowed in such wonderful areas, it is important to act as an ambassador for all canine owners.

Most of the trails within the park are strikingly underused. The ranger on duty agreed to that interpretation, and evidence of footfalls on the

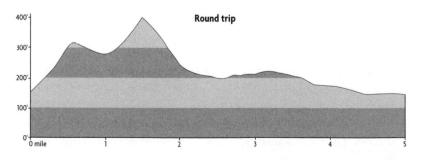

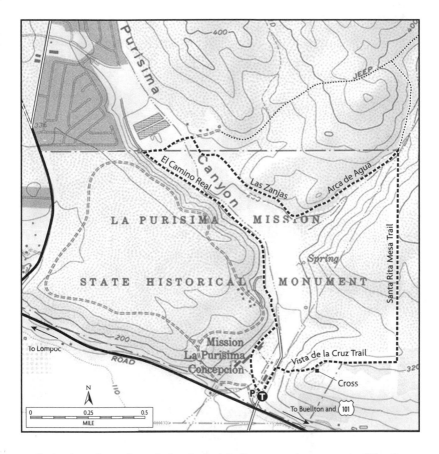

trails furthest from the mission is decidedly non-existent most of the time. If you desire to get "lost" and have solitude in the Purísima Hills, it is possible to spend the entire day in thoughtful contemplation. Straying off the main path and roadway will get you far enough into the "backcountry" that you may see no one else. Certainly, you are not in the middle of wilderness, but most people come solely to see the mission and only wander around the most heavily used portions of the park.

Make certain to check out the mission buildings and main grounds; after all, that's what you paid for. The architecture is both fascinating and beautiful. The loop indicated on the map specifies a trip made up of five trails in the park. The Vista de la Cruz climbs sharply to the large cross above the visitor center and affords wonderful views of the entire mission complex and valley. From there the Santa Rita Mesa Trail continues along the fence line of the property following an old sand road

An old bell hangs beneath the beams of La Purísima Mission with the hillside cross looming in the background.

through chaparral and coastal scrub. Arca de Agua (unsigned) turns back towards the mission and follows a creek bed that remains dry for most of the year. Poison oak is abundant in this area, so keep your dogs on the narrow single-track. The trail connects with Las Zanjas at a cistern where water pours into the well-constructed basin. Las Zanjas is a dirt road that follows the old stone aqueduct to a wonderful wetland area. The trail connects with paved El Camino Real, which is the original mission road that travelers followed from mission to mission in colonial times.

3. Nojoqui Falls County Park

Round trip: 0.6 mile
Hiking time: 1.5 hours
High point: 1000 feet
Elevation gain: 200 feet
Best season: Year-round
Difficulty: Easy
Paw comfort: Dirt and pavement
Water: Nojoqui Creek flows year-round in wet years
Map: USGS Solvang
Contact: Nojoqui Falls County Park (805) 934-6123, *www.sbparks.org*

Getting there: Take U.S. Highway 101 north from Ventura about 35 miles and exit onto State Street/San Marcos Pass (Highway 154) in Santa Barbara. Follow it through the mountains for over 23 miles past Cachuma Lake to the intersection with Highway 246 and head towards Solvang. As you enter the Danish section of town and pass Mission Santa Ines, turn left onto Alisal Road and follow it for 6.5 winding narrow miles to the entrance of Nojoqui Falls County Park. This road is beautiful and quaint. Alternatively, the Old Coast Highway exit is 3.5 miles north of the intersection of U.S. 101 and Highway 1 to Lompoc. The route is clearly marked for Nojoqui Falls County Park. Follow it for 1 mile to the park entrance on the right.

Nojoqui Falls is a jewel of Santa Barbara County that is relatively unknown to anyone not of local origin. Nojoqui is a Chumash Indian word that has lost its meaning. It is correctly pronounced "Na-hoo-ee" though those

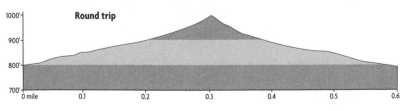

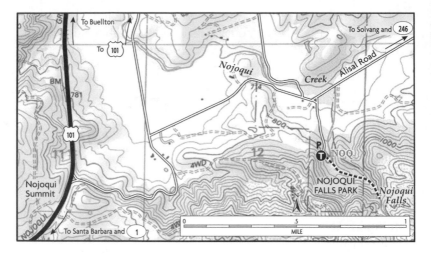

phonetics are certainly not intuitive. There is no sign in Solvang to mark its presence, and with past closings of the road directly off U.S. 101, this area is seeing less and less traffic. The park is massive, with three seemingly endless picnic areas that host multiple sites and barbeque grills, many of which can be reserved. There are two playgrounds, three restrooms, a baseball diamond and a soccer field, plus ample parking. That isn't even including the trail to the falls. This is a county park and dogs are welcome, but they must remain leashed at all times.

The falls trail begins at the end of the parking area. It follows babbling Nojoqui Creek along a nicely manicured path that is incredibly wide in spots. The path crosses a couple of footbridges and proceeds up some nicely landscaped stone stairs that might remind some of the elven cities from *The Lord of the Rings*. Someone should have told Peter Jackson to film here instead of New Zealand. It isn't quite as epic, but impressive nonetheless. Coastal live oak, white oak and California laurel trees line the sheltered path, which remains cool even in summer. Stringy bushels of lace lichen hang ethereally from the coastal live oaks, and wave in graceful time with the cool breezes that often gently blow down the canyon from the falls. The lichen is technically a parasite, but it does not harm the trees. The relationship is more symbiotic in nature, and it thrives in the pure central coast air. Most lichens are very delicate life forms. They are sensitive to slight changes in their ecosystems and will disappear with even the smallest of fluctuations. For this reason lace lichen is very rare or nearly extinct in the L.A. Basin due to smog, though it once was just as plentiful there.

A short but brisk ten minute walk uphill leads to the base of the 165-foot falls, which are best viewed in spring after heavy amounts of winter rainfall, or during and just after a rainstorm. The falls tumble down the travertine and drip off the Maidenhair ferns, five finger ferns, and radiant green mosses that line the towering cliff. During drier times, the falls will slow to a trickle but are impressive nonetheless. Even if the falls have slowed to a drip, the canyon, its solitude, and sylvan peacefulness are well worth the side trip. While most people are wine tasting, eating a danish in Solvang, or burning money at casinos, you and your pet can relish the natural wonder at this rarely frequented marvel.

An interpretive plaque is posted by the falls where you can read about the formation of the falls and how the falls continue to grow outwards due to the calcium carbonate in the water. The sandstone is continually being added to due to calcium deposits, much in the same way that a stalagmite forms in underground caves. There is further explanation of geology and plant life, but watching the falls and relaxing is probably the best way to spend your time here. Return the way you came and continue on to new adventures.

Water drips from the moss and ferns at Nojoqui Falls County Park.

4. Refugio State Beach to El Capitan State Beach

Round trip: 5.4 miles
Hiking time: 2 hours
High point: 100 feet
Elevation gain: 100 feet
Best season: Year-round
Difficulty: Easy
Paw comfort: Pavement
Water: Bring your own
Fees and permits: $8 parking/day use fee
Map: USGS Tajiguas
Contact: Refugio State Beach (805) 968-1033, *www.parks.ca.gov*

Getting there: From Goleta, take U.S. Highway 101 12 to 15 miles north and exit for either El Capitan or Refugio State Beach. You have to pay a parking/day use fee of $8 at either beach, although on the road right outside of Refugio, you can park for free and walk the extra quarter-mile if you so desire.

The first thing you'll see upon entering the parking lot is a big sign with a dog, a circle, and a slash. This means no dogs allowed on the beach. Unfortunately, there just aren't many beaches in Southern California where dogs are allowed on the beach. It is a shame, because this is a large enough coastline that it seems there could be some type of accommodation made for dog lovers, but alas, such is not the case. However, just because dogs are not allowed to wander on the beach does not mean that this is a trip taken in vain. In fact, there is a wonderful paved pathway between El Capitan and Refugio that covers the 2.5-mile distance between the beaches where dogs are allowed. The biking, walking, and jogging path travels atop the bluffs providing captivating views of the Pacific

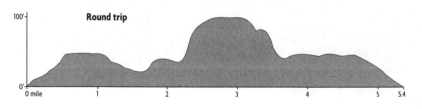

The coastal view of Refugio State Beach from the paved bicycle trail is impressive.

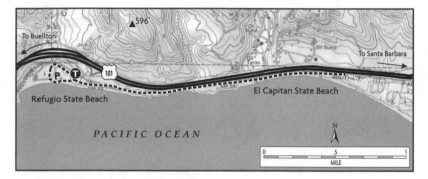

Ocean and the Channel Islands from a vantage point that is second to none. Of course, the dogs have to remain on a leash, but the easy walk is worth it, if only for the ocean overlooks.

About halfway between the parking areas, the trail dips down to a secluded section of the beach between El Capitan and Refugio that hardly receives any visitors at all. The occasional surfer who parks off the freeway and crosses the railroad tracks to scramble through the brush to the beach is the rare exception. This is a wonderfully idyllic spot that could easily be open to dogs, and there aren't any signs here, but this is still Santa Barbara County, which means the ordinance is still in effect, and technically this is state beach property. The walkway trail has a few ups and downs but generally runs fairly level and parallel to the freeway. The hum of the highway isn't horribly distracting, but it is constant and inescapable. Occasionally, a train whizzes by at nearly the speed of light, accompanied by the sound of rolling thunder. Telephone wires also run along the track, but these are only mild inconveniences that remind you that you are not on some isolated bluff overlooking a pristine unexplored beach.

Wandering along the path, one can only marvel at how this area must have appeared when the Chumash rambled here: unspoiled, tranquil, heavenly, and in places it still appears so. The beauty is otherworldly and tangible, with the Channel Islands sparkling like the gemstones they are, faraway lands removed from the development that is Southern California. The coastal waters sparkle blue and invite you and your dog to enjoy a sunset from atop the bluffs. Just don't linger for too long, because the parking area is only open until sundown.

LOS PADRES NATIONAL FOREST

5. Aliso Trail

Round trip: 3.25 miles
Hiking time: 1.5 hours
High point: 1800 feet
Elevation gain: 1000 feet
Best season: Year-round, hot in summer
Difficulty: Moderate due to steep elevation gain
Paw comfort: Packed dirt
Water: Aliso Creek flows year-round in wet years
Fees and permits: Adventure Pass required
Map: USGS San Marcos Pass
Contact: Los Padres National Forest, Santa Barbara Ranger District
(805) 968-6640, *www.fs.fed.us/r5/lospadres*

Getting there: From Ventura, take U.S. Highway 101 35 miles north to Santa Barbara, exit State Street/San Marcos Pass Highway (Highway 154)

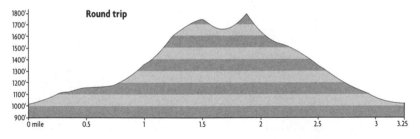

and follow the highway over the crest 10.5 miles to Paradise Road. Turn right and follow Paradise Road for 4.5 miles. Turn left onto the road marked with a sign for Sage Hill Group Camp. Park in the large parking area at the end of the lot beyond all of the campsites, and across from the campground host.

The Santa Ynez Recreation Area is a beautiful place to spend a spring or fall weekend. Even if you only have a half-day, there are wonderful opportunities for outdoor diversions. Campsites fill the valley, and the temperatures are moderate during the milder seasons. Trailheads are abundant both in the campgrounds and along the many roads that crisscross the forest. Hiking in the Santa Barbara coastal ranges is always a vigorous workout; steep canyons and rolling hills punctuate the landscape, and most of the routes through the forest regularly alternate between climbing and descending. The main hazards you should consider before hiking in this region are the abundant poison oak and the exploding tick populations. Both can be so pervasive that it is incredibly important to protect yourself and your dog from adverse effects before you ever set foot on a trail. Of course, mountain lions also prowl the area, and rattlesnakes lurk around too.

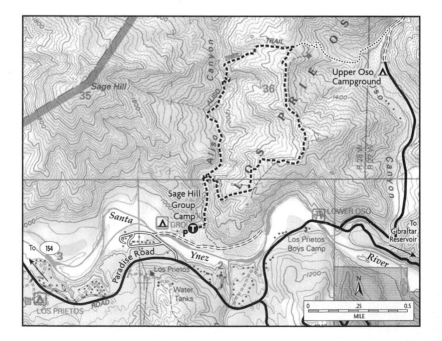

Socrates sniffs the wild grasses along the Aliso Trail.

A large trailhead kiosk marks the entrance to the interpretive trail. Pick up a trail guide, if there are any, so that you can find out information on local flora, fauna, and geology. The Aliso Trail is a short loop that is favored by horseback riders, so keep an ear open for the large animals, in case a troop is coming through. Keep the surprise at a minimum by always paying close attention to your surroundings. The trail is well maintained and traverses mostly dirt. As such, it is an excellent place for dogs that haven't had much hiking experience and also suitable for the dusty trail-hardened hound. Both sets of dogs will enjoy the trip equally.

A small tributary of the Santa Ynez River flows through Aliso Canyon. The riparian streambed is lined with California laurel, coast live oak and alder trees from which the ravine derives its name. Aliso means alder in Spanish, and the trees that line the creek are common throughout the west coast of the United States. When water is flowing, the area is a serene wonderland, suitable for lucid contemplation among the graceful water and gentle breezes that glide through the trees. In the dry season of autumn, the deciduous trees transform and lose their colors. The hues of gold, red, and orange display a vibrant pattern of periodic yearly life rarely seen in Southern California, which makes the area worth a contemplative stroll during a season of lesser usage.

The trail is easy to follow and surprisingly well signed. There are various side trails to hills and overlooks that are not maintained or labeled; however, these are easily distinguished from the main path. The trail climbs out of the lush canyon and along a dusty dry hillside where it turns upward and tops out on a high point overlooking Upper Oso Campground and the Santa Ynez River Valley. The views are superb extending back into the rugged San Rafael Wilderness. Follow the trail back around the loop in either direction and continue downstream to the parking area.

6. Knapp's Castle

Round trip: 0.93 mile
Hiking time: 1 hour
High point: 3000 feet
Elevation gain: 100 feet
Best season: Year-round, hot in summer
Difficulty: Easy
Paw comfort: Packed dirt
Water: Bring your own
Fees and permits: Adventure Pass required
Map: USGS San Marcos Pass
Contact: Los Padres National Forest, Santa Barbara Ranger District (805) 968-6640, *www.fs.fed.us/r5/lospadres*

Getting there: From Ventura, take U.S. Highway 101 north for 35 miles to Santa Barbara and exit State Street/San Marcos Pass Highway (Highway 154). Take Highway 154 north for 8 miles to East Camino Cielo. Make a right and follow it past Painted Cave Road, which branches off to the

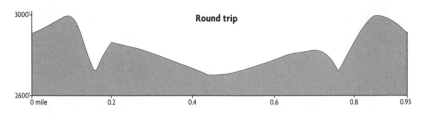

right. Continue on East Camino Cielo for nearly another mile. The "trail" to Knapp's Castle is unmarked. There is parking on both sides of the private road. Do not block the locked gate. Start hiking on the fire road that has a gate reading, "Right to Pass Revocable by Owner."

Knapp's Castle is one of those great little side trips that nearly everyone in Santa Barbara knows about. It's just long enough to be considered a hike, but short enough that even toddlers can make the distance there and back on their feet. The views are stunning to put it mildly. Camino Cielo has no match in all of Southern California. The road traverses the crest of the coastal mountains all the way from San Marcos Pass to beyond Montecito. On a clear day the four closest Channel Islands, Santa Rosa, San Miguel, Santa Cruz, and Anacapa, appear near enough to touch. The coastal views are unrivaled, and that goes without mentioning the vast panoramas that extend to the horizon in the north. For people who are unfamiliar with the geography of Southern California, the stretch of coast from Santa Barbara to Los Angeles runs mostly west to east. In fact, Los Angeles is only 30 miles to the south of Santa Barbara, and many of the major mountain ranges in this part of the state run east to west. The Santa Ynez Mountains are no different.

Technically, Knapp's Castle is only a ruin, but it is a wreck of magnificence. The foundation, some arches, and a few chimneys are all that remain after fire destroyed the lodge in 1940. It was completed in 1920 by George Owen Knapp, who was the founder and president of Union Carbide. The entrepreneur and philanthropist had settled in the Santa Barbara area and wanted a mountain cottage as a getaway from his large Montecito estate. One can only imagine how impressive the castle must have been in its heyday, and perhaps it is lucky that it was burnt to the ground. Surely if people still occupied the residence, there would be no public access at all, and it is a blessing that this area is open to the public.

Since this trail does cross private property, please be extra careful to behave yourself, and pay extra attention to your pets. It would be a shame to have this piece of history closed off, and as long as everyone does their part, Knapp's Castle will be open to people for generations to come.

It won't take long to view the ruins, and this walk can be done as a supplement to other hikes in the region, a stop along the road, or even as an afterthought. There are lots of trails and even just small outcroppings to check out along East Camino Cielo, but almost everyone that comes here will want to spend time enjoying the incredible views from the steps of the castle. So bring your lunch, drop some water for the pooch, and take your time. Relax on the sandstone and ponder the good life of mountaintop living. Your dog will love sniffing around, but do be careful of broken glass. Some visitors are not so conscientious, but most are. If you are willing, pack out some extra trash—it's only a short walk.

Cachuma Lake and the Los Padres National Forest sit below the ruins of Knapp's Castle.

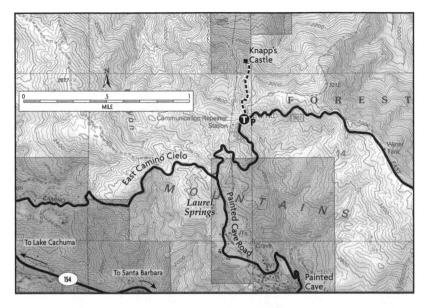

As many might guess, the castle is also a fantastic spot to watch a winter sunrise, if you are willing to brave the wind and cold. A midsummer sunset can be truly magnificent as the sun settles into the ocean for its nightly slumber from high in the west.

7. Coal Oil Point

Round trip: 1.5 miles
Hiking time: 1 hour
High point: 30 feet
Elevation gain: 25 feet
Best season: Year-round
Difficulty: Easy
Paw comfort: Sand and surf
Water: Bring your own
Map: USGS Dos Pueblos Canyon; USGS Goleta
Contact: University of California at Santa Barbara, Office of Planning and Design (805) 893-3971.

Getting there: From Santa Barbara take U.S. Highway 101 about 13 miles to Goleta and exit on Storke Road, turn left onto El Colegio, and make

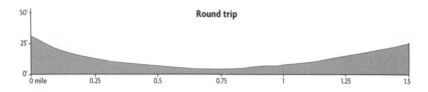

the first right onto Camino Corto. Turn right onto Del Playa and follow it until it dead ends at Camino Majorca. Park under the eucalyptus trees or wherever you can find a spot. If you wish to start at Coal Oil Point, veer right from Storke Road and follow Slough Road (unsigned) to the dirt parking area. The hike can be reached from the parking area by the University of California Santa Barbara (UCSB) dorms, but you'll have to pay to get onto campus and park there. Isla Vista has free parking.

A solitary cross stands sentinel overlooking Coal Oil Point and Santa Cruz Island.

The area north of Coal Oil Point through Sands Beach has been designated as critical habitat for the tiny Snowy Plover since 1999, and the dunes are now off-limits as the bird is listed under the Endangered Species Act. The beloved bird is making a comeback due to the efforts of the UCSB environmental studies department, and it is best to keep dogs entirely out of the area. An unleashed dog on this part of the beach can result in a hefty fine. Stick to the bluffs and Campus Beach to be safe; evidently the birds do not roost on the south-facing beach.

This is a combination beach and bluff hike that takes you along the beaches of Isla Vista from Campus Beach to Coal Oil Point. The hike can be lengthened and stretches all the way to Campus Point and beyond if you wish. Depending upon the tide, you may have to veer onto campus to avoid the lagoon runoff if you decide to travel that far to the east. You will see dogs of all sorts along the way. Students and people who enjoy taking their dogs to the beach bring their pets here. When dogs are allowed on beaches in Santa Barbara, they must be on a leash, but since this is UCSB, the land of iconoclasts and renegades, no one pays very much attention to rules, especially one that seems so inherently wrong and trifling. No matter what others do, unleashed dogs are prohibited on campus beaches to avoid an accidental encounter with a snowy plover.

Dogs love the beach, even dogs that don't like water. Something about sand, waves and unbounded freedom changes dogs into rampant scramblers. Taking a dog to the beach is akin to giving them a bowlful of energy drink. Even old dogs suddenly feel like and resemble dogs half their age when taken to the beach. Spontaneous sprinting is a common diagnosis for dogs on the beach. It is a shame that so many areas of Southern California restrict their movement. Most beaches between San Diego and San Francisco do not even allow dogs to set paw upon sand. At least you can bring your pet to this beach on a leash. He can have a taste of limited liberty by checking out tide pools, sniffing at

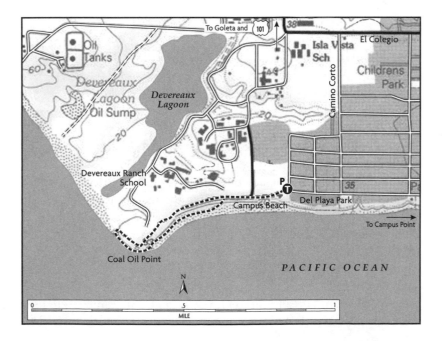

other dogs, and playing in the surf. There are many access points for the beach and the bluffs, so choose your route and enjoy the day at the beach. Pretend you are a dog and run a little.

After your outing, don't miss the fabulous fare of Isla Vista. There are plenty of places to gather your strength by eating a hearty meal. With a population of nearly 20,000 and a median age of twenty-one, Isla Vista is known for its eateries, among other things. Enjoy yourself and walk your pooch through the busy hamlet. Most places have outside seating and don't mind if your dog enjoys the atmosphere alongside you.

8. Reyes Peak

Round trip: 8.25 miles
Hiking time: 4 hours
High point: 7300 feet
Elevation gain: 800 feet
Best season: Summer, road and campgrounds are closed seasonally.
   The road may also be closed during wet periods, or fire danger
Difficulty: Moderate
Paw comfort: Dirt and duff
Water: Bring your own
Fees and permits: Adventure Pass required
Map: USGS Reyes Peak
Contact: Los Padres National Forest, Ojai Ranger District
   (805) 646-4348, *http://www.fs.fed.us/r5/lospadres*

Getting there: From Ventura, take U.S. Highway 101 north for 7 miles, then exit for Highway 33 north to Ojai. Follow Highway 33 for 45 miles to Pine Mountain Road. Turn right and follow it nearly 7 miles to its completion. Park in the large area and continue down the road to its end. The road will split and a trail will veer off to the left. Take the trail and follow it as it climbs and heads back around the other side of the ridge.

This is a wonderful area of the Los Padres National Forest; there are magnificent campgrounds in a splendid pine forest setting above 7000 feet in elevation. Fifteen years ago, the area and its camps were used relatively infrequently, but the secret is no longer quiet, and this region

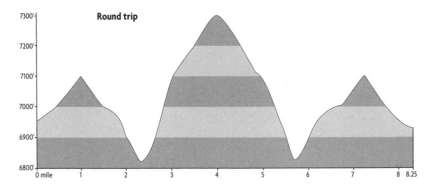

now gets a lot of use. Still, any one of the campgrounds is amazing and well worth the trip and an overnight stay. Pine forest is rare in this section of Southern California; much of Los Padres is coastal mountains and low-lying hills that don't reach elevations high enough to support large populations of conifers. The name of the hike is a misnomer, because the trail does not actually take you to Reyes Peak. Instead, the Reyes Peak Trail follows the crest of Pine Mountain Ridge.

The trail itself is rather straightforward. It stays fairly level while hugging the crest of the incredibly long spine of Pine Mountain. Due to this, there are quite a few areas that tend to stray up and down, so you are never moving in upward or all downward trends for very long. The constant ups and downs do not make this trail more difficult, but a leisurely pace is best, because the continuous shift in elevation gain and loss makes it hard to set a steady pace. The path itself is dirt, dust, and duff covered, and will be incredibly easy on your furry friend's paws. Even a relatively sedentary dog should be able to handle this one, maybe not all the way to the top of Peak 7431, but for at least a good majority of the way. If your dog is a regular hiker, he'll be running circles around you at the end of the trail entirely ready for another adventure.

Not only is this a good hike for beginner hiking dogs, but also beginning hikers. The 8 miles to and from where the trail begins its descent into Haddock Camp is a well-rounded, half-day outing that will test the legs of all but the strongest upper echelon of hikers. It's enough to make almost anyone feel that they had a great day of exercise out in the cleanest air and amidst some of the prettiest views in all of Southern California. On the clearest of days, wherever the trail offers a southern view, five of the eight Channel Islands are visible. On days obscured by lesser visibility, you might see only two or three, and even if the coastal fog has rolled in, the overlook is still quite heavenly. When the trail wraps its way around to the north side of the crest, the views into the Sespe Wilderness are spectacular. The rugged badlands of this section of the forest protect the endangered California condor. If you are truly lucky, you may get the chance to observe one up close soaring through the skies. If you do happen to see one, remember that these animals are endangered and federally protected. Do not approach or otherwise harass these majestic creatures. Their continued survival depends upon all of us who use these forests.

Once you've had a break for lunch and rest, return the way you came. However, there are other options to pursue for the avid hiker or backpacker. Haddock Camp is a wonderful place to backpack into, and if it is not being used by scouts, you should have the campgrounds all to yourself. The trip into Haddock Camp adds nearly 1.5 miles one way

Chewbacca and Socrates romp among the pines along the Reyes Peak Trail.

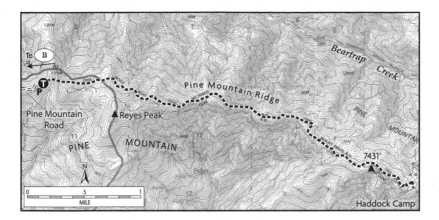

and a 1400-foot elevation loss to your trip. Attempting this as a day hike is doable, but it makes the trip very strenuous instead of a simple well-paced outing.

9. Piedra Blanca

Round trip: 2.5 miles
Hiking time: 2 hours
High point: 3225 feet
Elevation gain: 300 feet
Best season: Late fall through late spring
Difficulty: Easy
Paw comfort: Dirt, sand, stream crossing, and sandstone
Water: Sespe Wild and Scenic River
Fees and permits: Adventure Pass required
Map: USGS Lion Canyon
Contact: Los Padres National Forest, Ojai Ranger District
(805) 646-4348, *http://www.fs.fed.us/r5/lospadres*

Getting there: Take U.S. Highway 101 northwest from Los Angeles to Ventura. Head north on Highway 33 and follow it through the town of Ojai. Stay on Highway 33 at the Highway 33/Highway 150 split. After driving 14.5 miles from the split, you will see a right turn for Forest Service Road 6N31 which leads to the Rose Valley Recreation Area. Follow the road to its conclusion. There is no longer any camping at the old Piedra Blanca campsite, or the Lion campsite just below it, but you can park where the campsite used to be. If you want to make the trip longer, park anywhere along the road where there is a trail sign. They all lead to the rocks.

Piedra Blanca means white rock in Spanish, which should make everyone happy that the more aesthetic cultural moniker was retained instead of the English. The name truly belies the natural rustic beauty found in the Ojai Ranger District. First, you cross Sespe Creek, which was designated as a National Wild and Scenic River in 1992. The creek has been given this entitlement due to its unusual gorges, the interesting geology in the area, such as Piedra Blanca, and for its role as a critical habitat for the endangered California condor. The water flows year-round, and can be tough to cross after periods of heavy rainfall. The creek bed is home to some wonderful deciduous trees that show off the colors of autumn in a decidedly un-Californian fashion. However, don't expect much in the way of shade or any type of forest cover, because this is strictly a desert plant community hike after you find your way up out of the creek bed. There are plenty of reasons to scratch if walking bare-legged through this section of trail. Keep your eye out for spiny succulents and thorns that protrude in places where the trail is overgrown.

After crossing the creek a couple of times you have to turn left and fol-low the trail signs that lead to Piedra Blanca. As with any lower elevation brushy area, this region can be ripe with ticks during the cooler months, so be sure to have your pets protected, while also remaining vigilant over the humans in your party. When you come to the next junction, Piedra Blanca is conspicuously absent from the trail sign. Make a right and fol-low the trail that leads north into the extraordinary sandstone formation. Once you are standing amongst the smooth time-polished rocks, you

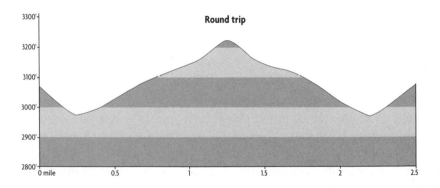

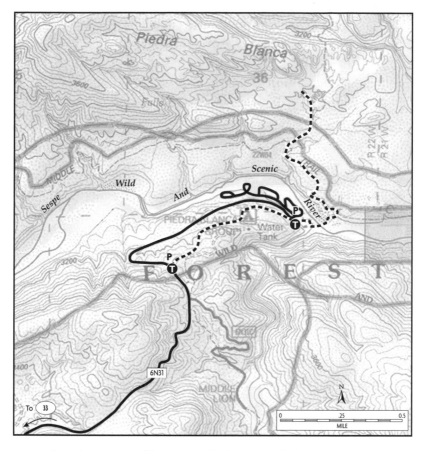

can truly gain a sense of how overwhelming and glorious the formation
is. Photo opportunities abound when the sky is overloaded with cloud
formations that mimic the downy look of the boulders. When the sun
hits Piedra Blanca, the true color of the appellation is apparent. From a
distance the appearance is blinding, but the close-up portrays an incredible spectacle. The contrast of stark whiteness against the cerulean blue
of an autumnal sky is nothing short of awesome. You may sense a need
to explore further just to gain more prospects for photographs.

Climbing on the slick rocks can be a wonderful diversion; the formations
pop out in mushroom-like protrusions all over the valley. You will want
shoes with good sticky tread to do this, and it should not be a pastime
for small children. Some of the rocks will prove a challenge to ascend and
may be even more formidable on the way down. Your dog might try to
join you as well, and it is not a good idea to get a dog into a situation that

Adam, Chewee, and Socs on the trail to the white rock formation known as Piedra Blanca.

involves tricky climbing from a human standpoint. Hiking around the stone outcroppings and exploring is the greatest way to see them. The best policy here is that if your dog can't make it, why do you need to go there? You and your dog can enjoy a wonderful half or full day just exploring. Bring the whole family so that everyone can join in the fun.

10. Rose Valley Falls

Round trip: 0.75 mile
Hiking time: Half-hour
High point: 3590 feet
Elevation gain: 150 feet
Difficulty: Easy
Paw comfort: Packed dirt
Best season: Year-round, but hot in summer
Water: Rose Valley Creek flows year-round in wet years
Fees and permits: Adventure Pass required
Map: USGS Lion Canyon
Contact: Los Padres National Forest, Ojai Ranger District
    (805) 646-4348, *http://www.fs.fed.us/r5/lospadres*

Getting there: Take U.S. Highway 101 northwest from Los Angeles to Ventura. Head north on Highway 33 and follow it through the town of

Ojai. From the Highway 150/Highway 33 split, follow Highway 33 for 14.5 miles. You will see a right turn for Forest Service Road 6N31, which leads to the Rose Valley Recreation Area. After 3 miles make a right turn and head toward the Rose Valley Campground. There are a couple of parking spaces at the end of the campground loop in spaces 3 and 4 where you can fit your vehicle. Don't block parking spaces for the campground. The trail is clearly marked to the southwest.

This is not a long trail and can be an easy destination for a child's first hike. Any dog should be able to take this walk, unless it is a dog without legs. The three-quarter-mile trip is barely enough to get your legs stretched or your heart racing, although there is a little bit of an incline. Some uneven ground marked with tiny stream crossings does not make this a good trip for the elderly or the infirm. However, anyone in even slightly well-maintained health should be able to make the pilgrimage to this marvel of nature.

The hike itself traverses through pretty oaken woodlands. It travels through a Tolkienesque fairyland with intertwining tree boughs crafting a living, breathing archway above your head. The interplay of light and shadow during the early morning or late evening can unlock wonderful photo opportunities. The trail is mixed dirt and rock, but easy on the feet, paws, pads, and claws. You do cross a small portion of the creek, and your dog should get a drink if he requires one at the moment.

Anyone paying close attention will notice the many small cascades along Rose Valley Creek. Some are quite splendid, and even have use trails that lead down among the tumbling water to the emerald pools that nestle below the tiny splashings of white water. While you might

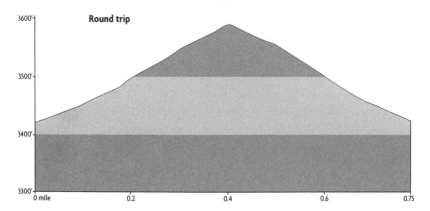

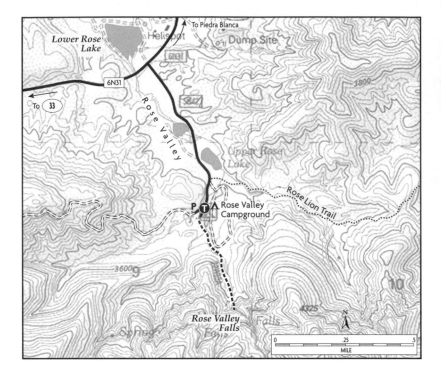

be tempted to take a closer look, you should at least wait until you have seen the main attraction.

Rose Valley Falls is awe-inspiring the first time you gaze upon it and each time thereafter. It might even strike you as surreal in its beauty. Frankly, it is just hard to imagine that such a shining, shimmering gem could be so close to a flat open circular campground that is hardly anything special. The area seems so arid that it appears nearly impossible that something so lush could exist in the midst of such heat and dearth of humidity. The falls drop over 70 feet down the face of a sandstone cliff. Even though the water technically only cascades over the edge, it still proffers an amazing sight. The upper falls are not visible from the viewing area and can be reached by much more difficult trails that are exposed and not advisable with dogs. Truly, you will be stunned by the sight, and if you are in need of more exercise, there are many trail options in the area, certainly not last among these is the Piedra Blanca rock formation a short drive to the north.

Opposite: Rose Valley Falls drops from a magnificent height amid a lush, sylvan setting.

Harbored under the shady canopy that guards this wooded wonderland, green mossy tendrils drip and ooze life-giving water. The lower falls is undoubtedly a rather extraordinary sight for the Ojai region, but it is only one of the many surprises that the nearby wilderness abounds in. This untamed and often starkly beautiful district is home to the rebounding California condor, so anytime you are traversing this section of the Los Padres National Forest, remember to keep one eye on what you are looking at and the other on the sky. Truly, this work of nature is only a beginning for what the Ojai Ranger District has in store.

Dawdle for a while by the falls, ogling and taking pictures. If you have a nice camera, this is a spot to use it. The lack of light beneath the trees and the tranquil character of the falls is one of a deliberate type of motion. To capture its essence, you will want a slower speed of film and the time required to set up that perfect shot. Then, you can always explore the pools and take a dip, especially on a hot summer afternoon.

Be aware that after a rainy season, this is prime tick country, so make sure your dogs are treated before coming here, and check yourself regularly as well.

SANTA MONICA MOUNTAINS NATIONAL RECREATION AREA

11. Satwiwa Loop

Round trip: 1.5 to 2.5 miles
Hiking time: 1.5 hours
High point: 1060 feet
Elevation gain: 260 feet
Best season: Year-round, summers are hot
Difficulty: Easy
Paw comfort: Dirt
Water: Satwiwa Culture Center
Map: USGS Newbury Park (does not show trails)
Contact: Santa Monica Mountains National Recreation Area (805) 370-2301, *www.nps.gov/samo*

Getting there: Take U.S. Highway 101 north from Los Angeles and exit Lynn Road in the city of Thousand Oaks. Turn left (south) and follow

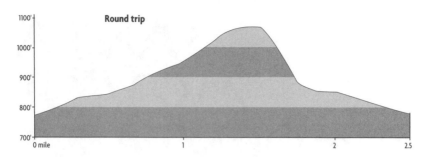

Lynn Road for 5.25 miles and look for the sign for State and National Parks. Turn left onto Via Goleta and park in the large parking lot next to the restrooms. Parking and admission are free. The lot is open from 8 am to sunset.

A solitary roadrunner struts through the tall grasses in the Satwiwa/ Rancho Sierra Vista section of the Santa Monica Mountains.

Satwiwa is a wonderful place. For being in such close proximity to city limits, the Rancho Sierra Vista/Satwiwa area feels incredibly wild. Encounters with roadrunners, prairie falcons, hawks, rabbits, deer, and even coyotes are quite common here. You are likely to see more wildlife in this small region than you will in all of the Santa Monicas, or any other mountain region in Southern California for that matter. The area itself is incredibly picturesque. The imposing stoniness of Boney Mountain lords above the rolling grasslands and verdant green hills of Satwiwa. From the parking area, a short walk takes you to the Satwiwa Native American Indian Culture Center, where you can learn about native life in the Santa Monicas and take part in scheduled activities, sans dogs, of course. A Chumash demonstration village sits across the trail from the cultural center. On Saturdays and Sundays a Native American guest host or park ranger is on hand to lead activities and answer questions. Satwiwa means "the bluffs" and was the name of a Chumash community in the area. Along with the Chumash, the Gabrielino/Tongva culture also flourished in the Santa Monica Mountains east of Malibu Canyon.

The park is quite popular even on weekdays. It acts as a quick getaway for the west-end cities in the San Gabriel Valley. Equestrians, mountain bikers, runners, and people looking to get outside enjoy the various uses the trails in the region have to offer. You are likely to see other guests at the center and on the main trail. There are many overlapping trails and quite a few areas to explore. The main loop itself can be lengthened or shortened with a couple of turns and side trips. Once you are here, this might just possibly be a place you might want to further investigate. The free handout includes a map that is not incredibly detailed, though you should be able to make your way around the park fairly easily.

The variety of uses in the park mirrors the historical assortment of culture that is woven through this region. Ranching began in the area in the early 1800s. Some of the buildings the park uses for infrastructure purposes come from the ranch days of Sierra Vista, and the horse trails in the park reflect this heritage. This is National Park Service (NPS) property, so it is nice to see signs that restrict horses and mountain bikes but allow dogs on leash. Having dogs on trails on NPS land is a treat and a real rarity, so it is imperative to be as respectful as possible in this place. Hopefully, the inclusion of dogs can be added to other parks throughout the nation.

There are other areas to explore in this magnificent place, but you'll have to be on the lookout for horse droppings and bicyclists. Also, the trails in Point Mugu State Park are off-limits for dogs, so any trail that crosses over the boundary is not one that you can travel upon. Keep that in mind when planning your outing. The good thing about the Santa Monica National Recreation Area is that there are many areas where dogs are welcome, so you can always visit another area.

12. Mishe Mokwa Trail to Mount Allen (Sandstone Peak)

Round trip: 6 miles
Hiking time: 3 hours
High point: 3111 feet
Elevation gain: 1550 feet
Best season: Year-round
Difficulty: Moderate
Paw comfort: Dirt, sand, and rocks
Water: Creek bed dry by early spring, so bring your own
Map: USGS Triunfo Pass (does not show trails)
Contact: Santa Monica Mountains National Recreation Area (805)
    370-2301, *www.nps.gov/samo*

Getting there: Take Highway 1, the Pacific Coast Highway, north of Malibu. A little more than 1.5 miles beyond Leo Carrillo State Park turn north into the mountains on Yerba Buena Road. Stay on Yerba Buena as it winds through the Santa Monica Mountains for 6.5 miles. Turn into the large parking area on your left and start up the trail.

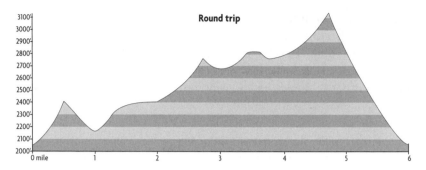

Dogs are allowed in a few areas of the Santa Monica Mountains, and the Circle X Ranch area is one of the largest. There is ample running room for dogs as long as they are leashed. Astoundingly, the area is managed by the National Park Service (NPS); it is almost unheard of for dogs to be allowed on trails operated by the NPS. Mishe Mokwa follows an unbelievable slice of the raised inland plateau section of this coastal park.

The Mishe Mokwa Trail begins by sharply climbing and meeting up with the loop split at a little over a quarter of a mile. The old fire road heads left up to Mount Allen (Sandstone Peak), whereas going straight takes you by Balanced Rock and later past Split Rock. You can take either direction, depending upon what type of hike you are looking for. If you continue forward, the trail climbs moderately up one thousand feet over a very evenly paced 4 miles; this is the more aerobic workout. If you turn left, the fire road continues sharply up to the top of Mount Allen, climbing the same 1000 feet in one mile.

For people not wanting to hike 6 miles, the trail can be turned into an end-to-end hike by ascending Mount Allen. The climb up Mount Allen makes this a short and steep 2.5-mile excursion, and an excellent elevation trainer. Either way, the trip is an enjoyable one, and most dogs should handle the trip fairly well as long as they are not entirely sedentary (6 miles is just about the right size trip for intermediately conditioned pets). The sand and dirt pathway forms an easy walkway for dogs to tread upon without roughing up their paws. Be cautious of poison oak and ticks, both of which flourish in coastal areas.

Mishe Mokwa traverses through a variety of habitats and past natural wonders in a relatively short amount of time. Balanced Rock is a cool formation that comes into view shortly after starting the hike. An enormous boulder is perched atop a tiny rock and looks as if it could totter over the edge at any moment. The trail climbs through coastal shrub and chaparral and then drops into a small canyon complete with flowing creek and mixed oak and riparian habitat. Crossing the stream brings you to Split Rock, which is a neat formation to grab the interest of small children. It looks as if an angry giant might have hit the rock with his fist and caused the enormous boulder to split in two. There is room enough to walk inside the split.

As you climb out of the creek bed and canyon, the trail begins to stretch up into the Boney Mountains. Strange volcanic formations loom above the trail as you ascend. They look like something out of *Land of the Lost* or a George Lucas film. You might expect to see a prehistoric animal or sci-fi monster lumbering toward you as you examine the strange cones and pinnacles. The geologic term for the rock is andesite breccia, although it looks an awful lot like sandstone. It has the same coloration as sand and from a distance appears to be made up of the compressed grains of rock. Up close, however, it is obvious that this is not the case and the somewhat strange geology of the area releases some of its secrets.

From here the path follows an old road that travels the ridgeline of the mountains to Inspiration Point and Sandstone Peak. The trip down to

The Inspiration Point marker highlights significant sights that can be spotted on a clear day.

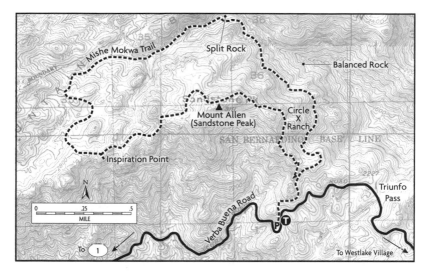

the parking area is steep, but the 6-mile loop will have been well worth the excursion. This area is also wonderful for viewing wildflowers. During peak times in the spring blossoms are abundant, but there are various blooming specimens present throughout the year.

13. Simi Peak

Round trip: 5 miles
Hiking time: 3 hours
High point: 2403 feet
Elevation gain: 1100 feet
Best season: Year-round, summers are hot
Difficulty: Moderate
Paw comfort: Dirt
Water: Bring your own
Map: USGS Thousand Oaks
Contact: Santa Monica Mountains National Recreation Area (805) 370-2301, *www.nps.gov/samo*

Getting there: Take U.S. Highway 101 north from Los Angeles for 35 miles to Westlake Village and exit on Lindero Canyon Road. Turn right and follow it for 4 miles into the residential area to the street-side parking and trailhead sign for the China Flat Trail.

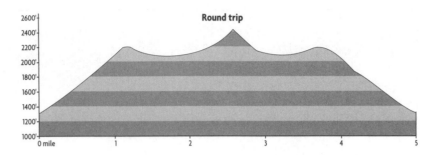

Brown and reddish volcanic rock make up the prominent cliff faces of the Simi Hills. These can be clearly seen from U.S. Highway 101 as you climb out of the valley. The resemblance to southern Utah is uncanny, and might be mentioned prominently if not for the smog and the overdevelopment of the area. It is very likely that many drivers passing through the vicinity have never even noticed the beauty surrounding them due to the pressures of modern city life. Certainly, it is hard to overlook the swarms of vehicles migrating up and down the highway when you are traveling amongst them. A quick detour off the beaten path takes you to several trailheads where you can start hiking up a canyon through chaparral-dotted slopes.

The trail to Simi Peak follows an old fire/maintenance/ranch road to the ridgeline of the Simi Hills. As you climb higher and higher, you come within a quarter-mile of the peak, but the sheer summit gradient makes it impossible to ascend vertically. Instead, the trail takes a long detour in the opposite direction and climbs to the backbone of

Early morning dew gathers on the flora of the hot, dry Simi Hills.

the range. Within a mile, the road gains 1000 feet of elevation, making this trip a serious workout. From the crest, you descend into the lovely wooded China Flat. Here, some shade provides a respite and escape from the sun, which shines prominently on the south facing slopes throughout the winter. The trail can be hot in the afternoon, and furnace like in the summer. As you walk through China Flat, turn left onto another fire road that twists and turns on its gradual climb to the top of Simi Peak.

   Simi Peak is the northernmost summit in the Santa Monica Mountains National Recreation Area. The peak is nestled above the expanding and mobile communities of the western San Fernando and Simi Valleys. Simi Peak and China Flat are located in the northern section of the Cheeseboro/Palo Comado unit, though the hike begins on land administered by Rancho Simi Recreation and Park District. The canyons are administered by the National Park Service. This area is just one of the many subdivisions of this atypical park unit. The recreation area is made up of federal, state, and local park agencies that work in conjunction with private preserves and landowners to protect the largest natural area around Los Angeles. Cheeseboro/Palo Comado is a huge parcel of undeveloped land just north of the town of Agoura Hills, and sits only minutes from busy U.S. Highway 101.

   The area was scorched in September 2005 by the 24,000-acre Topanga Fire. Many of the large and older valley oak trees made it through the fire and what burned were mostly grasses and non-native vegetation. In a few years, and after normal rainfall, the area will make a complete rebound, but at present is a great study in fire ecology. Look for abundant

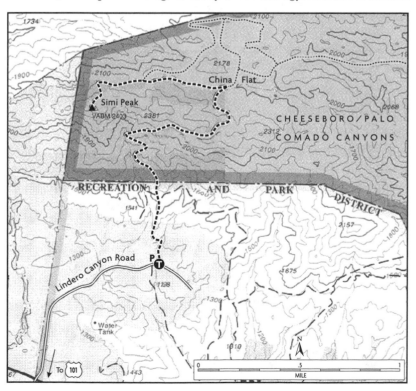

wildflowers in this area after winter rains. In the next few years, storms will provide many opportunities for the flora enthusiast. Currently, the area is a charred moonscape, and travel is restricted to trails and roads only. The restriction will most likely be lifted in the coming years, but not until the habitat has stabilized. Watch for raptors in the area. There are sizeable concentrations of nesting birds of prey.

14. Zuma Canyon Loop

Round trip: 1.85 miles
Hiking time: 1 hour
High point: 230 feet
Elevation gain: 150 feet
Best season: Year-round
Difficulty: Easy
Paw comfort: Dirt, sand, and stream crossings
Water: Zuma Canyon is seasonal, though puddles and trickles
   remain all year
Map: USGS Point Dume (does not show trails)
Contact: Santa Monica Mountains National Recreation Area (805)
   370-2301, *www.nps.gov/samo*

Getting there: Take the Pacific Coast Highway, Highway 1, north from Santa Monica through the long and wealthy coastal hamlet of Malibu toward Point Dume. One mile past Kanan/Dume Road, turn right onto Busch Drive, right again onto Rainsford Place, and left onto Bonsall Drive. (Turning directly onto Bonsall Drive off Highway 1 is dangerous due to a blind curve and the speed of traffic on Highway 1. The Park Service advises

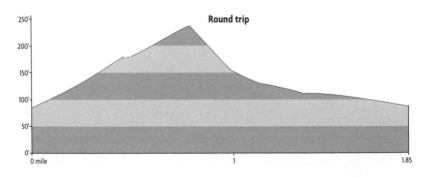

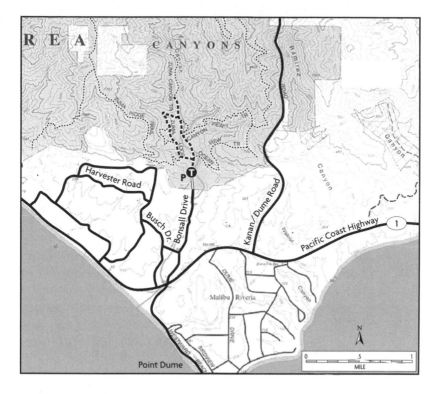

against it.) There are no national park placards directing the masses towards Zuma Canyon, so look out for the small roadway. Continue slowly down Bonsall Drive to its completion and park in the large dirt lot. The trail heads up the canyon directly from the parking area.

The creek that flows through Zuma Canyon runs year-round. In drier times it can be restricted to trickles and puddles. At the bottom of the canyon, the water is below ground. The change of seasons is ever evident here, which makes for a refreshing change from the usual amaranthine evergreen climate of Southern California. Sycamore, oak, willow, and black walnut trees line the canyon floor as it ascends towards the Castro Crest. Fall and winter can often be more colorful than the spring, with the perennial autumnal transformation of deciduous leaves and the rains that spawn forth new life in the form of wildflower blossoms. Zuma is derived from a word that means "abundance" in the Chumash language, and while the brush and foliage of the riparian woodland provide ample coverage for animals retreating at the sound of your approach, it is easy

Idyllic Zuma Creek, lined with sycamore trees, is lovely in the fall when the leaves turn colors.

to imagine the prevalence of wildlife living along the stream.

Wildlife is plentiful here, and if you arrive at the right time of day, you may spot any number of animals including coyote and bobcat. The place looks different year-round, and rain can make some areas of the canyon resemble a raging river. Arriving here just after a deluge can make for a beautiful outing, but you might get a little wet crossing the creek. Muddy trails can also be an issue; please do not make new trails if such is the case. Mud won't hurt your boots, but your boots can do damage that may take years to repair.

A variety of choices confront you upon entering Zuma Canyon. Many of the trails loop around and connect, so you can construct your own adventure depending upon the type of hike you are looking for. The Zuma Canyon Loop Trail outlined on the map takes you a hundred feet above the canyon bottom and then drops you back into a bountiful section of lush forest and stream. There you can stroll among the sycamores, rock hop, or relax and have a picnic lunch. There isn't anything stressful about this hike. On your way out, you can take the Scenic Trail, which varies only slightly in scenery from the main trail. Either way, your trip is sure to be enjoyable.

As this area is managed by the National Park Service, dogs must be on leash at all times. Please respect these rules; it is rare for dogs to be allowed on any trail in our nation's parks. The Santa Monica Mountains are the exception rather than the rule. This canyon isn't as heavily traveled as others in the recreation area. It has a much more local feel to it. Perhaps the lack of signs helps keep it more secluded, but it is possible to have this area to yourself, at least for a little while.

The more adventurous might want to take the steep Ocean View Trail nearly 1000 feet up and loop back around on the Canyon View Trail. This route has a distance of about 3 miles, but is substantially more difficult than the posted Zuma Canyon Loop Trail. For those wanting a longer hike, an all-day outing can be made using the Zuma Ridge Trail and connecting power company roads. Such a trip is very strenuous in nature and not recommended in the heat of summer.

15. Mount Hollywood

Round trip: 3 miles
Hiking time: 1.5 hours
High point: 1625 feet
Elevation gain: 650 feet
Best season: Year-round
Difficulty: Easy
Paw comfort: Dirt
Water: Bring your own
Map: USGS Burbank
Contact: Griffith Park (323) 664-6903, *www.laparks.org/dos/parks /griffithPK*

Getting there: Take U.S. Highway 101 north 2.5 miles from downtown Los Angeles, exiting onto Vermont. Head north towards the mountains.

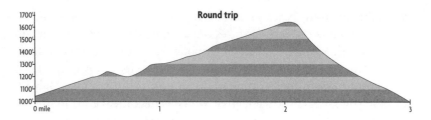

Follow Vermont until it ends. You can pick up the trail at the Griffith Park Observatory, or take Mount Hollywood Road. Mount Hollywood Road is permanently closed to vehicle traffic at the crossing with Vermont. Only foot and bicycle traffic are allowed.

Mount Hollywood is not the residence of Los Angeles' most famous landmark—that sits on top of Mount Lee. Nor is it the highest peak in Griffith Park—that title goes to Cahuenga Peak. This is simply the summit that offers the best wide-eyed views of the Hollywood sign and the Los Angeles Basin. On clear winter and spring days, the San Gabriels sparkle with snow to the north and east, while the ocean reflects glimmering sunlight to the south and west. This hike typifies all that is great about Southern California. The dream of stardom symbolized by the world's most famous sign intertwines with the natural beauty of one of the world's most heavily populated urban areas. From summit to sea, Griffith Park is the eastern terminus of the Santa Monica Mountains, and a beautiful place to recreate and get away from it all right in the middle of the city. The park belongs to the city and is not affiliated with the section of the mountain chain administered by the National Park Service. Entry is free.

The park's own website lists the region as "the largest municipal park and urban wilderness area in the United States." There are many wild stories, myths, and various legends surrounding the park and its famous sign. Griffith Park was donated by Colonel Griffith J. Griffith; his vision was to dedicate it for the recreation of the common person. Over 3000 acres were donated while he was living in 1896, with the remainder being willed to the city in 1919, along with a sizeable trust that provided for the building of the observatory and the Greek Theater. His benevolence was based upon his own good fortune and business success in the area. He bequeathed the land for the benefit of the community in which he had prospered, though many were skeptical of his generosity because of money he owed in back taxes.

Depending upon which story you read, the colonel is described either as a visionary altruist or a drunken madman. He was involved in a shooting/murder attempt on his wife at a Santa Monica hotel; she was wounded in the head, jumped down from the second story to escape, broke a leg, and lost an eye in the incident. The colonel was prosecuted and convicted of assault, although he maintained it was an attempted suicide. Purportedly, the incident came about because he believed the Catholic Church was attempting to "steal" his land, and his wife was a Catholic. While not much can top that story, rumor has it that at least one ghost haunts the park grounds to this day. One is Domingo Feliz, a murder victim from the old Los Feliz Rancho, and the other is Peg Entwhistle, an actress, who notoriously committed suicide by leaping from the top of the sign's letter H. Sightings of an historically dressed Peg have been accompanied with the scent of gardenias, her favorite perfume.

All trails in the vicinity lead to the top as long as you continue upwards. Dogs must be leashed, and most of the 53-mile trail system closes from 10:30 PM to sunrise. The Vermont entrance closes just after sunset. There are steep areas where people have cut switchbacks. Stay on the

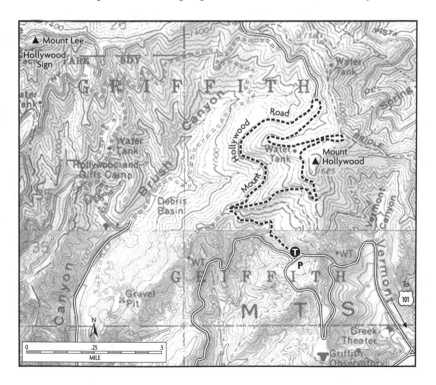

main trails or access roads; not only does this prevent erosion, but it will also make it easier on your pet. Return the way you came or make this trip into a loop. The fire hydrants in the park are numbered in case of accidents. Rangers can be reached on the park's emergency number, (323) 913-7390.

There is no hiking access to the Hollywood sign, though this fact dashes the hopes of many who visit. Urban legends state that there are helicopters, razor wire fences, hidden camera surveillance, loudspeakers that blast warnings of fines and/or imprisonment, and a host of other deterrents that ward away trespassing intruders. The reality is that there is a security system complete with motion detectors and a $283 fine with the possibility of jail time. The poignancy of the Hollywood sign being inaccessible is a stiff lesson that many who live in the city find out the hard way. Like the steep mountainsides that surround the sign, the road to stardom and fame is never easy.

Ta'Shara, Chewee, and Socs take a break atop Mount Hollywood to absorb the best view in L.A.

VASQUEZ ROCKS COUNTY PARK

16. Vasquez Rocks

Round trip: 1 mile
Hiking time: 1 hour
High point: 2600 feet
Elevation gain: 100 feet
Best season: Year-round, hot in summer
Difficulty: Easy
Paw comfort: Dirt and sandstone
Water: Bring your own
Map: USGS Agua Dulce
Contact: County of Los Angeles Parks and Recreation
(661) 268-0840, *parks.co.la.ca.us*

Getting there: From Los Angeles take Interstate 5 north for 25 miles to Highway 14 (Antelope Valley Freeway) north in Santa Clarita. Follow Highway 14 for nearly 15 miles and exit on Agua Dulce Road, turn left and follow the signs to Vasquez Rocks. Make a right turn onto Escondido Canyon Road and turn right into the entrance to the park.

Vasquez Rocks is a natural phenomena created by the San Andreas Fault. The upturned stones jut out at bizarre angles and are one of the most commonly used recognizable television and movie backdrops that you will ever see. The rocks have been employed in everything from the Austin Powers' movies to *Bonanza* to *Blazing Saddles*, but they are probably most famous for their use in the original *Star Trek* episode where Captain Kirk battled the Gorn. Remarkably, the entire episode was pretty much filmed in the parking lot. It is interesting what editing can do for a television show or movie.

The rocks will be instantly recognizable, even while you are driving up to them. The park is practically a must-see for movie buffs and for those who like to clamber along slick rocks. They can be fascinating for children and your dogs as well. It isn't recommended to take your pets to the very top; the angles can get a little steep for all but the best of rock-climbing dogs. You wouldn't want to have to carry a small pet down the steep angles, let alone a big dog; one misstep could be quite dangerous.

The most common thing to do at Vasquez Rocks is to scale the most famous and bizarre-looking angular rock, but there are numerous trails to be explored if you have the time, desire, and water. Your pets must be leashed at all times because this is a county park, and there are lots of horseback riders who frequent the trails. In the winter months the cloud formations can accent the rocks and complement them in astounding ways, while during rain and thunderstorms, the stones can also be strikingly beautiful set against the darkness.

Vasquez Rocks are named after the notorious outlaw Tiburcio Vasquez who was wanted throughout the state for murder, horse rustling, and robbery. After he and his gang committed some heinous murders and robberies in Central California, they fled to the Los Angeles area where he and his men hid out in the canyons, mountains, and valleys in and around Tejon Pass, with this rock formation being one of his favorite hideouts. From the rocks, they were able to rob stagecoaches traveling from Central California to Los Angeles. He is rumored to have hidden out all over the Angeles National Forest, especially in the area now known as Horse Flats. He was eventually captured in what is today the Hollywood Hills. He stood trial and was sentenced to death. He was hanged on March 19, 1875 in San Jose.

Despite or perhaps due to his notoriety, he was intensely popular

People scale the eerie and oft-filmed Vasquez Rocks. Be careful when climbing the slick rock.

among Mexicans and Californios. Californios were people who came from Spain or Mexico to settle in California, but who were often met with racism and discrimination. He believed that California rightly belonged to Mexico and claimed that his crimes were in part due to his desire to regain California for Mexico. Thousands of people visited his jail cell before his execution, and he was a sort of folk hero despite his horrendous crimes. He released a statement before his death explaining his actions: "A spirit of hatred and revenge took possession of me. I had numerous fights in defense of what I believed to be my rights and those of my countrymen. I believed we were unjustly deprived of the social rights that belonged to us."

His only word at the gallows was "Pronto."

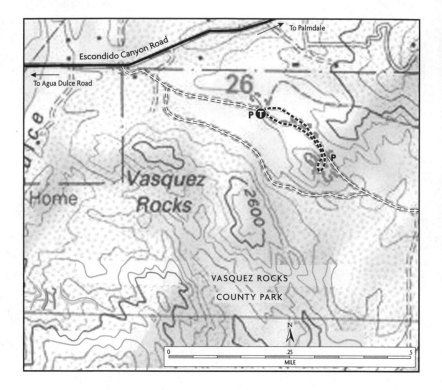

ANGELES NATIONAL FOREST— SAN GABRIEL MOUNTAINS

17. Strawberry Peak

Round trip: 6 miles
Hiking time: 3 hours
High point: 6164 feet
Elevation gain: 1600 feet
Best season: Late fall through late spring
Difficulty: Moderately difficult
Paw comfort: Dirt, gravel, and rocks
Water: Bring your own
Fees and permits: Adventure Pass required
Map: USGS Chilao Flat
Contact: Angeles National Forest (626) 574-5200, *www.fs.fed.us/r5 /angeles*

Getting there: From Pasadena, take Interstate 210 west for 5 miles to the Angeles Crest Highway (Highway 2). Follow it north for 13 miles to Red Box Junction. There is a large parking area and a ranger station on the south side of the road. Head east on the highway for less than one

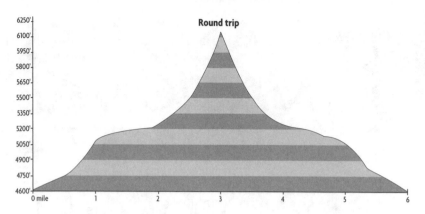

quarter of a mile and you should see the trail. A sand tower sits on the north side of the road; if you've walked past it, you've gone too far. The trailhead is not marked, but the start is an old gray dirt road that is clearly visible if you look for it.

Strawberry Peak is a fine hike, although it does get a good bit of foot traffic. At 6164 feet the peak is the tallest in this lower section of the San Gabriels. The only other 6000-foot peak in the front range is San Gabriel Peak, and therefore this is a fairly popular hike. Going on a weekday, or a day like Super Bowl Sunday, will take away the visitors and allow you and your dog to enjoy this trail to the maximum. This is a perfect winter climb, because the snow in the Angeles National Forest barely registers for long below the 6000-foot mark. Conversely, the afternoon in summertime can be scorching hot, and should not be attempted unless you are well equipped for that sort of undertaking. There are no berries to be had anywhere in the region, and the peak gets its name from its double-bump shape, which might remind you of an upside-down strawberry. Evidently in the days before easy travel into these peaks, imaginations ran wild with dreams of exotic fruits.

The view from the peak is obscured and unremarkable, but there are wonderful vistas to be had along the way, especially on the way down. The peak itself is somewhat of a disappointment and anticlimactic because you are not rewarded with a spin-around stunning view. On the other hand, there are quite a few Jeffrey pines and black oaks at the summit, which offer up the only shady relief from the sun to be had on the trip. Sign your name in the summit register and grab a quick bite to eat; chances are you'll spend more time gawking at the glorious view of Baldy from a notch about a half-mile below the summit than on the summit itself. If the day is clear, there are excellent perspectives of the urban landscape of Los Angeles; technically, you should be able to make out Dodger Stadium and the entire downtown area.

There are a few caveats, one being yuccas, that can poke you and your dog, and the other being the dry rocky climb, especially for the last mile. Also, there is a bit of scrambling involved, so if you or your pet aren't used to jumping from rock to rock, or either of you are uncomfortable with it, this is not a good hiking choice. The last mile is steep and somewhat strenuous for such a short hike, though it is a good proving ground for your pooch. If he can make this trail without

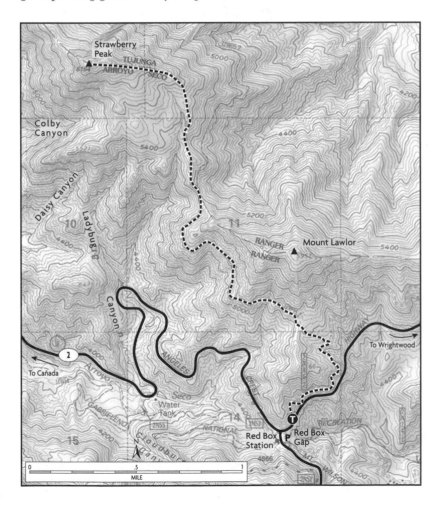

discomfort, then he is probably ready for longer outings. This was the first peak my dogs Chewee and Socrates ever bagged, and it wore them out. Their pads were badly cut, and I felt terrible for them afterwards. This is the hike that built my resolve to make them mountain-worthy canines. Remember that a dog can be conditioned easily if you take him for short walks of thirty minutes a day.

The front range of the Angeles National Forest is dry, gritty, and desert-like. There is not much in the way of shade, and there is very little water on this side. Make sure you pack extra water for your pets, and if you do decide to undertake this one on a Saturday, your pet should be leashed. The path itself follows the highway for a little more than half a mile. Stay on the old road until it intersects with an unmarked trail heading north, turn left and continue all the way to the saddle between Mount Lawlor and Strawberry Peak. From here you follow the ridgeline to the summit.

Mount San Antonio peeks through the clouds from the summit of Strawberry Peak.

The path is well worn and obvious, but be sure to keep a sharp eye on the yuccas as you climb.

The shrubbery in this area is notoriously scratchy and impossible to bushwhack through. This part of Southern California led John Muir to proclaim that the San Gabriel Mountains are "more rigidly inaccessible in the ordinary meaning of the word than any other that I ever attempted to penetrate." You'll soon see why, should you take a misstep off the trail and into the brambles and thorns that make up the scenery and vegetation. Indeed, it is a veritable briar patch filled with plants that cut, poke, and scar. You'll quickly gain an admiration for the Native Americans and trailblazers of this region who cut the paths and trails to these peaks and meadows. A definite plus is that this trail will also help you to train your dog to stay on the course and not meander off of it, because the brush is terribly unforgiving.

Attempting this peak from the Colby Canyon side with dogs is entirely inadvisable; there are some difficult Class 3 and 4 sections that will have your dog whimpering, especially on the way down. A day hike turned into a mountain rescue or a hitch-hike along the forest highway could quickly turn into a nightmare. There is no way to make a loop of the two hikes other than having a car shuttle waiting.

18. Mount Hillyer

Round trip: 2.75 miles
Hiking time: 1.5 hours
High point: 6162 feet
Elevation gain: 550 feet
Best season: Year-round
Difficulty: Easy
Paw comfort: Dirt and rock
Water: None, bring your own
Fees and permits: Adventure Pass required
Map: USGS Chilao Flat
Contact: Angeles National Forest (626) 574-5200, *www.fs.fed.us/r5 /angeles*

Getting there: Take Highway 2 (Angeles Crest Highway) north from La Cañada for 28.5 miles. Turn left at the Santa Clara Divide Road. The

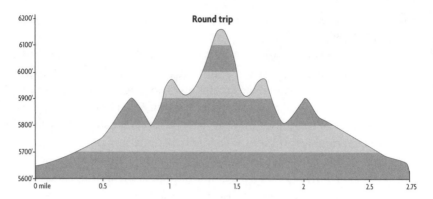

Round trip

paved and dirt road is a little over 2 miles past the visitor center at Chilao. In just under 2.5 miles turn left on the road signed for Horse Flats Campground. At the end of the loop, there is a trailhead sign and parking area.

Mount Hillyer is a short little trip that anyone can accomplish. There is a bit of elevation gain, but it is negligible, and this is really just a short walk up a hill. Surprisingly, the peak isn't named because it is "hillier"; it gets its appellation from Mary Hillyer, a clerk for the forest supervisor's office in the early days of the Forest Service. There isn't much in the way of a summit, but the scenery is nice and picturesque. There are

The marine layer, haze, and smog combine to give the sunsets from Mount Hillyer an ethereal quality.

giant boulders everywhere, some suitable for climbing. You might even spot climbers bouldering in this area.

This is a prize area for mountain biking in the Angeles National Forest, and it is used frequently for such pursuits. So much so, that the trail is rutted in more than just a few spots. The ruts can be easily avoided, and do not make hiking on the trail a hassle—just be certain you are careful and watch your footing. Most mountain bikers are courteous and pay attention for people. If your dog isn't under the strictest voice command, it might be a wise idea to leash your pet. Surprise encounters with bikes can lead to unpleasant situations for you, your dog, and bicyclists.

Hillyer is one of those places where the sunsets can be magical. As the evening begins to cool, the shadows dance and play. Perch yourself on any of the large boulders that rest on the flattened top of the summit plateau and look toward the sun as it wanes into the gloaming. Views open up into Alder and Tujunga Canyons, with Pacifico, Granite, and Roundtop Mountains hovering large in the north and west. The sharp contrast between canyon and summit ridge creates a beautiful interplay between the light, smoke, and haze that dazzles. The short hike out can easily be done in the dark when warm summer nights last into late evening hours. Be sure to bring a flashlight in case you have trouble finding the trail.

The trail can be enjoyed at any time of the day. There is enough forest cover to provide decent shade even on the hottest of days, and the boulders are fetching enough that your dog will have plenty to sniff and mark, while you will invariably enjoy the surroundings. Take your time and make the event into a pleasurable stroll. Bring the family and let them enjoy the great outdoors. The mesa can be a wonderful place

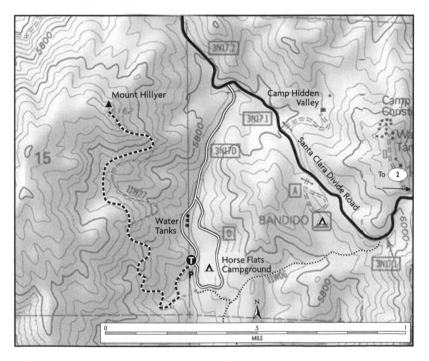

to bring a picnic basket and spend an afternoon throwing the ball and running with the pets.

19. Waterman Mountain

Round trip: 4.5 miles
Hiking time: 2.5 hours
High point: 8038 feet
Elevation gain: 1400 feet
Best Hiking time: Year round, snow in winter
Difficulty: Moderate
Paw comfort: Dirt and duff
Water: Streams are dry by early summer most years
Fees and permits: Adventure Pass required
Map: USGS Waterman Mountain
Contact: Angeles National Forest (626) 574-5200, *www.fs.fed.us/r5 /angeles*

Getting there: From the 210 split in La Cañada, take the Angeles Crest Highway (2) east for 34 miles just past the Waterman ski lift. Buckhorn Campground is too far. If you see it, you need to turn around. There are a lot of fire roads and pullouts along this section of the highway, so the trail is not the easiest to find. There are many places that look like they might be a trailhead, and there is no designated parking for the trail itself. There is a big rounded shoulder off the westbound lane, and this is the parking area. Park and cross the highway. There is a trail sign for the Waterman Trail. You can also start up forest road 3N03. The road meets the trail a little ways down.

This is a very pleasant hike. The area is wonderfully wooded and streams guard the lower reaches of the trail. According to the story of these mountains, this peak was originally named Lady Waterman's Peak. The Watermans, along with Commodore Perry Switzer, crossed the San Gabriels from Pasadena to Antelope Valley and back again during three weeks in May of 1889. Supposedly, Lady Waterman built a cairn on top of the peak, and the three intrepid trailblazers claimed and named the

Opposite: Mount Baldy and the old 39 on the horizon

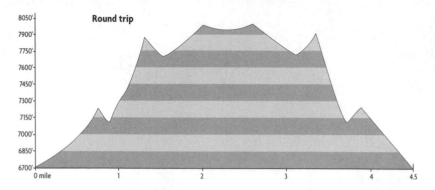

summit after her. No one else ever acknowledged or included Lady in the name, even though Robert Waterman tried until his death to have Lady kept as the moniker of the mountain. The name only passes to us through tales of old.

This mountain also holds a bit of unfortunate recent history. In 1964, Angeles Forest Supervisor Simeri Jarvi died of a heart attack while heading up this trail. The beloved ranger was memorialized with a vista near Islip Saddle that bears his name complete with plaque, nature trail, and parking area.

The trail itself skirts and enters the San Gabriel Wilderness as it quickly ascends away from the highway. The first mile gently climbs at a very steady pace and gains some elevation, but the majority of the altitude is to be had in the next mile, while the top is a large flat plateau. The trail is very well maintained until you reach the summit area. It disappears into a confusing mix of possibilities. At this point, you should look for the tallest rocks to the south in the broad expanse around you, and that is the peak. Although the actual high point of 8038' is a bit anticlimactic, there is a shelf 150 feet below to the south that affords incredible views of the San Gabriel Wilderness, including Twin Peaks, Bear Creek and Devils Canyon, not to mention the entire high country. The old 39 cuts a line across the horizon as you gaze at Islip, all three Hawkins, Baden-Powell, Baldy, Pine, Dawson, Burnham, the Three Tees, Cucamonga and Ontario Peak. If the day is clear, you can even gape all the way to San Jacinto, but even without this far crest the vista is awesome to say the least.

The trail shouldn't do any damage to your pet's paws, unless they've spent every waking minute on plush carpeting. It's fairly short, not incredibly rocky, at least some of the way is soft and duff covered. Much of the trail is shaded; the only caveat is to make sure to bring water. The later in the season, the less water there will be, and often there will not be any. Even when there is water, it is at the beginning of the trail, so as you climb and drink, give your dogs a drink, too. If a peak can be described as a beginner's hike, then this is it: less than five miles, fourteen hundred feet in elevation gain—what else could a hiker ask for? Take your pets on this one and see how they respond.

Since there is no true assigned parking for this hike, it is a little less traveled than some of the other peaks in the forest. During the week, you probably won't see anyone else, but on the weekends you can definitely expect to see other hikers, and probably some people from the campground, since this is a relatively easy peak to bag and close to camp. Still, you shouldn't have to worry about too many people on this one, and it is a good place to let the dogs roam free.

Look for enormous Jeffrey and ponderosa pine, along with incense cedar trees all along the route. There are fantastic granite boulder outcroppings almost the entire trip, and the area has a very Sierra-esque feel to it, unlike most places in the Angeles. The trail affords views the entire way, and this is a trip you won't regret taking. Although there are roads and ski lifts close by, you'll feel a long ways away from the city. This is a refreshing short half-day hike that can have you back in time to watch the afternoon football game, or take a night on the town.

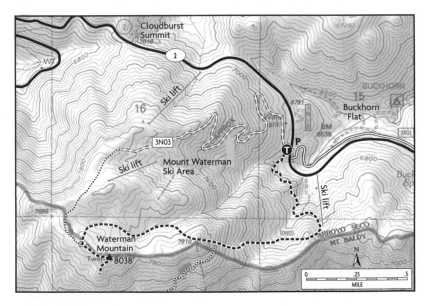

20. Devils Punchbowl

Round trip: 1.2 mile
Hiking time: 1 hour
High point: 4800 feet
Elevation gain: 300 feet
Best season: October to late spring
Difficulty: Easy
Paw comfort: Rocks and dirt
Water: Bring your own
Map: USGS Valyermo
Contact: Devils Punchbowl Natural Area (661) 944-2743,
    www.devils-punchbowl.com

Getting there: From Highway 14 in Palmdale take the Pearblossom Highway (138) east. Turn right onto Longview Road (N6) and follow the signs to the county park. This includes a left turn onto Tumbleweed Road, which becomes Punchbowl Road.

Devils Punchbowl is a remarkable piece of organic handiwork. Mother Nature did herself proud in the production of this area. The San Andreas Fault meets the Pinyon and Punchbowl Faults, and the resulting uplift has not only produced the Pleasant View Ridge and the San Gabriel Mountains to the south, but a striking sandstone formation where the rocks thrust out of the earth at bizarre angles. Over millennia, runoff water from the surrounding high peaks has exposed the sheer faces of the giant rock structures.

The area surrounding the county park is quite fascinating. It exists in a transition zone between the Mojave Desert, or High Desert as it

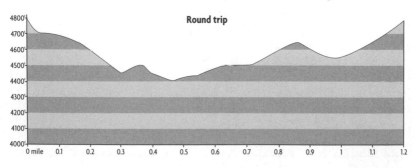

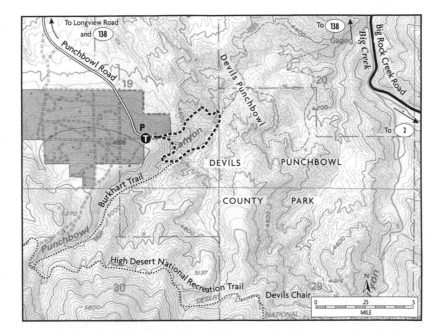

is known to residents and Southern Californians, and the San Gabriel Mountains, the imposing tops of which soar some 5000 feet overhead less than 4 miles away as the hawk flies. The northern slope of the San Gabriels is incredibly sharp and rugged. A dramatic incline provides a stirring backdrop for the arresting aesthetic of the natural outcroppings of this earthquake prone landscape. The trail and starting point are high enough to provide vistas north into the vastness of the Mojave Desert and south into the yellow pines of the Angeles National Forest.

Dogs must be on a leash, due to the fact that this is a small mile-long loop. Most nature trails require leashes due to frequent visitation and small children. The trail is short and not at all strenuous; anyone and any dog can handle the difficulty and the mileage.

The Devils Punchbowl shares features with other nearby seismic architecture, such as Mormon and Vasquez Rocks. The Mormon Rocks, located just off Interstate 15 in the Cajon Pass region, are a comparative twin formation to the Punchbowl. Both are made of relatively young geologic rocks and the result of geologically recent processes and activity. The sandstone was formed in each region between the late Miocene/early Pliocene epochs. These formations are equally striking in appearance. The Punchbowl, however, is significantly larger, less developed, more

The rock formations of the Devils Punchbowl jut out at extreme angles.

picturesque, and away from the traffic and noise of one of California's busiest mountain passes. Vasquez Rocks are the result of much older processes, but the skyward protrusions resemble the tectonic counterpart regions that lay thirty and fifty miles farther east along California's main fault line.

The plant community around the Punchbowl is made up of shrubs such as manzanita, yucca, sage and other high-desert plants. The mountain flora communities that reside high above this desert wonderland can be seen from the trail, but not close up unless you are ready to do some climbing. Scattered juniper and pinyon pines can be found along the trail as this is the beginning of the first transitional climactic zone heading up into the mountains. The seasonal stream that dries up in the blistering summer heat can be a winter or spring treat, depending on rainfall. Nice cascades and icefalls stick around until the temperature begins to heat up. When the mercury is just right, the atmosphere in this remote desert park is more than pleasant; it is enchanting.

21. Devils Chair

Round trip: 5.5 miles
Hiking time: 3 hours
High point: 5050 feet
Elevation gain: 1600 feet
Best season: October through late spring
Difficulty: Moderate
Paw comfort: Dirt and rock
Water: South Fork of Big Rock Creek and Holcomb Creek (not reliable)
Fees and permits: Adventure Pass required
Map: USGS Valerymo
Contact: Devils Punchbowl Natural Area (661) 944-2743, *www
.devils-punchbowl.com* or Angeles National Forest (626) 574-5200,
www.fs.fed.us/r5/angeles

Getting there: From Cajon Junction take Pearblossom Highway (138)
for nearly 30 miles west from Interstate 15 past the town of Llano. Just
before the tiny burg of Pearblossom, turn left onto Longview Road. Make
another left onto W Avenue (there's a sign for Valerymo Road). W Avenue
will veer right and become Valerymo Road. Follow for nearly 7 miles until
you see the sign for Big Rock Creek Road. Turn right and follow for 2.25
miles to the signed turnoff for South Fork Campground. Turn right and
follow it to its end. If you are traveling east from L.A., take Highway 14
to just after Pearblossom, make a right onto Longview Road and follow
the above directions. The High Desert National Recreation Trail will take
you into Devils Punchbowl County Park, a Los Angeles County park.

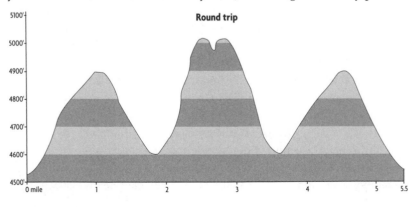

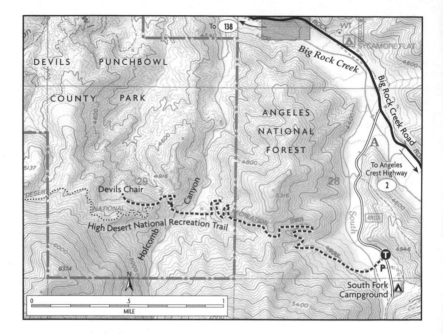

This is a magical yet secluded area of the Angeles National Forest. Chances are you and your dogs might be the only civilized life on the trail, even on weekends. The main reason for seclusion is that this is the backside of the forest, and coming from L.A., you have to travel pretty far around to reach it. Even from San Bernardino, this trip is out of the way. If there is water in the creek and people staying in the campgrounds, you can almost lay odds that they are fishermen and not hikers. Perhaps the greatest reason this is a seldom traveled route is that it is primarily a winter hike; situated at 4500 feet where the mighty Mojave Desert meets oak and pine means that this area can cook any time of year. Needless to say, coming here in summer and expecting free flowing water and cool temps would be the very definition of insanity. Even in March, temperatures can be well above 80 degrees, so check the weather before setting out, and if it is hot, bring extra water for you and your dogs.

As you start the hike, you'll boulder-hop across the creek and begin a 500-foot ascent. Fantastic views await you at the top, and then you quickly descend back to your starting elevation on the way into Holcomb Canyon. When the water is flowing, this is a lovely shaded arbor. It is also a prime water and rest stop for the way back. The next quarter mile is an incredibly steep climb to the Devils Chair; you'll gain nearly 600 feet. The chair itself is a cliff that falls away on three sides, and is sheltered from disaster by the iron bars that have been erected to keep those who don't know any better away from the slick and steep drop-offs. The guardrails extend for a good way onto the chair and do not ruin the view or picture opportunities, although they are particularly ugly and out of place in the forest. From atop the fiendish throne, you'll oversee the high desert and the Punchbowl. If you're feeling impish and your dogs are game, there's no telling how long your particular reign will last.

The High Desert National Recreation Trail will take you through several different ecosystems. The entire walk takes place in a transitional desert to forest environment. One minute you'll traverse next to pointy yucca and other desert shrubs; a short climb later you'll be among pinyon and juniper trees. In the watery areas you'll even spot ponderosa pines among the oaks. The trail itself is mostly dirt, well marked, and well maintained. There are a few dicey spots that may make those fearful of heights wish they had have stayed in bed, but these are short and infrequent. This

Socrates on the trail with confidence; his upright tail slightly curled behind his back shows that he knows what he is doing and is happy.

one should be easy on your dog's paws; just be wary of the spiky desert plants on the lower parts of the path.

The Devils Punchbowl is a bizarre formation caused by the San Andreas Fault. Exposed slabs of sandstone and slate jut out of the ground at wicked angles. Perhaps the combination of heat and the bizarre look of the place led some early settler to designate this wondrous area with its current demonic moniker. You might enjoy this one enough to return with friends. Make sure they bring their pooches as well.

22. Mount Williamson

Round trip: 5 miles
Hiking time: 2.5 hours
High point: 8248 feet
Elevation gain: 1600 feet
Best season: Year-round (Angeles Crest Highway is closed in winter at Islip Saddle)
Difficulty: Moderate
Paw comfort: Rocky dirt
Water: Bring your own
Fees and permits: Adventure Pass required
Map: USGS Crystal Lake
Contact: Angeles National Forest (626) 574-5200, *www.fs.fed.us/r5 /angeles*

Getting there: Take Highway 2 (Angeles Crest Highway) north from La Cañada and follow it for 39.5 miles to Islip Saddle. Parking is on the north side of the roadway. Head north on the Pacific Crest Trail (PCT) at the front end of the parking area.

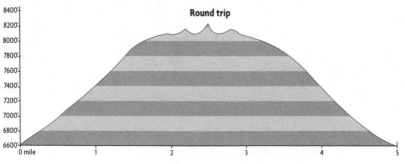

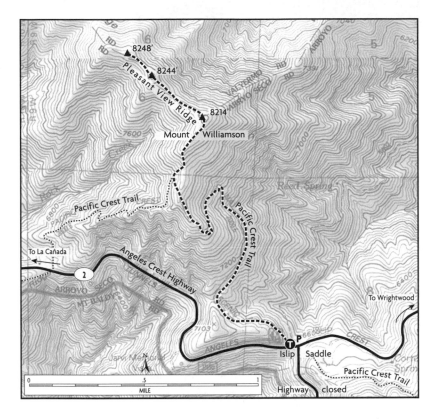

Mount Williamson is the northern complement to Mount Islip (see next hike). In many regards the two hikes are almost identical. The distance, elevation gain, and even summit elevation are virtually the same. One peak is on the south side of the Angeles Crest, and the other on the north. Truly, these twin trails seemingly lead to twin peaks. Statistics and data are where the comparison begins, but these are also where it ends. Williamson and Islip are about as different as two mountains in the same area can be.

The trail up Williamson is mostly unshaded through chaparral, with sparse covering from lodgepole pines. The south-facing climb is hot and arid, as is the general rule with south-facing slopes in the transverse ranges. What is unusual about it is how much more rocky the slope is. Certainly, many mountains in the back range of the San Gabriels are rocky. The trails are lined with granite chips in spots on most hikes, but this trail is almost entirely made up of rocky ground cover. Islip, in contrast, is relatively dusty and duff covered. This should be taken into

With Mount Islip and the Angeles Crest Highway in the background, Cameron makes his way up to the top of Mount Williamson.

consideration before taking a pet up Williamson. Islip is the better choice for beginners; even though both trips are approximately the same, this trail will be more than rough on your pet's paws. Even though the distance is fairly short, the wear and tear is much greater here.

Another difference between Williamson and Islip is the summit area. Islip is well defined and comes to a nice point that affords full 360-degree views. The apex is distinct and hovers above the remains of an old lookout cabin and base supports. When you reach the top of Mount Williamson, you won't be sure which bump is the actual peak. The topo shows the third bump as the high point, but the second notch seems higher when you are on top. It is really difficult to tell, however, and climbing from one protrusion to the next sets up a grass-is-greener situation that would confuse even Abbot and Costello.

Pleasant View Ridge continues from the summit bumps all the way beyond Will Thrall Peak and Pallett Mountain into the hills above the high desert community of Little Rock. The farther north you continue, the more parched the trail becomes. The transition from lush pine forest to Mojave Desert is readily apparent. These mountains are a remarkable study in contrasts. In fact, the disparity between the two would probably make for a good ecology or environmental studies doctoral thesis.

Mount Williamson is worth a look, and the trail is steady and even. It only gets steep as you veer off the PCT and head up the easily seen path to the summit ridge, and then only for a short while. There is a nice broad area for a picnic that includes incredible views of the high desert and Cajon Pass. A look back at the Angeles Crest Highway and the highest summits in the Angeles National Forest is awe-inspiring. The vista may motivate you to further explore the wonderful ridge that leads from Islip to Mount Baden-Powell, a captivating and beautiful section of the PCT that gets less usage than many areas along the trail.

The main advantage of this trail over the one up Mount Islip is the smaller proportion of people that climb Williamson. On any given summer day, there will be numerous people headed for Islip. Chances are that even on weekends, hikers visiting the top of Williamson will be minimal to nil. If isolation, desert views, and neverending summit ridges are what you are looking for, Mount Williamson has it all.

23. Mount Islip

Round trip: 5.5 miles
Hiking time: 2.5 hours
High point: 8250 feet
Elevation gain: 1600 feet
Best season: Year-round (Angeles Crest Highway is usually closed in winter at Islip Saddle)
Difficulty: Moderate
Paw comfort: Dirt and rocky dirt
Water: Bring your own
Fees and permits: Adventure Pass required
Map: USGS Crystal Lake
Contact: Angeles National Forest (626) 574-5200, *www.fs.fed.us/r5 /angeles*

Getting there: From Interstate 210 in La Cañada take Highway 2 (Angeles Crest Highway) north into the Angeles National Forest. Follow it through

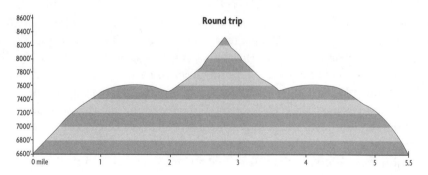

the forest for 39.5 miles to the Islip Trailhead. Often, after winter storms and well into spring, the highway will be closed at Islip Saddle. There is a large turnout, and parking on the north side with signs marking the Pacific Crest Trail (PCT). Walk across the highway to the clearly visible switchbacks that lead up the mountain to the south.

Mount Islip, pronounced "I-slip," is a wonderful destination for people who want to get to the top of a major peak but don't want to spend an entire day of hiking to get there. Islip sits above 8000 feet and is the stout eastern stalwart in the back range of the Angeles National Forest. The mountain gets its name from George Islip, an early homesteader who made his way in the San Gabriels. He cleared earlier Indian paths into trails and also prospected and explored the area of San Gabriel Canyon. It is believed that he spent a good amount of time around and atop the summit that shares his name.

The trail's first mile is the most difficult as it ascends through chaparral up into shady forest. The area is filled with enormous Jeffrey and sugar pines. You follow the PCT toward Mexico as it switchbacks across old fire roads and into Little Jimmy Campground. Early in the twentieth century, the campground was frequented by one of America's pioneers in cartooning, Jimmy Swinnerton. He created many characters for King Features Syndication starting at the young age of sixteen, and was featured extensively in William Randolph Hearst's newspapers. He moved to New York when his illustrations became highly successful, working not only on strips, but opinion comics and magazine cartoons. Some consider Swinnerton to be the "father" of comics; at the very least he was one of the medium's earliest innovators.

Swinnerton moved back to the West to escape chronic tuberculosis in his thirties. At the site of the present day campground, he painted the character of Little Jimmy on a tree with a sign that said Little Jimmy Camp; the name stuck and was printed on USGS maps by the year 1920. He was not expected to live beyond a month, but he lived to be nearly 100 years old, retorting to a friend that he had forgotten to die. In the early twentieth century, his presence was commonplace in the camp, where he routinely drew cartoons for the campers and hikers.

Today, Little Jimmy is a favorite place to camp for Boy Scouts, thru-hikers, and people out for a weekend getaway. The camp is also a favorite of black bears, who frequent the area. In the past couple of years there have been conflicts between bears and campers when humans do not adequately store their food. A highly publicized incident happened in 2003 when a camper left his full pack unattended, despite the kiosk that warned of recent bear activity in the campground. The bear knocked the man down and was subsequently killed for its aggressive behavior. Sadly, humans are to blame for socializing bears improperly and introducing human food into their diets by improper storage of food and disposal of waste. If care is not taken, bear altercations will become more and more frequent.

As of now there are no bear lockers at Little Jimmy, so if you do decide to camp, make sure you protect the bears and yourself. Hanging food is not the best way to keep it out of a bear's paws; in fact it is rather ineffective. The best method is to bring along a bear canister. While it has been reported that bear populations in California are growing, the

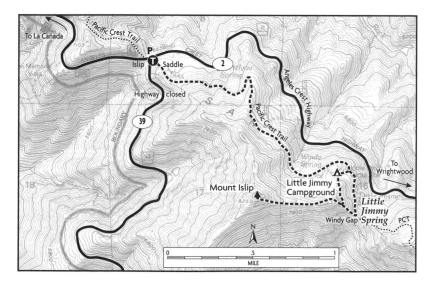

Adam moves along the Pacific Crest Trail (PCT) near Mount Islip.

forests are increasingly under more and more pressure, and bear habitat is shrinking.

From Little Jimmy Campground, there are two options for going up Mount Islip and either is fine. You can continue along the PCT to Windy Gap, where a plastic marker will direct you to make a right onto the peak trail. The other way is to follow the old trail through the campground and up. Both trails meet up in about a half-mile, but the small loop does create a little variety in the hike.

An old stone shelter still stands on the peak. There used to be a fire lookout atop the mountain in the days when people were paid to watch and protect the natural heritage of all Americans. The lookout was abandoned in favor of a better spot on top of South Mount Hawkins. The stone relic is a neat reminder of the past, and the view from the top is spectacular. The peak is rather sharp; on clear days the vista into the high desert is awe-inspiring, and the view back into L.A. can be breathtaking. The tiniest tip-top of Mount Baldy is barely visible just above the Pacific

Crest and when snow-covered, it resembles a tasty bowl of ice cream. Return the way you came or make this a backpacking adventure.

The trail is short enough and not so rocky that most dogs should have little or no trouble summiting, although any trail can tear a dog's pads if they are not conditioned enough. As always, be watchful when hiking with pets.

24. Mount Baden-Powell

Round trip: 9 miles
Hiking time: 5 hours
High point: 9399 feet
Elevation gain: 2800 feet
Best season: Late spring through late fall
Difficulty: Difficult
Paw comfort: Dirt and rocky dirt
Water: Bring your own
Fees and permits: Adventure Pass required
Map: USGS Crystal Lake
Contact: Angeles National Forest (626) 574-5200, *www.fs.fed.us/r5 /angeles*

Getting there: From Interstate 210 in La Cañada, take Highway 2 (Angeles Crest Highway) north into the Angeles National Forest. Follow it through the forest for 39.5 miles to Islip Saddle. Continue 5.5 miles east of Islip Saddle on Highway 2 to Dawson Saddle. The Angeles Crest Highway is usually closed winter through spring east of Islip Saddle, so for a portion of the year this trailhead is unreachable. If you are coming in from the east, Dawson Saddle is a little more than 8.5 miles beyond Vincent Gap.

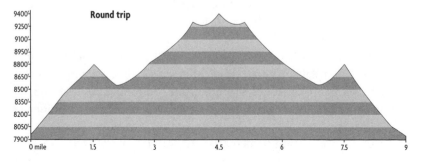

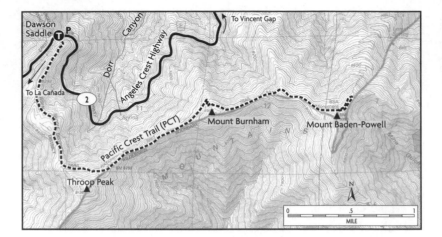

The Angeles Crest Highway is also frequently closed until spring on this side of the forest at Vincent Gap. At Dawson Saddle, there is unmarked turnout parking on either side of the highway. A fire department shed sits on the north side of the road. Do not park in this lot.

This is Angeles National Forest high country, above the smog, and nearly above everything else in Southern California. You'll start this trek at Dawson Saddle, which is the high point on the roadway topping out at 7900 feet. There are a couple of trailheads here, but both meet up at the top of the ridge a short distance in front of you. One is newer and the other is more obscure and thus harder to find. If you are not used to elevation, you might feel its effects as you tromp directly upwards from the outset of the hike. You'll climb 1000 feet in the first 1.5 miles, but the trail is gradual and well graded; once you set a pace, the climb is steady and relatively easy going. Dawson Saddle Trail is nicely forested with stands of Jeffrey and lodgepole pine, which shade the sun through mid-morning. This is a pleasant bonus to diffuse the effects of heat and sweat as you ascend. An early start is ideal to enjoy the crisp and invigorating mountain air.

At the junction with the Pacific Crest Trail (PCT), turn left and follow it to Mount Baden-Powell. From there the trail mostly follows the ridgeline with considerably less shade. You can follow the trail and go around Mount Burnham or opt to go over it via a faint mountaineer's path. You can also make a side jaunt from the junction to Throop Peak, pronounced "troop" and named after the founder of Caltech.

Though this track is well traveled, it is less frequented than some of the more popular paths in the forest. Even this section of the PCT is visited less often than other parts of the trail. The fashionable and shorter but much more crowded way to climb Mount Baden-Powell is from Vincent Gap with its many switchbacks. It boggles the imagination as to why this slice of forest is so infrequently used. It is a blissful parade of gorgeous vistas. You can take in the high slopes of Mount Baldy and the simmering desert of the Mojave; all along the way you will be afforded 360-degree views that are nearly unmatched in any other part of the Angeles National Forest. The solitude is wonderful in and of itself. It also affords a perfect opportunity to give your dogs some running room. This is an ideal place to allow your pets to travel off leash; there is sniffing and sprinting area aplenty atop the ridge.

Taking pictures of and watching dogs as they scuttle along the mountaintops is pure pleasure. They seem to enjoy the openness and the spirit of freedom that this environment lets loose within them. The trail ahead is clearly visible for great distances, so with this in mind your dogs can have greater latitude to run the trail.

The peak of Mount Baden-Powell is marked with a concrete and iron

Chewee enjoys the ridge-top breeze along the trail near Mount Baden-Powell.

obelisk to honor Lord Baden-Powell, founder of the Boy Scouts. The summit itself is broad and open. Here you can take a well-deserved rest under a limber pine. These trees are hardy stalwarts that only grow above 9000 feet in Southern California. They prefer dry windy slopes and cling to the rocky soil. You can enjoy this gnarled lifeform, take in the vistas, and return the way you came.

25. Big Horn Mine

Round trip: 3.5 miles
Hiking time: 2.5 hours
High point: 6850 feet
Elevation gain: 850 feet
Best season: Year-round (Angeles Highway is sometimes closed before Vincent Gap in both directions during winter)
Difficulty: Moderately easy
Paw comfort: Rocks and dirt
Water: Water seeps from the mines, but you might want to bring your own
Fees and permits: Adventure Pass required
Map: USGS Mount San Antonio; USGS Crystal Lake
Contact: Angeles National Forest (626) 574-5200, *www.fs.fed.us/r5 /angeles*

Getting there: Take Highway 2 (Angeles Crest Highway) from Los Angeles for 51 miles to unmarked Vincent Gap, or from the east, go 8 miles west of Wrightwood where the pullout on the south of the highway is marked. There is an incredibly large parking area on both sides of the highway. Park in either one and head to the south side of the road.

The trail is an unsigned wagon road to the left and below the path for Mount Baden-Powell/PCT. It is easy to find—just look for the "road closed" sign. This is the old mine road that used to convey wagons loaded with ore and dreams of the miners of yore. The path follows the wagon-carved road the entire way to the mine, so the trail is especially easy to follow and well maintained. It is a bit rocky, but as long as your dogs are relatively conditioned, this short trail should be no big deal. The 8-mile round trip up the PCT to Mount Baden-Powell is

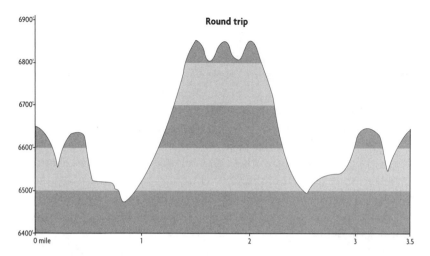

also dog friendly, but you will see quite a few more humans traveling up the many switchbacks to the summit. Instead, take the route to the mine, which is considerably less frequented, although it too sees its fair share of people.

This is a fun family hike; watch your small children on some of the loose spots, but older kids and teens are usually more dexterous than us old folks anyway. There are lots of historical leftovers, so keep your eyes peeled, and you might spot some cabins and traces of settlements that not everyone gets a chance to investigate.

There are a few mines (gated off) along the way, and the roadway is severely washed out in places, so you will need to watch your footing at these drop offs. There is a little bit of water seeping out of one of the mines, and if you hit this area at the right time of year there may be trickles of water coming down the mountain side, but generally it might be a good idea to bring your own water for your pets. I wouldn't trust water that percolates out of mines due to the historical nature of con-taminants and pollutants, such as mercury, that also ooze from mines. Do not count on water from other sources, but this trail is so short that there is no reason to necessitate extra water. The mines that are blocked off are closed for a wealth of reasons; looking inside, you can see the se-verely rotted timbers and an entrance that is sunken into the mountain, totally covered in water.

The views from this hike are spectacular. You can see Vincent Canyon and Mine Gulch and along the entire Pine Mountain ridgeline all the way up to the San Antonio massif. Half of the hike is shaded and wooded through a mixed pine and oak forest, and the other half is exposed on the side of the mountain with lots of desert plants, chaparral and yucca. The first view of the old stamp mill is quite spectacular, and on the approach it looks nearly pristine. However, upon closer inspection, the graffiti is abundant, but the ruins are still standing; the workings themselves look quite wonderful, albeit in an increased state of disarray. The mines are explorable; there are several miles of tunnels and at least six levels; the mine is vast and quite large. The entrances are very wet and it isn't advisable to enter any mineshaft with dogs. If you are not a trained spelunker, stray no further than the entrance. There are many hazards in any mine from gas pockets to hanging timbers and rusty nails, so if you do decide to enter, use caution and bring a headlamp. Please leave your dogs at home.

The stamp mill is a good shady place for a picnic lunch or simply to bask in the view. In the late spring and early summer, the snow pack

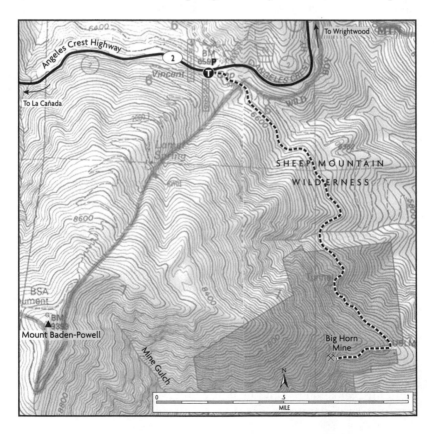

Remnants of the old mine at Big Horn are extensive. Be careful around old mine equipment and shafts, and be especially mindful of dogs and children.

glistens atop Baldy, Pine and Dawson; it dwindles as the summer progresses, but sitting in the heart of the San Gabriels, you can imagine what life must have been like for the mountain men who first worked this area through sun, snow, wind, and rain. A bedroll, a mule, and a lonely view of the open smogless sky are a long way from hydration systems, Gore-Tex and neoprene, not to mention the modern highway that snakes its way along the old trail that once meant an adventurous journey through foothills and mountain alike. No matter how you look at it, the lives of these people must have been difficult, lonely and backbreaking. Toiling for minerals in these rough mountains with dreams of striking it rich must have made for many broken lives. How many dreams died in these highlands with nothing but bleached bones as reminders of the souls who believed in them?

Remoter still are the Gabrielinos, Cahuillas, and Serranos who eked out a living in these unforgiving Southern California desert peaks and valleys, subsisting on edible plants, berries, and roots, hunting game that is largely nonexistent in our time. To enter this place is to cross the threshold of another era; a bygone time when campfire stories and horse trails connected these mountains, a time before conservation was needed to keep and preserve historical structures such as these. Please tread lightly here, and do not remove any objects you find. Not only is it akin to vandalism, it is illegal.

With your help, we can keep this building and the other edifices of past human ingenuity around for many generations to come. Unfortunately, there is always some trash along this trail because of the easy access. I always pick up what I can, please try and do the same. Do your part to protect this trail and the historical structures along it. This land is beautiful, even when stark; it is our heritage. We have a responsibility to preserve it for those who will come after us.

26. Mount Baldy—Manker Flats Loop

Round trip: 11.6 miles
Hiking time: 8 hours
High point: 10,084 feet
Elevation gain: 4000 feet
Best season: Late spring to late fall
Difficulty: Very difficult
Paw comfort: Very rocky
Water: San Antonio Creek
Fees and permits: Adventure Pass required
Map: USGS Mount San Antonio; USGS Telegraph Peak
Contact: Angeles National Forest, Mount Baldy Visitor Center
(909) 982-2829, *www.fs.fed.us/r5/angeles*

Getting there: From Highway 60, Interstate 10, or Interstate 210, take the Mountain Avenue exit in Chino, Montclair, or Upland respectively. Follow it north to its conclusion where it merges left with Euclid Avenue. Turn right onto Mount Baldy Road and follow it a little over 9 miles to where the road splits at Manker Campground. Park in the large open area between the roads.

This trail traverses one of the grandest loops in Southern California. It has everything: pine forest, streams, waterfalls, a Sierra Club ski hut, and a grand view from atop one of the region's highest mountains. Though it is wildly amazing, Mount Baldy is not for everyone. The ski hut trail is high altitude, steep, extremely rocky, and difficult. The Devils Backbone is incredibly steep and rocky as well, and it is also precipitous. If your dog is not used to alluvial drop-offs and wobbly rock-strewn ground, this is not the place to bring your pet. At the same time, for people who hike continuously, the clear day views are among the best in all of California. Even the not-so-clear days are pretty darned close to magnificent. And, for dogs whose pads are tougher than tank treads, this trail will be nothing but another fun all-day outing in the mountains.

Please be careful and sure of your own limitations, and always be aware of weather conditions; more people die on this peak than any other in Southern California. Every year, unprepared, under-prepared, and well-prepared hikers and climbers of all creeds and nationalities set out for a snow trek on this easily accessible trail never to return. Should you encounter anything you or your dog cannot handle, always do the smart thing and return the way you came. Ten thousand feet is nothing to sneeze at, and without a doubt this mountain is more powerful than you are.

With that mentioned, Mount San Antonio (which is the proper name for Mount Baldy, although nobody calls it that) is invigorating, exciting, and spectacular. Certainly none of this should scare you away. Being prepared and being smart are one and the same. Underestimating any mountain can get you into trouble; this peak just has more than its fair share of people who partake in such folly. Mount Baldy is susceptible to heavy foot traffic. It is the postcard peak of Los Angeles, and as such the weekends can be horribly overcrowded, especially between the summer holidays of Memorial Day and Labor Day. People flock here; it's popular, well known, highly visible, and ripe for bragging rights. Weekdays are

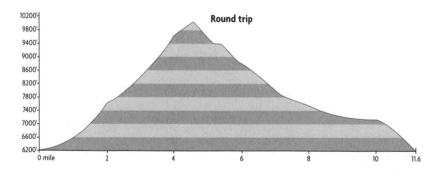

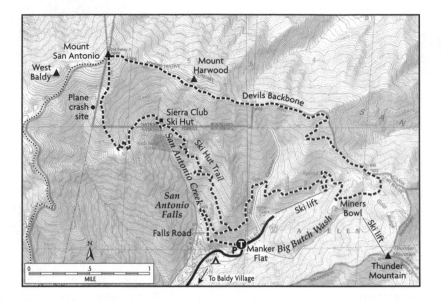

your best bet, and non-holiday Sundays are also better than Saturdays.

It is not required that you keep your pet on a leash, but you should always have one with you, especially when you have a trail that gets more than a fair amount of usage like this one.

Begin your ascent on a paved road to the west of the parking area. There is a locked gate and portable toilets at the start of the road. Falls Road traverses a steep incline and comes within a couple hundred feet of San Antonio Falls. If you've come at a time when the water is flowing, you will hear the falls in the distance when you begin your hike. Continue walking directly away from the falls up the road and as soon as you round a corner, begin looking for the Ski Hut Trail on your left. It rises steeply up the side of the hill, and some people who aren't observant miss it entirely. It isn't hard to see, though, and there is a register at the top of the rise. The trail from here to the Ski Hut will be easy on the dogs. It is dirt- and duff-covered with a few rocky places here and there. San Antonio Creek runs right by the Ski Hut and offers not only a halfway respite but a 2.5-mile turnaround point for those less inclined to scramble up the rocky slopes of the summit. This can be a rewarding adventure in itself, and lots of people who start on the trail end it here. Wildflowers, mule deer, and bighorn sheep are sighted often on this portion of the trail. The high ridge keeps the sun off the slopes until mid-morning, which is a great bonus on hot days.

From the Ski Hut, you cross the boulder strewn and rocky expanse of the Baldy Bowl. The trail can be a little tricky here for some, but if you look across the bowl, you should be able to easily spot where the trail picks up again amongst the trees. Here is where things start to get really rocky. You climb up to the ridgeline behind the jagged fang-like rocks looming above you.

Once you reach the top and take a rest to commence enjoying the views, you will need to head east down the Devils Backbone. There are lots of trails on top and if you are the slightest bit confused, go back the way you came. You wouldn't want to end up in Baldy Village, or on top of Dawson Peak. Head towards the ski runs, which should be obvious as they are cleared-out areas with ski lifts running up them. When the trail ends, follow the road down and back to Falls Road.

The Devils Backbone provides some of the most jaw-dropping scenery that Southern California has to offer. Some spots are not for those afraid of heights.

27. Ontario Peak

Round trip: 12.5 miles
Hiking time: 7 hours
High point: 8693 feet
Elevation gain: 3900 feet
Best season: Summer through late fall; spring is discouraged due to bighorn sheep mating in the area
Difficulty: Extremely difficult
Paw comfort: Very rocky
Water: Icehouse Canyon, Columbine Spring
Fees and permits: Adventure Pass and wilderness permit required
Map: USGS Cucamonga Peak; USGS Mount Baldy
Contact: Angeles National Forest, Mount Baldy Visitor Center (909) 982-2829, *www.fs.fed.us/r5/angeles*

Getting there: From Highway 60, Interstate 10, or Interstate 210, take the Mountain Avenue exit in Chino, Montclair, or Upland, respectively. Head north towards the mountains and follow the road to its conclusion. Veer left as the road curves around and merges with Euclid Avenue. Turn right onto Mount Baldy Road. Follow it for nearly 6.5 miles and turn right into the recently refurbished Icehouse Canyon parking area. There is plenty of room for parking and restrooms are located at the trailhead.

Icehouse Canyon is definitively among the most popular areas in the San Gabriels. Easy access to the flowing stream, trickling cascades, old ruins, and tranquil forest beauty offer quick rewards to families, couples, and

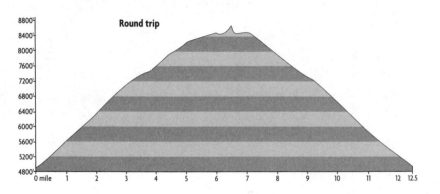

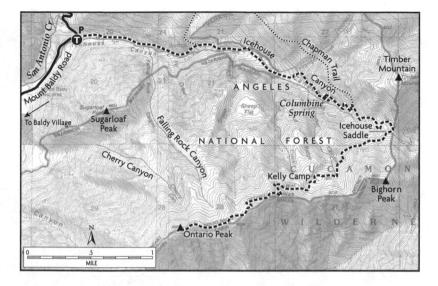

anyone wanting a little away time from the pressures of the city. The splendor here is undeniable with everything you would expect to see in a forest, including wildlife and towering trees. On the weekends, it is not uncommon for the trailhead parking lot to be overflowing. You will find people picnicking, playing in the stream, and even taking a very frigid soak in some of the larger pools along the way. The steepness of the Icehouse Canyon Trail discourages all but the hardiest of hikers in continuing on to one of the many peaks in the vicinity, but the variety of options at the top guarantee plenty of outdoor types on the trail. Getting an early start or taking a weekday excursion is the best way to ensure solitude.

The trail begins on pavement and passes many summer cabins that are still in use and the ruins of the old Icehouse Lodge. The lodge was destroyed by a flash flood in late February and early March of 1938. More than thirty inches of rain fell over a five-day period, inundating much of Southern California. This period is still regarded as one of the worst floods on record for the region. The deluge actually prompted the building of many reservoirs and spillways around Los Angeles, Riverside, and San Bernardino Counties to protect residential areas from future torrential mountain runoff.

A short distance from the parking area brings you to lush Icehouse Canyon, where an unnamed tributary of San Antonio Creek flows year-round. Alders, coast live oaks, big cone spruce, incense cedar, sugar pines,

The view from Ontario Peak reaches from the back ranges to the Pacific Ocean. An old fire wiped away most of the tallest trees, though mighty remnants still stand.

and fir trees line the wash. A mile of hiking takes you past the final cabin retreat and the majority of people on the trail. Quite a few people do make the trip to Icehouse Saddle, though only the most determined will venture on to the three "T's" (Timber, Telegraph, and Thunder), Cucamonga, Bighorn, or Ontario Peaks. The elevation gain remains constantly steady and steep throughout the hike. Icehouse Canyon is a workout, no matter how you slice it. The trail is rocky most of the way, and has the ability to do severe damage to your dog's paws, pads, and underbelly. Be sure to check frequently for signs of injury or distress. Even the most tried and true hiking dog can take punishment on a trail like this one.

Obviously an area such as this presents all sorts of options. There is no need to go all the way to the peak or the saddle should you choose not to. The area offers plenty for you and your dog to do along the way. Soaking in a pool, exploring the creek, or searching the ruins can provide a day's worth of enjoyable activity that will while away an idle afternoon. The Chapman Trail presents another alternative. Although it adds nearly 2 miles to the trail each way, it is substantially less frequented than the main trail and does not cross the wilderness boundary for an additional mile. The trail is a bit more arid than that through Icehouse Canyon, and slightly less shaded. Dogs must be leashed in all wilderness areas, and although it is not mandatory below the wilderness boundary, it is recommended due to high volumes of people.

The trail climbs steadily through incense cedar, Jeffrey, sugar, and lodgepole pine toward Icehouse Saddle. Vistas open up immediately, and the magnificence of the forest becomes more austere and rugged. Trees grow taller and straighter; the trail becomes more of a sloping ascent, which can be very dangerous under wintry conditions. From Icehouse Saddle, there are four trail options. The path farthest to the right will take you to Kelly Camp, Ontario Peak, and the splinter trail to Bighorn Peak.

There are numerous opportunities for backpacking and camping in the area. Cedar Glen campsite sits 2.5 miles into the hike off the Chapman Trail. Kelly Camp rests just below Bighorn Peak and offers easy access to both Bighorn and Ontario Peaks. Commanche Campground is nestled along the Middle Fork of Lytle Creek, 1600 feet below Icehouse Saddle on the east side. Any one of these spots guarantees solitude and serenity during summer outings.

SAN BERNARDINO NATIONAL FOREST

28. Cleghorn Mountain

Round trip: 10 miles
Hiking time: 4 hours
High point: 5333 feet
Elevation gain: 1700 feet
Best season: Late fall to early spring, scorching hot in summer
Difficulty: Moderate
Paw comfort: Dirt and rocks
Water: Bring your own
Fees and permits: Adventure Pass required
Map: USGS Cajon
Contact: San Bernardino National Forest, Arrowhead Ranger Station
(909) 382-2782, *www.fs.fed.us/r5/sanbernardino*

Getting there: From Devore, take Interstate 15 north for 7.5 miles up Cajon Pass. Exit to Highway 138 east; follow it for exactly 4 extremely curvy miles, and turn right on unmarked dirt road 2N44 (the road is signed as Elliot coming from the other direction, so if you drive beyond 4 miles and have to turn around, this is your turn). Follow the dirt road to the locked gate and park alongside the fence. After the fires, this area was closed to off-highway vehicle use. As a consequence, it is not a bad place for winter hiking. Follow the road past some noisy electrical towers and the junction with the Pacific Crest Trail, veer left to stay on the main road, and follow it to the top of the ridge and mountain.

This is a straightforward hike on a dirt road. You head in and up to the top of a very impressive ridgeline. The gain is steady and actually makes for an exceedingly enjoyable climb. This area was completely devastated in the Old Fire of 2003, and fell victim to firestorms of the recent past as well. The flora of the region is beginning to make a recovery due to the massive rainfall of 2005, but it is still a shadeless, waterless, and barren burnt-out chunk of land. It is doubtful that this section of the forest will ever regain its former glory. It will probably remain a victim of desertification; it is doubtful that even the junipers will grow back, let alone the pinyon pines that graced these slopes more than a century ago.

Being a scorched wasteland doesn't make this area a place entirely without merits. As stated before, there is an incredibly slight amount of travel in the region. People avoid burn areas when recreating, so this is a perfect place to take your pups for solitude. The views, when they are present and unobstructed by smog, are magnificent. The tallest peaks in the San Gabriels sparkle with snow across the lowest reaches of the Cajon Pass. The summits juxtaposed to the gap appear close enough that a grasping hand could reach out and clutch the snow from atop the jagged ridgelines and summit saddles. The western half of the San Bernardinos, Mormon Rocks, some scattered badlands, and the historic Cajon Pass are also within view as you ascend and summit. You can see the original pass where the California Southern Railroad came through as early as 1885. The railroads still travel via this historic route; once it was the only accessible route to the growing L.A. region from the rest of

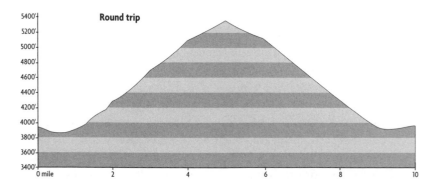

Round trip

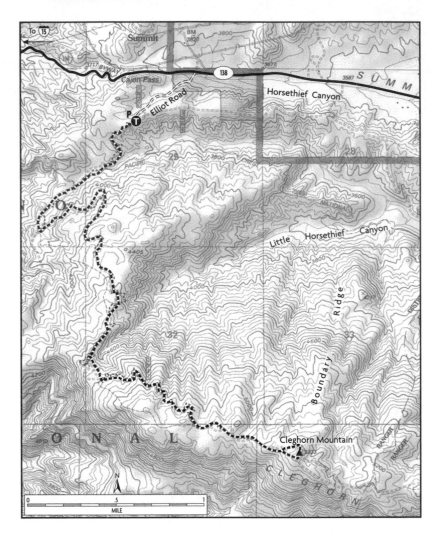

the United States. Separated by the San Andreas Fault, the Cajon Pass is the dividing line between the San Bernardino and San Gabriel Mountain ranges. It is still a busy thoroughfare transporting people from the lower basin into the high Mojave Desert.

Your pets will enjoy this trail for more than just the solitude. Birds, such as quail, seem to thrive in areas that have been burnt and throughout the gullies that surround them. What dog doesn't love to sniff out birds from their hiding places? In a case such as this one, there are no hiding places, and Fido is free to roam, hunt, and track. The dirt on the road is soft and shouldn't present a problem for pads. You will not be traversing rocks or rocky soils, and this could be used as a training trip to toughen up pads for longer voyages over harder surfaces.

This area can also be hot in winter, so be sure to bring lots of water. It is a short enough medium-sized trip to the top, but it can seem much longer than that if conditions are unfavorable, especially if you or your pooch is without water for long distances. It might not only be uncomfortable, but dangerous. Also, please be aware before undertaking this trek that it is most pleasing to the eye when the air is clear. If it is smoggy, or even slightly hazy in San Bernardino, you will not be seeing much of anything except fire damage, hills, and dirt road. It is possible that you won't even be able to see the peaks of the San Gabriels that are only separated from you by the country's most famous fault line. The smog in this area is horrible; even the Native Americans knew it as a place that gathered the smoke from all the fires in the entire Southern California

Cleghorn Mountain still suffers the scars of careless fires. Once upon a time this area was loaded with high desert scrub brush and pinyon pine and juniper forest.

basin. Planning ahead and watching the weather patterns will make this trip much more enjoyable if you take it at the right time. However, the sense of solitude, freedom, and adventure can make up for scenery almost any day, and your dog will not know or mind the difference. This trip is a guaranteed dog pleaser.

29. Little Bear Creek

Round trip: 3.8 miles
Hiking time: 2 hours
High point: 5350 feet
Elevation gain: 800 feet
Best season: Year-round, hot in summer
Difficulty: Easy
Paw comfort: Dirt and duff
Water: Little Bear Creek usually has some water year-round
Fees and permits: Adventure Pass or $5 day use fee required
Map: USGS Lake Arrowhead, USGS Harrison Mountain
Contact: San Bernardino National Forest, Arrowhead Ranger Station
(909) 382-2782, *www.fs.fed.us/r5/sanbernardino*

Getting there: Take Highway 30 east from Interstate 215 in San Bernardino, exit on Waterman (which becomes Highway 18) and follow the road north into the mountains for 18 miles. Turn left when you reach the junction with Highway 173 to Lake Arrowhead. Follow Highway 173 for over 4 miles around the lake to the North Shore turnoff. You can follow the hospital

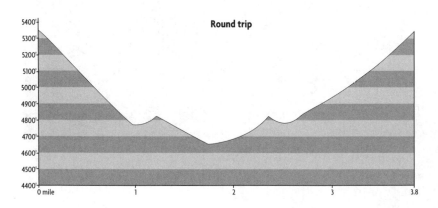

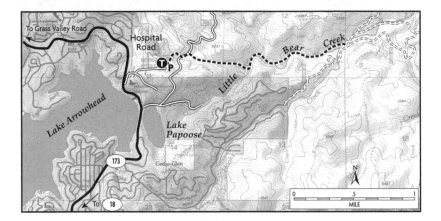

signs and turn on Hospital Road, and that will take you directly to the North Shore Campground where the hike begins.

You must stop at the campground host and pay a $5 day use fee or you will be given a ticket for $25. An Adventure Pass is not required when paying the day use fee. There is a parking area at the far east side of the campground for day use, and this is where the trail begins.

The hike descends through a once lovely wooded glen that has now seen epic damage due to the Old Fire of 2003. Firefighters protected the community around Arrowhead Lake, and this area was one of the final battlegrounds utilized in combating the blaze. Though singed, the area is still worth a trip. Studying fire ecology can be a fascinating endeavor on its own, but this trip will take you up close and personal. A firsthand assessment can be made of what happens due to carelessness, negligence, and sheer stupidity on the part of humans. The area is bouncing back very well despite bark beetles and years of drought before the blaze. Spring rains produce wildflowers galore in this region especially in the seasons just after a fire.

The trail is used rather infrequently, even on weekends, probably even less so now after the conflagration destroyed much of the surrounding forestland. You and your pet can share in the solitude and unruffled wildness of the area. The trail crosses Forest Service Road 2N26Y, which is the turnaround point listed on this hike. Your hike can be extended by following the road north and then west to Splinter's Cabin and on to Deep Creek. Much of this area burned too, but you will begin to see some of the area's former glory if you continue for a short trip along Deep

Socs takes a rest break along Little Bear Creek.

Creek, one of the finest streams in the lower San Bernardinos.

The hike is an easy outing although it is an inverse trip. In the summer months, temperatures can exceed the 90s. It is advisable to bring lots of water and to realize that much of the shade along this trip is gone. Hike out the way you came, or set up a car shuttle at any one of the various other trails or roadways that traverse this lovely area of the forest. Deep Creek is billed as a "special" area, and indeed it is.

30. Grays Peak

Round trip: 7 miles
Hiking time: 3.5 hours
High point: 7925 feet
Elevation gain: 1200 feet
Best season: April to November (trail is closed in winter)
Difficulty: Moderate
Paw comfort: Dirt, duff and some rock
Water: Streams intermittent, bring your own
Fees and permits: Adventure Pass required
Map: USGS Fawnskin
Contact: San Bernardino National Forest, Big Bear Discovery Center (909) 382-2790, *www.fs.fed.us/r5/sanbernardino*

Getting there: From Interstate 10 in Redlands, take Highway 30 west (the direction you'll actually be going is north) to Highway 330 north.

Follow it all the way up the mountain, and then continue east on Highway 18 to the dam at Big Bear Lake. Turn left onto Highway 38. Follow it for nearly 3 miles to the Grout Bay Picnic Area. There is parking in the picnic area and a large lot across the highway, just before you reach the tiny hamlet of Fawnskin.

Important: The trail is closed from December 1 to April 1 in order to protect bald eagle nesting sites.

Grays Peak is a fantastic adventure on the north side of Big Bear Lake. The trail begins by climbing up and away from the lake, eventually wrapping around the backside of the mountain. The water views that begin to open up abruptly disappear, but so does the sound of cars, boats and any other noise emanating from the most heavily populated national forest in America. This is a very good thing. All that is left is granite, sky and forest. Open vistas lead beyond Fawnskin Valley into Holcomb Valley and farther into the high desert, which more than make up for the missed opportunities to look at the lake.

Walking up to Grays Peak is a pleasant trip. You climb 1200 feet in 4 miles, and almost all of that is evenly spaced out, with the final push to the top ascending a little steeper than the rest of the trail. The climb feels less like a summit climb and more like a short uphill jaunt. Black oak, white fir, ponderosa and Jeffrey pines surround the granite and gravel filled trail. In spots the chaparral is very thick; ceanothus and manzanita line the path, making it impossible to travel cross-country along the ridgeline. This is not a big deal though, because the trail itself is very picturesque. Outcroppings of granite boulders touch the sky, and

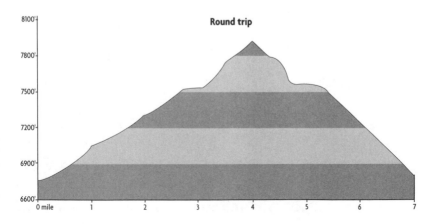

can provide for some impromptu scaling should the desire arise. Picture taking is a viable second alternative, especially if fall clouds are rolling in. The contrast of granite on white clouds and skies of azure is a spectacular sight. This might even begin to derail you from your original purpose. No matter, though, the trail is best traveled in a leisurely manner. There is really no purpose in quickly getting to the top; there is much more to enjoy along the way.

The gravelly trail is unusual for the north side of Big Bear Lake. It is possible that the rocky soil may wreak havoc upon your dog's pads, but the length is short enough that if your dog is somewhat hardened, it shouldn't present much of a problem. The distance, grade, and destination make this a perfect beginner hike for humans, but dogs should be in at least moderate shape and toughened pads are a must.

This area is strangely reminiscent of the Sierra Nevada; tall ponderosa pines soar above looming granite towers that emerge in all directions. Once you reach the summit, an obscured view of Big Bear Lake opens with the enormous summits of Sugarloaf and San Gorgonio looming on the horizon. If you didn't know better, you might think you had been teleported to Northern California, complete with a blissful escape from smog, exhaust, and the hum and drum of the L.A. Basin. Big Bear might exist

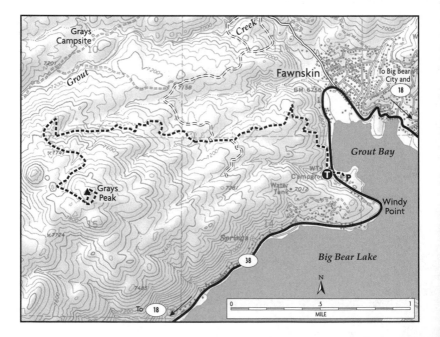

as a glacial tarn beneath beautifully cruel peaks that require mountaineering skills year-round. It could be, but it is not. Instead, the panoramic playground is situated virtually in your own backyard. Why not enjoy it more often?

This trip is generally overlooked for other trips in the area, such as Cougar Crest and the Big Bear Discovery Center. The lakeshore is a much more popular draw, and a weekday hike virtually guarantees seclusion. Summer weekends have a little more bustle, but the area will never be overcrowded. You and your dog will have plenty to take pleasure in. Sign the register and return the way you came.

Striking granite monoliths line the trail to Grays Peak.

31. Cougar Crest–Bertha Peak

Round trip: 6.2 miles
Hiking time: 3 hours
High point: 8201 feet
Elevation gain: 1600 feet
Best season: Year-round
Difficulty: Moderate
Paw comfort: Dirt and rocks
Water: Bring your own
Fees and permits: Adventure Pass required
Map: USGS Fawnskin
Contact: San Bernardino National Forest, Big Bear Discovery Center (909) 382-2790, *www.fs.fed.us/r5/sanbernardino*

Getting there: From Interstate 10 in Redlands, take Highway 30 west (you'll actually be going north) to the connection with Highway 330 north. Highway 330 ends at Highway 18 in the town of Running Springs. Take the Rim of the World Highway (18) east towards Big Bear,

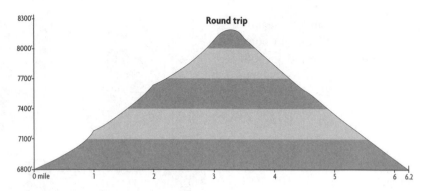

and continue for nearly 13 miles. At the dam, veer left onto Highway 38 and head toward Fawnskin and the Big Bear Solar Observatory. At 6.5 miles there is a large trailhead parking area on your left. Park here and start down the trail.

The Cougar Crest is a well-traveled beginners' trail. The first mile used to be an old fire road. The trail gains only a minimal amount of elevation until reaching the end of the old road. You will probably see lots of people of differing athletic abilities and different purposes. There is a good chance you'll come across runners, families, older people, and people with their dogs should you venture out on a busy summer weekend. On the other hand, during the week, there will be relatively few people and you should have the trail mostly to yourself.

The area is nicely forested with lodgepole and Jeffrey pine and some mixed chaparral. There are also quite a few western junipers on this trail. They are hard to miss with their distinctive red bark and their twisted and gnarled look. They are hardy survivors much like bristlecone or limber pines, subsisting on lower amounts of rainfall and rocky soil. Since this is the north side of Big Bear Lake, the area is considerably dryer than the southern side. The snow melts quicker here and the streams dry up much earlier as a result, so there won't be much water. There is plenty of shade however, and the trail is mostly dirt with some rocky areas. It should be easy on you and your faithful friend. The only issue with this trail is its heavy usage. Due to that fact, there is a requirement of leashing your pet. Make sure you follow this guideline.

Cougar Crest is one of those trails that need not be completed to be enjoyed. Once the trail starts gaining altitude, it does so at quite a rapid pace. The views of Big Bear Lake quickly open up about 1.5 miles into the trail. This is a good stopping and turnaround point for those who are not quite conditioned for a longer outing. What can be better than getting outdoors, reveling in the fresh mountain air, and swallowing a breathtaking view of a crystalline lake reflecting the highest mountain range in Southern California? From this point on, the trail climbs its way up to the Pacific Crest Trail (PCT). The climb is not bad and anyone in good shape should be able to make it easily (this includes pets with toughened pads). Many people opt to continue on towards Bertha Peak, although Delamar Mountain is also an option, albeit a much longer and tougher one.

At the PCT, turn right (east) and follow the trail until it intersects with the service road that goes to the top of Bertha Peak. Head right again and climb the road until you reach the pinnacle. There is no trail register or marker, because of the radio repeaters that are stationed on top. The towers are conspicuous from anywhere in the Big Bear area. They form an obvious landmark that is easy to follow.

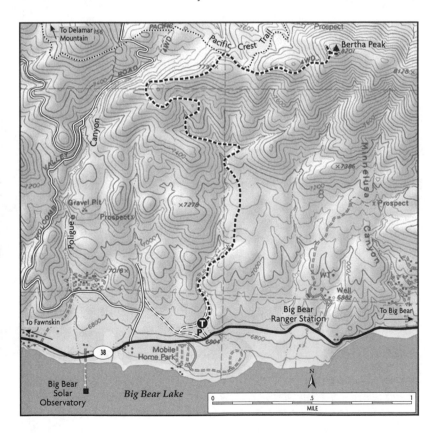

The views are magnificent from the summit. You can take in sweeping vistas of Holcomb Valley, the entire Bear Valley, and much of the Mojave Desert. The expansive vantage over Big Bear Lake is also much more pronounced than it was at lower elevations on the trail. The shimmering blue provides a welcome foreground to the often snow-spattered peaks in the San Gorgonio Wilderness. "Old Greyback," another name for 11,502-foot San Gorgonio, rises majestically, like a protector, above the valley, and beckons anyone with the stamina to come and attain its high crown. Return the way you came, enjoying the wallflowers and lupine that often grace the sides of the trail. You will also be much more suited to enjoy the unrestrained views of the lake and mountains as you head down and out.

Western wallflowers grace the gorgeous views that adorn Cougar Crest. Big Bear Lake and the San Gorgonio Wilderness offer a stunning backdrop under cloudy skies.

32. Castle Rock

Round trip: 1.6 miles
Hiking time: 1 hour
High point: 7400 feet
Elevation gain: 700 feet
Best season: Year-round; snow in winter
Difficulty: Easy, but a steep and short elevation gain
Paw comfort: Dirt and rocks
Water: Streams may run into summer
Fees and permits: Adventure Pass required
Map: USGS Big Bear Lake
Contact: San Bernardino National Forest, Big Bear Discovery Center
(909) 382-2790, *www.fs.fed.us/r5/sanbernardino*

Getting there: From Interstate 10 in Redlands, take Highway 30 west to Highway 330 north. Follow it and Highway 18 east at Running Springs for 26 miles and continue across the dam to the south side of the lake. Go a little over a mile past the bridge and you will see the signed trail on your right and a small turnout on your left 20-40 yards around the turn. There is room for more than a few cars to park. Walk down the road, keeping a careful eye out for traffic as you cross with your pets.

This trail is classic Big Bear. Towering lodgepole pines sway in the wind well more than a hundred feet overhead. The air is crisp and vibrant here; this is one Southern California vale that routinely escapes the smog and haze. Lake views open up almost immediately, and the final destination

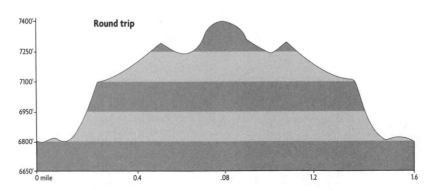

sits less than a mile from the trailhead. Large granite boulders crop up everywhere; this is the reason the area nearby is fittingly called Boulder Bay. A small stream trickles by and deposits water in the lake from alongside the trail throughout late spring and during the rainy/snowy part of the year. If the trail were flat, this would be a perfect place for ambling through the forest. It isn't flat, though, and most people would be hard pressed to call this strolling of any sort.

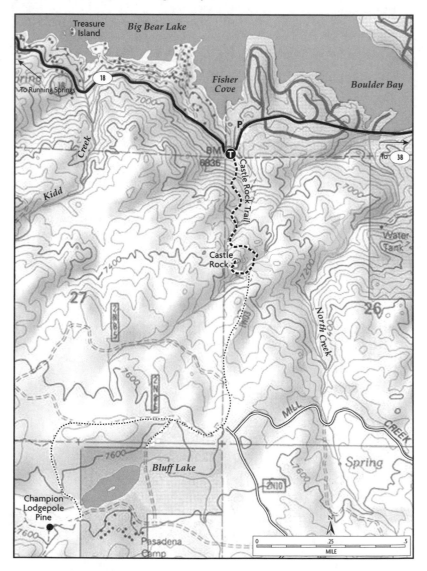

Though the hike is short, it is incredibly steep, so steep in parts that older people or anyone with knee problems might want to steer clear of ascending and especially descending this trail. It is brief, though your muscles and lungs will get a good workout if you push yourself up the mountainside. Actually, this is a perfect training hike for both you and your dog. For one thing, it takes a lot less than an hour to ascend and descend if you are doing it for exercise and training alone, and you gain 700 feet very swiftly. Conceivably, you could go up and down several times to train for greater distances and elevation gains. It will get your dog's paws used to rocky soil and boulders; they will toughen up in this environment rather quickly. Hiking rapidly up and down will be an aerobic exercise for you and your pet. And finally, this is a popular trail, so you will be bound to run into other hikers.

There is no better way to get your pets used to a trail and a leash and other hikers than taking them to an area that is frequented by other hikers. As with most trails in Big Bear, dogs should be leashed. This is mainly a courtesy, rather than a law, but there are signs directing you to have dogs restrained. Big Bear is a densely populated mountain town, and one can only imagine what it would be like if everyone let their dogs run roughshod over the trails. In actuality, the San Bernardino Mountains are the heaviest populated forested area in the United States. Many areas like this could be closed to dogs if owners aren't responsible. A few complaints of dog harassment and the forest supervisor could shut dogs out permanently, which has happened before. Remember, even if Fido is the friendliest pooch in the world, some people have an irrational fear of animals, and his friendly approach may mean deadly fear to an advancing stranger.

The trail winds through granitic switchbacks and is thoroughly marked. If you ever do feel as if you are wandering off-trail, stop and look for the arrows, as they are placed almost everywhere a person could look. You'll know you have nearly reached the end when you see the large east face of Castle Rock, which is strictly Class 5 climbing. You have to circle around the back to find the trail up to the top. Your dogs might not be able to make it all the way to the climax because some Class 3 scrambling is required to reach the summit block, but there are lots of little places to stop on the rocks and admire the lake views and the larger mountains to the south and east.

If you feel like exploring further, this is a great area to do it. There may be people on the Castle Rock Trail, but it is almost assured that you will

The trail to Castle Rock is loaded with boulder outcroppings and towering pines.

see no one if you carry your travels further. Once you meet up with the next trail or road, there is no reason to not let the dogs run freely. There is ample space and opportunity to do so. You can connect this trail to the Champion Lodgepole Pine Trail and a number of other forest roads and trails. You can even continue to the edge of beautiful Bluff Lake, which is currently operated by the Wildlands Conservancy, a charitable organization dedicated to returning lands to wilderness and protecting endangered plants and animals. It is illegal to enter without a permit, but there are lots of trails that go around it.

While hiking in this area, you may sense something reminiscent of old *Bonanza* reruns; that's because a lot of filming for the show was done on the south side of the lake. If the area looks familiar, it is. Many Hollywood westerns used the Big Bear area as the setting for their mountain adventures. There is no doubt as to why: the area's beauty is nearly unmatched, the south side gets considerably more snowfall, and is generally more lush, greener, and pleasant. When spotting the peaks of the San Gorgonio Wilderness, and glancing over alpine lakes, it is hard not to think of more northern climes. The Castle Rock area is truly a gem of our forests.

33. Grand View Point

Round trip: 6 miles
Hiking time: 3 hours
High point: 7784 feet
Elevation gain: 1400 feet
Best season: Year-round, snow in winter
Difficulty: Moderate
Paw comfort: Dirt and duff
Water: Springs and streams intermittent, so bring your own
Fees and permits: Adventure Pass required
Map: USGS Big Bear Lake
Contact: San Bernardino National Forest, Big Bear Discovery Center
(909) 382-2790, *www.fs.fed.us/r5/sanbernardino*

Getting there: From Interstate 10 in Redlands, take Highway 30 north to
Highway 330 west, follow it as it merges with Highway 18 east to Running
Springs for a total of 26 miles. Continue across the dam to the south side
of the lake. Stay on Highway 18 through the town of Big Bear Lake, turn
right onto Mill Creek Road and follow it a short distance to the Aspen
Glen Picnic Area. Park here to hit the full six miles of trail.

After the picnic area, Mill Creek Road becomes Forest Service Road 2N10
(Skyline Drive). This road will take you very near the point; the trail crosses
the road a short distance below the summit. A quarter-mile walk leads to
the top. This is an option for people who do not want to hike the entire distance of the trail. A small sign marks the short trailhead from the road.

The trailhead is situated in the northeast corner of the picnic area, almost on the roadway. The trail is rocky at first. The way starts wide and is

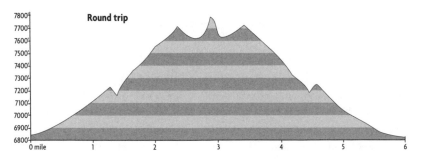

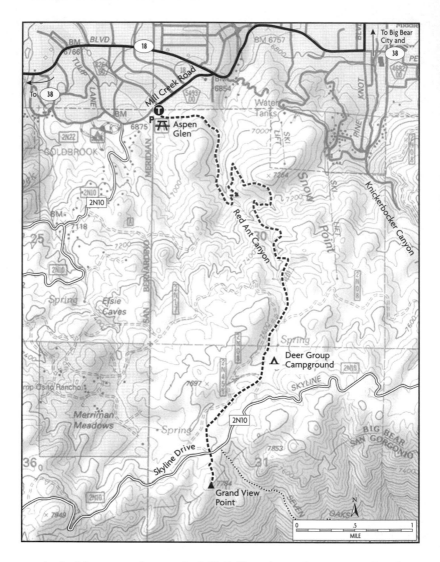

marked with posts going up the hill. Follow the trail as it ascends a short hill and then descends along an old forest road to Red Ant Canyon. The trail continues along this dirt road for a short while and crosses over creek beds that will be dry at certain times of the year. You start your ascent up the canyon shortly after you enter it, and travel through a wonderful forest of white fir, ponderosa and Jeffrey pine. The south side of Big Bear Lake is more verdant than the northern side, due to the transverse east-west direction of the mountains. Snow melts much more slowly on these north-facing slopes, due to the tilt of the earth. This condition is about as close as Southern Californians can get to understanding winter's effect on the landscape. Due to later snow melt and prolonged moisture, the area stays greener longer and is more resistant to drought and pestilence, such as bark beetles. There is a preponderance of healthy trees. Dampness in the area also creates an opportune environment for wildflowers. The usual fare of the mountains can be seen here along with wild irises, penstemons, baby blue eyes, an assortment of lupines, and other lovely blossoms.

At times the correct trail can be difficult to follow. There are confluences everywhere where the trail meets a side trail, or one that is not maintained. The trail crosses several dirt roads, and it is not always clear what direction to follow. The good news is that most of these paths will take you to the top and some of them will get you there faster, but those can range from steady up to perilously steep. Many of these side trails have been created by mountain bikers and equestrian users who have gotten off the trail and who also frequent these parts. When you do cross dirt roads, most of them lead to 2N10 eventually. If you have good map and compass skills, you will always know where you are and can follow any one of various paths to the top. Although the trail system is convoluted, a watchful eye will keep you on course, and should you stray too far out, just remember the way you came and follow it back down.

Your pets should remain on a leash in these areas. Mountain bikers and horses are not overabundant, but they are common enough that you

Grand View Point presents spectacular views of the San Gorgonio Wilderness and the canyon cut by the Santa Ana River.

may have a surprise encounter with one or the other. Sometimes bike races are held here as well. Since the area is a mecca for things other than hiking, it might be wise to keep your dog leashed, in case you need to restrain him or keep him out of harm's way. There are rocky areas and sections on the trail, but a moderately conditioned dog should be able to handle this trail's minimal impact on the pads. Most of the way is rather easy going. There is never a tick season this high up, and poison oak is non-existent.

Grand View Point was named for a reason. The view from the "summit" is magnificent. You can have a look at the work the Santa Ana River has done on the valley between Big Bear and the San Gorgonio Wilderness. The river is much different than its Inland Empire complement—up here it is wild and flowing, and not the concrete storm channel you drive by in Riverside. Speaking of the wilderness, the views are up close and personal. San Gorgonio appears nearly touchable above the clouds. The rounded cap of Old Greyback is as inviting as any of the mountains in California. Hearing its call is something that can drive you back to these spots again and again. A clear day will allow viewing of the entire Los Angeles Basin and beyond.

34. Sugarloaf Mountain

Round trip: 7 miles
Hiking time: 3.5 hours
High point: 9952 feet
Elevation gain: 1500 feet
Best season: Year-round
Difficulty: Moderate
Paw comfort: Dirt and rocks
Water: Bring your own
Fees and permits: Adventure Pass required
Map: USGS Moonridge
Contact: San Bernardino National Forest, Big Bear Discovery Center
(909) 382-2790, *www.fs.fed.us/r5/sanbernardino*

Getting there: From Interstate 10 east exit University Avenue in Redlands. Make a right off the exit, and then turn immediately left at the light onto Citrus. Hang another left onto Judson/Ford. Follow it to Lugonia Avenue,

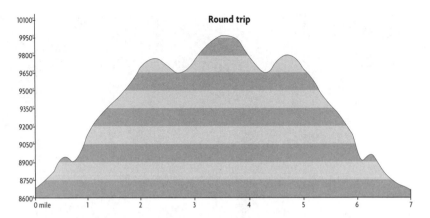

which is Highway 38, then make a right. You will stay on Highway 38 as it changes from Lugonia to Mentone Boulevard and then to Mill Creek Road. Keep on Highway 38 as it veers north toward and past Angelus Oaks. About 2 miles beyond Heart Bar Campground is Forest Service Road 2N93. Turn left and follow the road for 5.75 miles. This trailhead is tricky to find. If you come to a large open area with a locked gate to the left, you have gone too far. You can take the road in, but it will add distance to your trip.

This is the highest peak outside the wilderness in the San Bernardino National Forest. You do not need a wilderness permit, but you will be afforded all the views of the San Gorgonio area you can possibly imagine. This trek is a pretty straightforward journey through high alpine forest nearly topping out at 10,000 feet. The short distance and relatively light altitude gain would seem to make this an ideal outing with dogs, and it is, provided that they are well conditioned before you go. This is by far one of the rockiest trails you can take in Southern California, and consequently can be extremely hard on your pet's paws. There is no water along this route either, so bring plenty.

The forest here is beautiful, quiet, and secluded. Most hikers eschew this area and head for the wilderness instead, even on weekends. The 5+ miles of dirt forest road is also enough to discourage many day-trippers from driving to this trailhead. Should you run into other hikers, it is likely that they have made the trip from Green Canyon just outside of the city of Big Bear. Although this is an option or a loop via car shuttle, it adds 1000 feet of elevation gain, and the lower elevation trail is bleaker and dryer. The first few miles are not as lush as the higher forest out of Wildhorse Meadows; I've even heard the lower section described as "boring."

Mountain views abound on the trail to Sugarloaf Peak, the highest mountain in the San Bernardino National Forest outside of wilderness areas.

If you time this trip right, you may be in for quite a wildflower show. Lupine, Spanish paintbrush, western wallflower, and California blue-eyes are common, especially just after snow melt in early to late spring. You might even find some wild iris, penstemon, or snow plant among the more common flora of the area. However, even if the flowers aren't in bloom, this trip is an excellent choice. The high country air is vibrant and cool, even on the hottest summer days. It is a short and steady climb that can be accomplished by hardy older children, though it is steep.

The only letdown of this hike is that there is no real 360-degree summit view. The peak is covered with lodgepole pines. The vistas of Big Bear Lake aren't clear either, despite the fact that you lord over it by more than 3000 feet. There are some lesser peaks along with the trees that obscure your view; however, if you head off to the south side, there is a small shoulder that provides a picturesquely stunning panorama of the entire San Gorgonio Ridge. Grab a seat and some granola and revel in the splendor of the mountains. The best lookout point on the trip can be found about a mile east of the peak on top of unnamed USGS marker 9775. The area on this nub is nearly devoid of trees, and if the peak itself wasn't towering above this little notch, it would be quite easy to actually mistake this mound for the summit.

Sugarloaf is quite the generic name; there are four summits with this name in Southern California. Apparently, it comes from the mound-like shape of the mountain, which resembles how lumps of sugar were sold before the modern era. The Serrano Indians gave this peak a much more romantic name, Ata'npa't, and it was a sacred place to them. Chances are, it will become a sacred place for you and your canine companions.

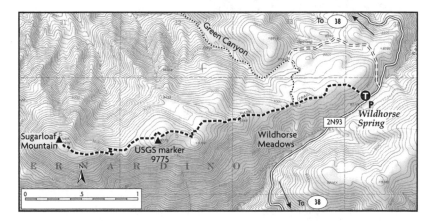

SAN GORGONIO WILDERNESS

35. Shields Peak

Round trip: 12.2 miles
Hiking time: 7.5 hours
High point: 10,680 feet
Elevation gain: 4000 feet
Best season: Late spring through late fall
Difficulty: Extremely difficult
Paw comfort: Dirt, duff, and rocky dirt; sharp boulder scrambling at the peak
Water: Jackstraw Springs and Trail Fork Springs are usually reliable
Fees and permits: Adventure Pass and wilderness permit required
Map: USGS Big Bear Lake
Contact: San Bernardino National Forest, Mill Creek Ranger Station (909) 382-2881, *www.fs.fed.us/r5/sanbernardino*

Getting there: Take Interstate 10 east to Redlands, then exit at University Avenue. Make a right off the exit, and then turn immediately left at the light onto Citrus. Hang another left onto Judson/Ford. Follow it to Lugonia Avenue, which is Highway 38, then make a right. You will stay on Highway 38 as it changes from Lugonia to Mentone Boulevard, and then to Mill Creek Road. You'll need to pick up a first-come, first-serve wilderness permit at San Gorgonio Ranger Station for Forsee Creek; on summer weekends, you might want to apply in advance. Head east again past Mountain Home Village, and follow Highway 38 as it turns to your left up the mountain. After 5 miles you'll pass Angelus Oaks. In another 5 miles turn right onto Jenks Lake Road West. Follow the signs for Forsee Creek Trail and turn onto Forest Service Road 1N82. A high clearance vehicle is recommended for this dirt road, but it is not necessary. Park at the trailhead.

This trek takes you up and up into the San Gorgonio Wilderness. There is no easy way into this high country; every trail to the tallest crest in Southern California gains at least 3500 feet, and the shortest way to the top is just under 7 miles. Anyway you slice it, getting to the San Bernardino Divide is an all day workout. Make sure your dogs can handle this type of trip before setting out on this one. Even the best-conditioned dogs can wear out at this distance, elevation, and duration. My dogs and I have bagged Shields, Anderson, and San Bernardino East in a day, and by the end of the trail, they were in misery. The trail is a good one, dirt- and duff-covered a majority of the way, but gravelly in parts. Shields Peak itself is a short, rocky semi-scramble to the summit; your pooches can make it, but check their paws before the final push up the peak. There is normally very little water along this trail, except at the two springs, so make sure to remember the little guys and pack in quite a bit extra. When you reach the San Bernardino Peak Divide Trail, turn left. Follow it to the rocky base of Shields Peak. The summit push is off-trail, due to the boulders leading to the peak.

In all wilderness areas, dogs are required to be leashed. Technically, the wilderness guidelines say you are in violation if possessing a dog not on a leash or "otherwise" confined. Your dog must be under leash control at all times, so if you do happen upon wildlife or people, you can quickly rein the dog in.

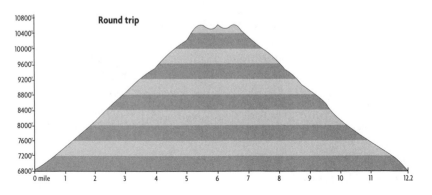

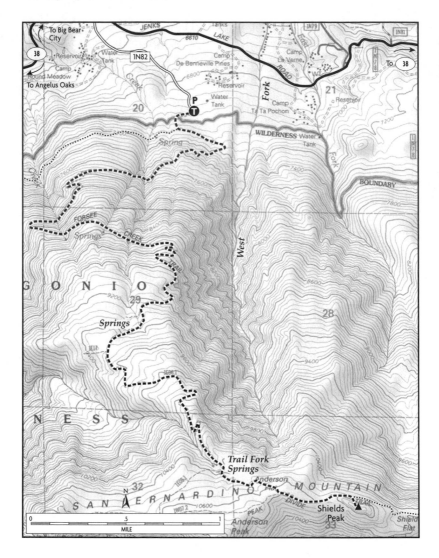

The rewards of the San Gorgonio Wilderness are ample. In this most lush area of the San Bernardinos, the views are breathtaking, and it's not just the altitude, although the 8 miles between San Bernardino Peak and San Gorgonio Peak only drop below 10,000 feet at Dollar Lake Saddle (9975 feet). On a clear day, you can see beyond Big Bear to Charleston

Opposite: Chewee practices "stay" in order to pose for a picture with Big Bear Lake in the background.

Peak near Las Vegas, the entire Angeles National Forest, and even the Pacific Ocean. You should even be able to glimpse the southern Sierra under perfect conditions. However, even under normal, more realistic smog-shrouded views, the scenery will leave you stunned in awe of these beautiful forests.

Hiking along the ridge is easy once you get there, and you'll want to spend extra time just taking it all in. If you plan to bag more than one peak, prepare to be pooped, and store enough energy for the way back down, as it is a long way out. There are lots of great resting spots along the divide to eat lunch with your canine companions.

36. Dry Lake

Round trip: 11 miles
Hiking time: 6.5 hours
High point: 9100 feet
Elevation gain: 2400 feet
Best season: Late spring/early summer through first snowfall
Difficulty: Very difficult
Paw comfort: Dirt, duff, and some rocky areas
Water: Dry Lake, Lodgepole Spring, several creeks run through
　　summer; check with the ranger when you get your permit
Fees and permits: Adventure Pass and wilderness permit required
Map: USGS San Gorgonio; USGS Moonridge
Contact: San Bernardino National Forest, Mill Creek Ranger Station
　　(909) 382-2881, *www.fs.fed.us/r5/sanbernardino*

Getting there: From Interstate 10 east exit University Avenue in Redlands. Make a right off the exit, and then turn immediately left at the light onto Citrus. Hang another left onto Judson/Ford. Follow it to Lugonia Avenue, which is Highway 38, and make a right. You will stay on Highway 38 for 12.5 miles as it changes from Lugonia to Mentone Boulevard and then to Mill Creek Road. Continue on Highway 38 as it turns sharply left, heading north 5 miles toward and past Angelus Oaks. Continue on Highway 38 for another 5.5 miles and turn right onto Jenks Lake Road West. Follow Jenks Lake Road for 2.5 miles and park in the enormous South Fork Trailhead parking lot on your left. Head toward the restrooms to find the start of the trail and wilderness information. Pack your leash;

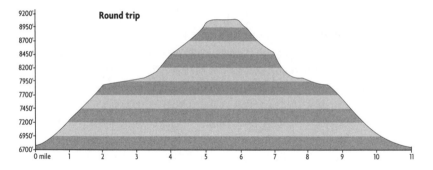

this is a wilderness area and dogs are to be leashed at all times. This trail is a favorite of equestrians, and you might share it with some horses, especially on the weekend.

This route is the turnpike of the San Gorgonio Wilderness and with good reason. The sheer beauty and magnificence of this region can be reached relatively easily from this mostly shaded and well-graded pathway. In fact, this is the most undemanding way to reach the high country wilderness. You will know that this area is abundantly traveled when you see the size of the parking lot and the number of cars parked here even on weekday afternoons. The access is simple, no four-wheel drive necessary, and the rewards are ample almost immediately after clearing the asphalt. You enter riparian woodlands of oak and pine nestled beside creek beds. In spring and early summer, the creeks are flowing, and nearly spilling over during heavy rain years; later on in the year, however, bet on dry arbors. After the heavy rainfall of 2004 and 2005, the water level was still at a commanding roar into late July and wildflowers were everywhere.

This area was reworked in 1988 to prevent damage and overuse of the Poopout Hill entrance to San Gorgonio. The trail is a wide thoroughfare and climbs steadily to Horse Meadows, an old facility for horse camping, and then on to the border of the wilderness area. There is a grandiose but not pretentious sign and monument to The Wilderness Act and a general history of the San Gorgonio region on top of Poopout Hill. A short side jaunt (less than 0.1 mile) from the main trail takes you to said overlook, which is marked by a sign with a picture of a camera. This impressive view is not to be passed by, and once you've seen it, you'll probably want to return on the trip out. The high ridge to the left of San Gorgonio is your destination on this hike, so you can take a peek to see where you will be traveling.

The 1.5 miles from Poopout Hill to South Fork Meadows is a fairly level walk; this acts as a nice reprieve for the midpoint of the hike. Here the lodgepole and ponderosa pine trees grow tall, many reaching incredible heights and girths. A signed turnoff for Lost Creek and Grinnell Ridge means that your hearty climb is beginning. The next trail junction, which is just a short hike away, is where you veer left and cross several tributaries of the South Fork of the Santa Ana. The upward march remains as steady as the lower section, but it is an intensifying journey through increasingly thin air. The South Fork offshoots of the Santa Ana River can be raging at times, but as the season of summer marches on, they slow to a trickle and eventually become dried-up ravines with perhaps intermittent remnants of water here and there. As you climb, the trail becomes progressively rockier, mostly loose gravel that can wreak havoc

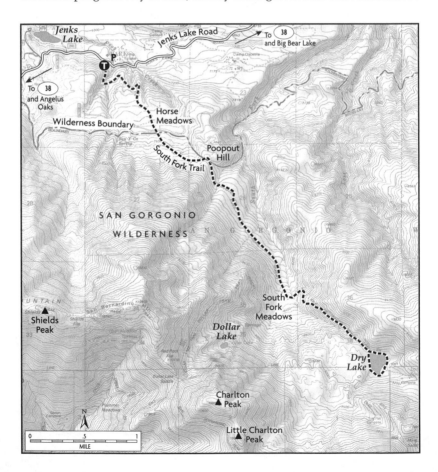

Jepson Peak glistens in the reflecting waters of a not-so-Dry Lake.

on your companion's paws. Make sure that you monitor them closely, and take care not to push too hard. Be watchful as this is a strenuous trek for all but the most experienced of hikers. The beginnings of altitude sickness can raise their head at this elevation, and if you begin to notice signs such as nausea, headache, and lightheadedness you should descend immediately.

If you've timed your hike to coincide with a full lake, you'll be greatly rewarded. The reflections of San Gorgonio and Jepson Peaks in the tarn afford some of the most majestic scenery south of the Sierra Nevada. Indeed, you may have to remind yourself of your latitude and your proximity to Los Angeles to even believe such a scene exists here. Even if you visit Dry Lake when it is only a swamp, pond, meadow, or dry grassland, the view, air, and aura of the place is magical. There's nothing quite like this area anywhere else in Southern California. Return the way you came, downhill the entire way, and make sure to leave nothing behind but footsteps.

37. San Gorgonio Mountain

Round trip: 16 miles
Hiking time: 9.5 hours
High point: 11,499 feet
Elevation gain: 5600 feet
Best season: Late spring in low snow years to early fall
Difficulty: Extremely difficult
Paw comfort: Dirt, duff, and very rocky above 10,000 feet
Water: Vivian Creek, High Creek
Fees and permits: Adventure Pass and wilderness permit required
Map: USGS San Gorgonio Mountain; USGS Forest Falls
Contact: San Bernardino National Forest, Mill Creek Ranger Station
(909) 382-2881, *www.fs.fed.us/r5/sanbernardino*

Getting there: From Interstate 10 east in Redlands, exit onto University. Make a right off the onramp and an immediate left onto Citrus. Turn left again at Judson/Ford and follow it to Lugonia Avenue. Lugonia Avenue is Highway 38. It changes from Lugonia to Mentone Boulevard and then to Mill Creek Road. Follow it for 12.5 miles as it bends and enters the San Bernardino National Forest. Stay straight at Mill Creek Road; do not go up the mountain on Highway 38. You need to veer right onto Valley of the Falls Road and follow the road to its completion in Forest Falls and park at the end in the nearly stadium-size parking area. Once you have parked and secured your Adventure Pass to your mirror, follow the dirt road until it droops to the left and crosses Mill Creek. You'll see the sign for the Vivian Creek Trailhead.

This is one of the most intense hikes you will ever take on a well-developed, highly traveled trail. Many people use this as a training hike for Mount Whitney. The first half-mile after crossing Mill Creek is enough of a proving ground to turn around lots of average folk who think besting this mountain will be an easy task; the trail gains a full thousand feet in that short distance, switchbacking up into the San Gorgonio Wilderness. The first section is rather rocky and you should always check your dog's pads when walking over rocky terrain. You would not want to get halfway or more along in this trek, only to find out you need to carry your pet out on your shoulders.

Once you reach the wilderness the trail levels off a bit, but the verdant fertility of Vivian Creek is what will strike you the most. You enter fern-filled pine woodland that has no equal in Southern California. For the less ambitious, this can actually be a wonderful destination. You won't wear yourself or your dogs out, you will have gotten in a good workout (it is impossible not to on the opening switchbacks), and you will be surrounded by the beauty of this tranquil arm of primeval forest. There are several campsites along this trail that can split up the grueling nature of this bestial hike should you so desire. A lot of people trek the wilderness this way, and it makes the entire adventure more enjoyable for you and your pet. However, this trail can be done in one long day and you will most likely meet people fast packing or trail running, trying to improve their record time up and down the mountain.

The trail itself is very well maintained and steady after the opening switchbacks, when the rockiness subsides, until the last mile and a half before the summit. From Vivian Creek Camp to well after High Creek Campsite, the route is mostly broken gravel and dirt. Much of the way is shaded through morning and should be easy on your pet; there is water available year-round on this section, albeit intermittently as summer progresses. There will always be a puddle or two spaced fairly evenly around the camps and where the trail crosses the creek even in the driest of years.

The final summit push is both figuratively and literally a breathtaking slog over a stony, unshaded, steep alpine landscape completely above tree line and slightly reminiscent of slopes in the Andes or Alps. A solid 2 miles of uphill hiking lies ahead of you when the first looming view of San Jacinto attacks your senses; you might almost feel as if you can throw a stone across the pass and hit the peak with it—after all, San Jacinto's summit is only a measly 20 miles away. Aside from the initial

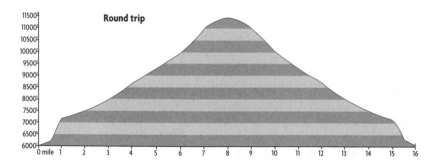

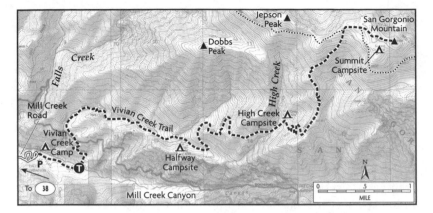

switchbacks, this is the steepest section of the hike. You gain 800 feet per mile, all above 10,000 feet. This is another good point to check your pet's pads for signs of wear, because the remainder of the trail will be rough, and coming back down it will not be any easier. The viewpoint is reached after you have ascended the switchbacks from High Creek Camp; enchanting vistas open wide over the Coachella Valley, Palm Springs, and most of the Inland Empire. If you are lucky, Southern California will not be having a bad air day, because the views can be downright spectacular. Here, the serenity of the wind whispers sweetly and offers the only escape from the mid-day sun. Be wary of summer thunderclouds. Lightning strikes and summer storms are very dangerous at this elevation; you should be ready to descend at the first signs of approaching bad weather.

This is not a trip to undertake if either you or your dogs are underconditioned. This will be an exhausting trip for even the most experienced hiker. I have never completed this trail without feeling like I was beaten up by the mountain. The trail gains more than a mile in vertical elevation, and even though the forest officially lists the distance as 17 miles, it feels like 20 or more. I know people who have registered over 20 on their GPS, so the topos and the mileage from all sources may not be the most accurate. Regardless, the trip off the mountain seems strangely longer than the trip up to the peak. This is a brutal trek and in my humble opinion, tougher than climbing Whitney. There are many climbs in Southern California that are more arduous, but none of them are straight maintained routes; instead, those trips take you off trail, or over other peaks to get to your ultimate destination. This trip is straightforward—it does not even junction with a side trail until you are almost at the summit. You do not need to be an off-trail bushwhacker for this one, but you will need to be in great shape.

Many people view the San Gorgonio Wilderness as the crown jewel of Southern California, and with good reason. There is no easy access to any of its peaks or high elevation lakes and streams. Riff raff and the hoi polloi do not frequent this quarter of the forest because it takes too much of an investment. Wildlife, including bears and bighorn sheep, still roams these wilds. Even on a well-traversed trail such as Vivian Creek, it is still possible to escape the masses and find serenity amid the woods. Please make sure it stays that way. This is a wilderness area, so your pets must be on a leash at all times. You can be ticketed if your pets are not leashed or otherwise confined. This place is fragile, so always be sure to tread lightly.

Lush grasses, ferns, and incense cedar trees line the most verdant meadows along Vivian Creek.

38. Kitching Peak

Round trip: 8 miles
Hiking time: 5 hours
High point: 6598 feet
Elevation gain: 2700 feet
Best season: Year-round, snow in winter
Difficulty: Difficult
Paw comfort: Dirt and rock
Water: Millard Creek is intermittent through summer
Fees and permits: Adventure Pass and wilderness permit required
Map: USGS Whitewater
Contact: San Bernardino National Forest, Mill Creek Ranger Station
(909) 382-2881, *www.fs.fed.us/r5/sanbernardino*

Getting there: Take Interstate 10 east about 85 miles from Los Angeles past the town of Banning, and take the Fields Road exit. Make a left under the underpass and then left again at the stop. Turn right onto Fields Road (there is a guard station limiting access onto the Reservation). Immediately turn right onto Martin Road. Follow it to the cattle guard and make a left-ish turn onto the dirt road. Follow the main road until you see the sign for the turn to Kitching Peak Trail. Access to Kitching Peak and the Millard Canyon area is sometimes limited. The Morongo Band of Indians owns the land that allows access to the forest roads that will take you to the trails. In times of fire risk, the tribal council will shut down the area to all usage, so definitely call ahead on this one. A high-clearance vehicle might be necessary to make it to the trailhead, although any automobile should be able to make it within half a mile with little or no difficulty.

Note: As of this printing, Kitching Peak is closed. Please contact the Mill Creek Ranger Station for information about when it will open.

Kitching Peak is a half-day jaunt to the isolated farthest reaches of the San Bernardino Mountains and the final peak in the nearly 16-mile summit string of the San Gorgonio Wilderness. From the top, you can survey the dropoff to Banning and the San Gorgonio Pass region, while looking backwards at Southern California's highest peaks. Across the

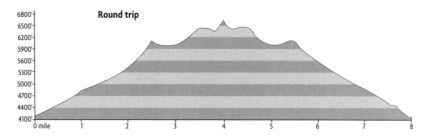

divide, San Jacinto Peak seems hardly a hop, skip, and a jump away. The harsh verticality of its rise from the desert floor is incredibly pronounced from this vantage point. Casino Morongo rises like a modern day monolith and is the most easily recognizable landmark in the area that is not a mountain.

Since this is federal wilderness, you will need a wilderness permit to enter the region, and the only place to get one is at Mill Creek Ranger Station, which is completely on the other side of the range near Redlands. Do yourself a favor and plan in advance and have the permit mailed to you. It will make your driving less and your day easier. This is not an area that receives much traffic, although you might see a few people on the trail on the weekends. Since this is more of a winter hike, you may also see hunters out and about rather than hikers.

The region is heavily wooded and was added to the wilderness in 1984; its resource as a valuable watershed to the high country is the main reason for its inclusion. The area itself is pristine mixed-oak woodland, with stately conifers gracing some of the upper reaches of the peak and residing within the confines of lush and lovely Millard Canyon. Chaparral also makes an appearance on some of the more sun-exposed portions of the trail.

Dogs will love the journey to Kitching Peak. The trail is not very rocky, except in spots, and a good portion of it is shady, complete with a well-worn dirt path. The trail is steep, but evenly graded. The elevation gain is substantial for a trail of this distance, but is nothing you won't get used to after hiking for a while. There is no down-slope until you come to the junction with the trail that leads to The Sink. From here you will want to take a right and head the remaining distance to the top of Kitching Peak. This is where the trail makes a few descents and ascents that are steep and rather challenging if snow and ice are present. If the area has received heavy amounts of snow, you would be well advised to bring along crampons. It can get quite vertical and slippery here. Even though the Millard Canyon region is significantly lower in elevation than the rest of the wilderness, the area is highly prone to sudden shifts in weather, and the same weather changes that occur higher up happen here due to proximity. If the weather changes suddenly for the worse, it is wise to descend immediately. This area can get plastered with snow and rain in the wintertime.

Finding the summit can be a challenge. Near the peak, there are trails that meander off in different directions. The Sierra Club has actually de-listed this peak, calling it "too difficult," probably due to routefinding. Someone has yellow-flagged the trail, which is technically a no-no in wilderness areas, and following the flags will keep you on the trail when you reach the most difficult spot. There has also been a more-than-adequate trail carved out of the brush by animals (and other hikers) where you

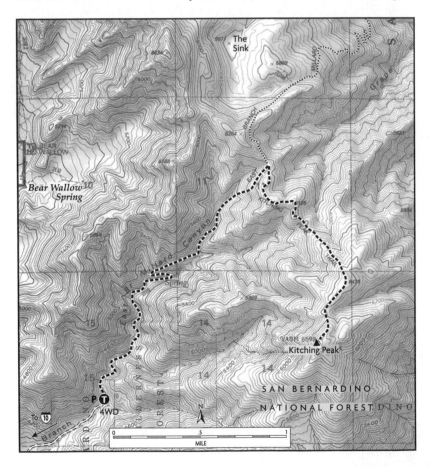

Hiking to Kitching Peak is best saved for cold weather adventures. Summers get very hot, and the area is not heavily frequented in winter.

literally scramble through a canopy of whitethorn and manzanita. This is not the correct way to go, though. The correct trail follows the lowest part of a small mini-canyon through a pine tree clearing and continues by veering up to the right. If you use your instincts and patience, it will not be too tough, even if the flags have been removed. The ambiguity in the trail comes right before the final stretch to the summit. The trail becomes obscured less than a quarter of a mile from the top. Persevere and you can enjoy the great rewards the top of this remarkable wilderness peak has to offer.

LAKE PERRIS STATE RECREATION AREA

39. Terri Peak

Round trip: 3.5 miles
Hiking time: 1.5 hours
High point: 2550 feet
Elevation gain: 1000 feet
Best season: Year-round; summer is very hot
Difficulty: Moderate due to steep elevation gain
Paw comfort: Dirt and rocks
Water: Bring your own
Map: USGS Perris
Contact: Lake Perris State Recreation Area (951) 657-0676, *www.parks.ca.gov*

Getting there: Take Highway 60 to the Moreno Beach exit, and head south toward Lake Perris State Recreation Area (SRA). Follow the road as it becomes Iris Avenue and passes a growing number of stoplights and stop signs. Turn left onto Grande Vista just before Lasselle and follow the road to its end. Walk up the dirt road past the water tanks and the soccer field, and begin ascending once you reach the top of the small hill. This trail enters from outside the park, so there is no entrance fee to be paid. The road to the trail is owned by Riverside Community College and access is available to all. New housing tracts are constantly limiting access to this trail, but it can still be reached via Cahuilla Drive in the college.

Terri Peak is a great workout and altitude trainer in the Perris Lake SRA. Most of the elevation you gain occurs in a little over three-quarters of a mile, so the trail is incredibly steep in sections. While you won't be acclimatizing to alpine oxygen at two thousand feet above sea level, the gain will make your body accustomed to the demands of higher altitude hiking. There are several smaller off-shoots that all meet up with the main trail; many are cut switchbacks or deer paths that gradually appear as the season gets drier and much of the thicker foliage dies away. The trail is well marked and easy to follow, though not heavily traveled.

The area is most beautiful in the spring or a few days to a couple of weeks after a rain shower. Many varieties of desert wildflowers bloom, and the area can become quite alive and lovely. However, any time of year is pleasant, especially at sunset. Even in summer, the temperatures cool down just enough to allow for delightful hiking an hour before twilight or just before dawn. The best views occur in winter when the smog is minimal. In summer, smog can impair even the closest of viewpoints.

Once on top, a large plateau covers a sizeable amount of ground that is unperceivable when viewed from below. In the middle of the mesa, the only visible landmarks are the looming mountain ranges of Southern California, the San Bernardinos—including eye-opening shots of the entire San Gorgonio ridgeline—the San Jacintos, the San Gabriels, the Santa Anas, the Palomars/Agua Tibias, and the Lagunas. All of the major

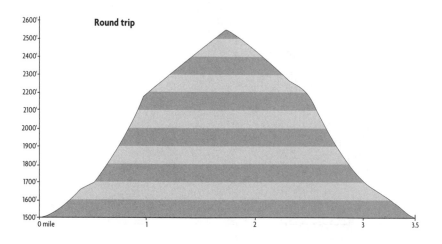

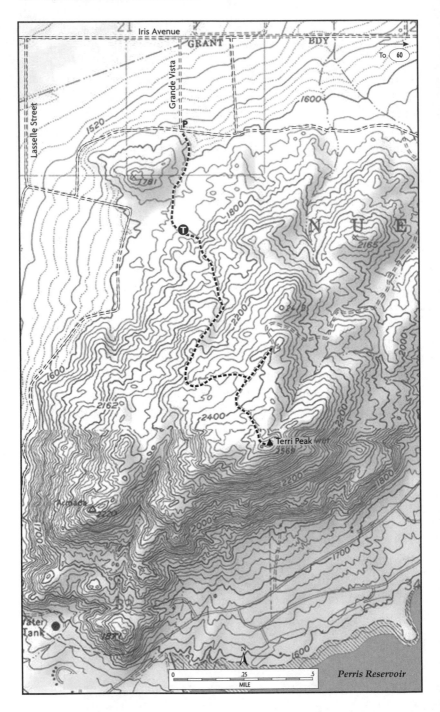

Perris Lake sits boldly beneath the shoulder of Terri Peak. The long, flat mountaintop area to the back is the Palomar chain.

Southern California peaks can be seen from this vantage point on a clear day. Since the area is primarily a desert, the best time to hike is in winter. When the summer heat and coastal breezes have stopped blowing the smog inland, the skies are pure and the views are outstanding. From the summit the perspective is even better, and the straight-down look into Perris Lake is amazing. Due to the arid nature of the region, high fire danger is a constant threat. Always be careful and aware.

Rabbits, coyotes, quail, deer, skunk, owls, red-tailed hawks, rattle-snakes, and mountain lions can all be seen here, though infrequently. This is an arid desert environment that is rapidly being encroached upon from all sides by housing and urban sprawl. Be aware that evening is a critical time for the predators in this group and stay away from encounters by always making your presence known. Coyotes have attempted to lure dogs away from the trail, so always be on alert.

The vertical nature of a trail such as this can increase endurance and boost your uphill workouts tremendously. If you can find something similar close to home that you can do three nights a week with your pooch, you will be ready for anything the mountains can throw at you. A training hike like this is invaluable to prepare you for long backpacks, treks to the eastern Sierra passes, or even easy summit attempts of the 10,000-footers in this neck of the woods.

HUNTINGTON DOG BEACH

40. Huntington Dog Beach

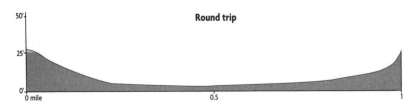

Round trip: 1-2 miles
Hiking time: 1 hour
High point: 30 feet
Elevation gain: 25 feet
Best season: Year-round
Difficulty: Easy
Paw comfort: Sand
Water: Water fountain on the bluff above the beach
Map: USGS Newport Beach
Contact: Preservation Society of Huntington Dog Beach (714) 841-8644, *www.dogbeach.org*

Getting there: From Interstate 405, exit Goldenwest Street and head south. Follow Goldenwest as it curves west towards the Pacific Coast Highway (Highway 1) and park in the lot or along the roadway. The beach is open from 5 am to 10 pm every day of the year, but the parking lots close at 8 pm. Parking is $.25 for every 10 minutes. On weekends, representatives for the beach are stationed at the entrances to answer questions, offer assistance, or accept donations.

Round trip

50'

25'

0'
0 mile   0.5   1

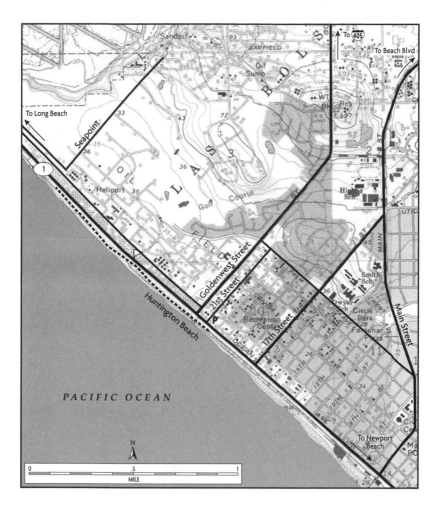

Huntington Dog Beach is the one place in Orange County where dogs can freely run over the beach. And run they do. You will find dogs of all breeds and sizes gamboling in the water and sand. The area where dogs are allowed on the beach extends between Seapoint on the north and 21st Street on the south. Roughly a mile of shore and surf exists solely for the pleasure of dogs and their proud owners. On any given weekend the beach is full of dogs running to and fro. No leashes, no restraints, just tennis balls, sticks, Frisbees, and canines aplenty. Those who enter the beach do so at their own risk.

Nothing too scenic here—a boulder-strewn seawall provides protection for the city streets in case of extremely high tides or waves. Offshore oil platforms sit in the distance, slowly extracting the final remains of long since decayed dinosaurs. Fittingly, the least scenic area has been reserved for the dogs, but the dogs don't seem to mind in the slightest. There are a few rules to keep in mind. Your dogs must be on leash before you enter and as soon as you leave the beach. They must be in control at all times, though no one will notice if they are not. Dogs literally jump and zoom about everywhere. This seems to be the place dogs come to get out of control, though they all have a purpose that has little or nothing to do with humans. You will see dogs running up and down the sand with reckless abandon. They will jump into waves for carefully tossed sticks and balls. The site is quite impressive.

Whether you hike on this one or not, you are sure to get exercise running with your pooch. It is possible to walk from one end of the beach to the other, but that is up to you and your dog. Your pet will thank you for coming here in more ways than one. Simply watching the dogs ride a wave and exert limitless energy on the beach is well worth the price of parking. Huntington Dog Beach is sure to put a smile on you and your dog's faces.

SAN JACINTO MOUNTAINS

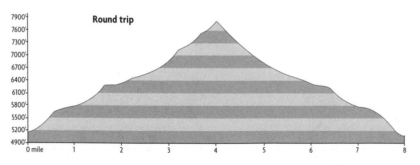

41. Black Mountain

Round trip: 8 miles
Hiking time: 4 hours
High point: 7772 feet
Elevation gain: 2700 feet
Best season: Year-round, but summers can be hot
Difficulty: Difficult
Paw comfort: Dirt, duff, and some rocks
Water: Hall Canyon Creek through early summer
Fees and permits: Adventure Pass required
Map: USGS Lake Fulmor
Contact: San Bernardino National Forest, San Jacinto Ranger District (909) 382-2921, *www.fs.fed.us/r5/sanbernardino*

Getting there: From Los Angeles, take Interstate 10 east 85 miles to Banning and exit onto Highway 243. Follow the signs for Highway 243, making a left and then a right, and drive up the San Jacinto massif. Thirteen miles out of Banning and just beyond the Vista Grande Ranger Station

Round trip

and Girl Scout Camp, you will see a sign for Black Mountain Trail. Park in the pullout on the east side of the road.

The San Jacinto region is a favorite of many Southern Californians. Most who visit here enthusiastically proclaim its resemblance to the Sierra Nevada, and this hike shows off many of those endearing qualities. The area is strewn with large granite boulders and enormous lodgepole pines. The many open-air vistas offer magnificent views of the Inland Empire, the San Gorgonio Wilderness, the San Gabriels, the Palomars, the Santa Rosas, and Mount San Jacinto itself. This hike takes place outside the Mount San Jacinto State Park and the wilderness area, so no permit is necessary other than the Adventure Pass needed for parking.

The Black Mountain Trail itself is straight to the point; you gain nearly 3000 feet in less than 4 miles. It contours near and along a ridgeline most of the way and then follows a wash through Hall Canyon close to the peak. At the top, turn right onto the road and follow it up to the lookout. There are no ups and downs, just ups, but the climb very steadily gains 600 to 700 feet per mile. Once you get moving and into your rhythm, the incline just doesn't seem as steep. Indeed, if you are used to this type of trail and like to move fast, you can make it to the top and back in little more than 2 hours. The trail begins at the highway and crosses through a mixed oak and pine forest, quickly ascending into the San Jacinto high country. Though rocky in some areas, this trail is nearly perfect for dogs—it is mostly dirt- and duff-covered, and just long enough to get them used to and trained for hiking. There are a few places where you might have to look for the trail, but it is very well maintained and a few seconds of searching will have you on the main passage in no time.

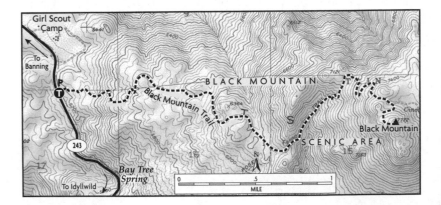

Socs likes to hop on rocks, and there are plenty along the way to Black Mountain.

Since the trail is outside the park and the wilderness, it is not one of the more popular trails in the area. So if seclusion for you and your dogs is what you are looking for, this is the trail for you. In addition, if you make it out early enough, there is abundant wildlife. The wildflowers bloom along Hall Canyon Creek and the haze is greatly reduced through the San Gorgonio Pass, which makes for epic photo opportunities.

Winter is the best time to take this trek because the views are wide and vast, the air is crisp and cleansed of smog, and solitude is everywhere. Be wary of ice patches on the path, though. For some reason winter ice is always present at the most dangerous sections of trail, so use extra caution. Dogs are much better at avoiding slippery ice and falls down the mountainside. There is a road (generally closed in winters) to the top of Black Mountain, so there is an easy way up, but what fun would that be? From Memorial Day through the October or November snow closure of Black Mountain Road, the lookout tower atop the peak is staffed by friendly volunteers. It receives few visitors due to the long dirt drive one must take to reach it. If you do make this trip when the lookout is staffed, make sure to stop in and say hello. You can sign your name in the visitor book in lieu of a register, and the volunteers will answer any questions you have about the forest. Enjoy your view from one of the many boulder outcroppings, have a snack or a meal, and head back the way you came. A last word of caution: don't try getting your pooches up the metal-latticed steps at the lookout, unless you enjoy carrying them down steep flights of stairs.

42. Tahquitz Peak

Round trip: 6 miles
Hiking time: 4 hours
High point: 8846 feet
Elevation gain: 2500 feet
Best season: Year-round, snow in winter
Difficulty: Difficult
Paw comfort: Gravelly dirt and rock
Water: Bring your own, no water
Fees and permits: Adventure Pass and wilderness permit required
Map: USGS San Jacinto Peak
Contact: San Bernardino National Forest, San Jacinto Ranger District
(909) 382-2921, *www.fs.fed.us/r5/sanbernardino*

Getting there: Head south on Highway 243 from Idyllwild and turn left on Saunders Meadow Road. Turn north (left) onto Pine Avenue (you can only turn north) then turn right onto Tahquitz View Drive, follow

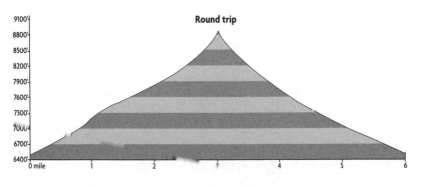

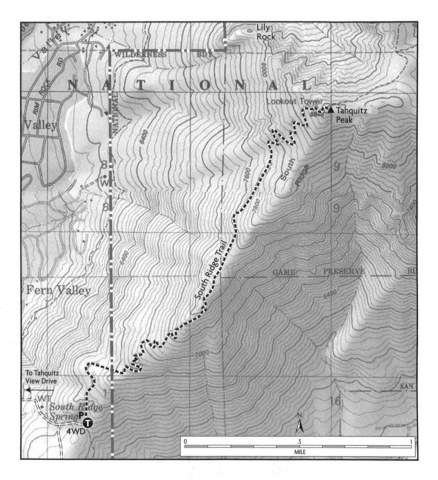

it until you see a sign for South Ridge Road. There isn't really a sign for the road, but it lists the trail as an option on the sign. Turn right and follow it to its completion. The road is a bit rocky and can be muddy and washed out after rain or in a particularly wet year. You might need to stop and park a quarter-mile lower than the trailhead if you do not have four-wheel drive. If you are heading north into Idyllwild, be aware that Saunders Meadow Road is a loop. If you take the southern leg, you will turn right onto Pine Avenue after looping around.

The South Ridge Trail is the "easy" way to get to Tahquitz Peak, depending upon who you talk to. Generally, this route is hotter and dryer than the route up the Devils Slide from Humber Park in Idyllwild. The South Ridge

Trail is also "less" visited than the other route, and is the best choice for dog owners. Fido will probably get a chance to meet other dogs along the way, as many dog owners bring their pups up to the highest fire lookout in the San Bernardino Mountains via this route. This trail does traverse entirely through the San Jacinto Wilderness and your dog will need to be leashed. In wilderness areas, leashing is required by law. Travel this trail on a weekend and it may be busy; even so, it won't feel crowded.

Unless you are attempting this summit at the very beginnings of spring, do not expect water. The water on this side dries up before the snow leaves the peak, so make sure you bring lots of extra water for your pooch, and for both of your sakes get an early start. If you are on the trail by seven or eight in the morning, you should be fine, but later than that in the summertime can get extremely hot. The lower part of the trail is partially shaded through oak and mixed pine forest, but as you traverse upwards the trail becomes chaparral covered and highly exposed. About

The fire lookout atop Tahquitz Peak was built in 1937 and is now a national historic lookout. It has been consistently manned by courteous volunteers since 1998.

halfway along, you'll reach a "window" rock where you can look thro
at the lower San Jacintos and the Desert Divide, and then quickly you
come to a plateau that makes a nice rest stop. This is where the trail be
gins to get the majority of its sun exposure and you'll be climbing fairly
steeply for the remainder of your voyage. The walkway becomes rockier
at this point, changing over from a mostly dirt- and duff-covered trail. It
isn't as bad as some trails, but as usual, you will want to make sure your
dog's paws are conditioned for such use.

The trail is easy to follow and very well-maintained. There are a few
places where it converges with an old fire road that was built for the
first lookout on the mountain. Most of these can be followed and meet
up with the main trail, so if you are looking for adventure or off-trail
investigating, you can always take an offshoot and explore. The trail only
has one junction and that is near the very top; make a slight right turn
and head up to the fire lookout. Remember the turn and sign, because
you will be returning to Idyllwild, not Saddle Junction. It is possible to
make a loop out of these two trails, but it requires traversing the Ernie
Maxwell Trail and walking along two separate roads, which adds another
6 or 7 miles to your hike.

The fire lookout on the summit was built in 1937 and has been operated by a courteous and dedicated staff of volunteers since 1998. The
tower is open from Memorial Day until the first snowfall of the season,
and it is open as often as volunteers can fill the slots. Dogs are not allowed
into the tower and may be frightened climbing down the steps, so be
careful if you take them up. The hosts can answer any questions about
the numerous peaks, lakes, and valleys around you and about the forest
itself—all you have to do is ask. The views are spectacular; Catalina and
San Clemente Islands are visible on the clearest of days, as are all of the
major peaks of Southern California except those in the San Gorgonio
Wilderness. The Salton Sea glimmers like a mirage in the distance at the
end of the Coachella Valley. Garner Valley rolls underneath as the lower
peaks of the San Jacintos settle to the south and join the Santa Rosas. The
air up there is a bit thinner and folks used to sea level may have a bit of
a problem due to the lack of oxygen. At 8828 feet some people may be
susceptible to altitude sickness, and anyone feeling dizzy, nauseated, or
disoriented should descend immediately.

An interesting side story about Tahquitz is the legend surrounding
the name of the mountain. Takwish or Daquish was a demon who stole
the souls of people who disappeared in the forest. He was notorious and

ndary among most of the natives of Southern California, and nearly ... tribes attribute menacing stories to him. Takwish would devour his victims after taking them back to his home within a boulder located somewhere on the mountain. He created lightning and thunder, as well as earthquakes, and his mere appearance was enough to strike a person dead. Any people who disappeared in the mountains, especially young females, were believed to have been captured and eaten by Takwish.

43. Palm View Peak

Round trip: 9 miles
Hiking time: 4 hours
High point: 7160 feet
Elevation gain: 2200 feet
Best season: Fall through spring
Difficulty: Difficult
Paw comfort: Rocky dirt and gravel
Water: Bring your own
Fees and permits: Adventure Pass required
Map: USGS Palm View Peak
Contact: San Bernardino National Forest, San Jacinto Ranger District (909) 382-2921, *www.fs.fed.us/r5/sanbernardino*

Getting there: Take Highway 74 east for 2 miles past Lake Hemet. Turn left onto Fobes Ranch Road. The turnoff is only marked with a small sign on the fence, so keep a watchful eye out for it. Fobes Ranch is a dirt road that has many offshoots and lesser-use roads connected to it. Stay on the main road, and when in doubt turn upwards. Nearly 3.5 miles down the road, there will be a sign that indicates you should turn right.

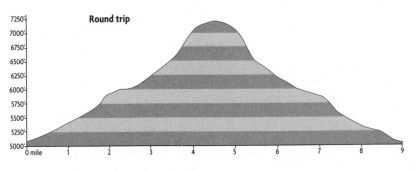

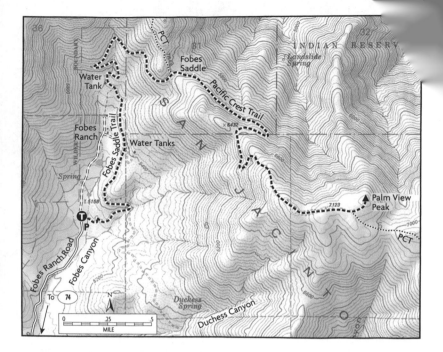

The trailhead is 0.5 mile farther. Park in the turnouts. There is an incline ahead with a locked gate at the end. Do not go up the road any farther; it is steep, rough, and blocked. The trail begins by the parking area.

A man named Dick Wakale signed the peak register on top of Palm View Peak with this crafty witticism: "No Palms, No View, No Peak." While his quip of a comment is true and taken, this does not mean the hike is completely without merits. The view from the top may be nonexistent. There aren't any palms or even a viewpoint that might allow you to see the distinctive desert trees in the valley below. The peak itself is little more than a pile of rocks that were possibly erected solely to house the summit register amid a thick cluster of pine trees. The old adage that half the fun is getting there is erased by a hike to Palm View Peak, because all of the fun is getting there and getting back, none of it is about being on top. The summit itself is really without value and difficult to find without a GPS. With a good map and some trail sense, you will eventually find the peak and the register filled with signatures that date back to the early 1980s; that is, if you spend some time working at it.

Your dog will love this area. The trails are mostly gravelly sand

The snow-covered San Jacinto massif affords excellent picture-taking opportunities.

that can punish sedentary dogs, but rewards active dogs already equipped with tough pads. The Desert Divide is a completely under-utilized area of the San Jacintos. Many people avoid this region, because pines are found only on the uppermost section of the trails. The preponderance of weekend hikers will make the trip to Mount San Jacinto State Park in Idyllwild and ignore the lower section of the mountains entirely. When most people choose to get out and hike, they go only once in a while and want the easiest access to lush pine forest. That is not a description of the Desert Divide, which makes this place great for anyone who hikes with off-leash dogs and likes to explore without swimming through herds of people on the trail.

The west- and south-facing trails can be ingloriously hot even in winter, if you haven't gotten an early enough start. The converse of this is that an early start can mean frigid mountain temperatures that can send a chill to the depths of your toes. The good thing about chills is that walking briskly gets them out of your mind almost immediately. Another bonus is that winter is hardly the most popular time to hike. Since this area is primarily a cooler-weather adventure, many people are not even aware of its potential.

The trail climbs and climbs up to Fobes Saddle, where you are greeted with incredible vistas of the Coachella Valley, Lake Hemet, and the highest reaches of San Jacinto Peak. An old wooden sign marks the junction with the Pacific Crest Trail (PCT) and the route to both Cedar Springs

and Palm View Peak. Turn right at the junction and follow the
it ascends through manzanita, whitethorn and other mixed cha
Eventually you'll see some pine trees amid the granite outcroppings,
once you reach a high plateau with fantastic views of Toro and Sar
Rosa Peaks in the distance to the south, the peak is not very far away. The
path becomes a little more obscured up here, but this high country has
an austere beauty all its own. If you live for beautiful places to rest and
relax when hiking, do it here and forget about the summit. This is the
wonderful viewpoint, and the open area is a great place for your dogs to
run if you've come in wintertime. The dry grass will not be harmed by
them trampling it; it's already dead for the season.

Peak-baggers will of course want to continue on to the summit, which
is nearly an eighth of a mile off-trail to the east. After experiencing the
anti-climactic peak of Palm View, return the way you came for breathtaking views in the opposite direction that you may have missed on the
way up.

44. Pyramid Peak

Round trip: 7 miles
Hiking time: 4 hours
High point: 7035 feet
Elevation gain: 1700 feet
Best season: Late fall through late spring
Difficulty: Moderate
Paw comfort: Rocky dirt and gravel
Water: Morris Creek unreliable, Cedar Spring into summer
Fees and permits: Adventure Pass required
Map: USGS Palm View Peak
Contact: San Bernardino National Forest, San Jacinto Ranger District
(909) 382-2921, *www.fs.fed.us/r5/sanbernardino*

Getting there: Drive about 4.5 miles east of the Lake Hemet Store on
Highway 74. Turn left onto Morris Ranch Road. Follow it for a little more
than 3.6 miles. The road is paved and parking is the wide turnout lot on
the right hand side. You have to walk a tenth of a mile up the road to
reach the trailhead. The no trespassing signs are not for hikers; just make
certain to respect the private property you cross to get to the trailhead.

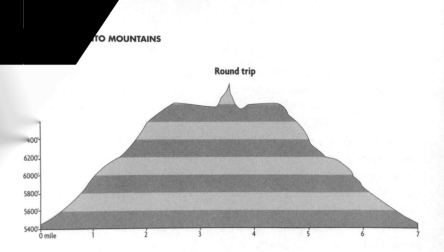

Round trip

Pyramid Peak lies along a relatively obscure section of the Pacific Crest Trail (PCT) known as the Desert Divide. The views here arc from horizon to horizon, and the scenery is some of the most spectacular in all of Southern California. The San Jacinto massif commands the northern sky while the Santa Rosa range blankets the south; Lake Hemet rests in Garner Valley below, and the Coachella Valley expands endlessly to the Salton Sea in the west. On the clearest day, Catalina and San Clemente Island, jutting out of the Pacific, can be spotted from atop the crest. Despite all this, the entire lower section of the San Jacinto Mountains is sparsely used, even on weekends. There is a good reason for this, however. Take this hike on a hot summer afternoon, and you'll never come back, maybe literally. The climb to the crest and summit is sun-exposed the entire way, which means temperatures in the upper 90s and beyond by mid-morning during the hottest time of year.

The best ways to avoid the sun are to get an incredibly early start, or take this trip on a brisk wintry morn. Even with temperatures dipping into the 40s, having the sun on your back while you climb in fresh desert air is exhilarating, and your dogs will love it. This is a perfect off-leash area, but be sure to keep a leash handy. You may share this trail with horses, and your pups might not know how to react to these rather strange, enormous, and unfamiliar beasts.

This is a high-elevation desert hike, and you'll be hiking through a transition zone into the remote beginnings of pine forest. Consequently, there is very little water on the trail. There is rarely more than a mud puddle in the stream, and Cedar Spring is a little out of the way if you are going to Pyramid Peak. Please keep this in mind for your dogs and bring along extra water. There are no shade trees on the climb and only

a couple along the crest. You'll be sharing this trail mostly with
ranean chaparral of the dry variety.

The first half-mile alternates between trail and road. As you e
cross, and exit private land holdings, there are gates that should
closed behind you. The trail follows the creek bed for a bit through oaker.
woodland. Soon, you will reach a picnic area and the switchbacks. The
slope is constant yet gentle. A good pace will have you up to the crest in
no time, and you'll have received a great workout along the way. It is a
bit rocky, so wear strong boots, and watch the paws.

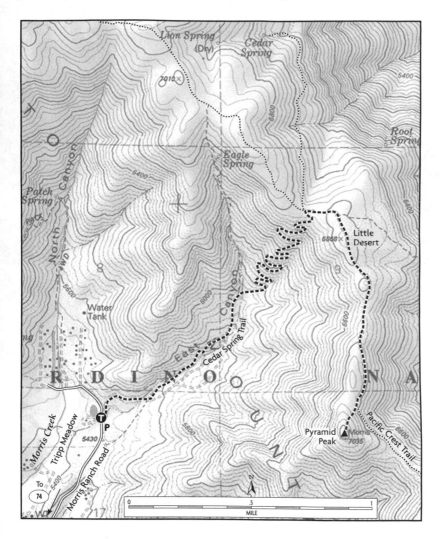

Pyramid Peak slightly resembles its namesake. The off-trail scramble through chaparral will more likely be rougher on you than on your dog.

After 2 miles you'll reach the PCT. From here other options are available, all of them good, and the hidden forested splendor of Cedar Spring cannot be overstated should you choose that route. The junction is where you'll find the trail's solitary shade tree, and you can take a rest or just take a right to the peak. Follow the trail until you almost pass the peak. A ducked cairn will lead you to the top, although you may have to scramble through the bramble a bit to reach the zenith. Chewee, a twenty-pound chihuahua/terrier mix, has made this summit easily several times.

From the rocky top, you have a full 360-degree panorama and everything around you comes into crisp vibrant view.

45. Thomas Mountain

Round trip: 12 miles
Hiking time: 6 hours
High point: 6825 feet
Elevation gain: 2300 feet
Best season: Year-round; hot in summer, snow in winter
Difficulty: Difficult
Paw comfort: Rock and dirt
Water: Tool Box Spring year-round; streams are dry by late spring most years
Fees and permits: Adventure Pass required
Map: USGS Idyllwild; USGS Anza
Contact: San Bernardino National Forest, San Jacinto Ranger District (909) 382-2921, *www.fs.fed.us/r5/sanbernardino*

Getting there: Drive 25 miles east of Hemet on Highway 74 to the turnout for the Ramona Trail/Toolbox Springs parking lot, or from the Palm Desert intersection of Highways 111 and 74 drive south and west on Highway 74 for nearly 29 miles to the same parking lot. The parking lot has recently been reworked and it is large with ample space for parking. Many of the trails in the Santa Rosas are infrequently used, so the lot is often wide open. Once again, most people who frequent this area prefer the higher regions of the San Jacintos. The parking area is on the south side of the road, and the trail begins among a convoluted maze of roads. Head left and up the hillside for the correct trail/road.

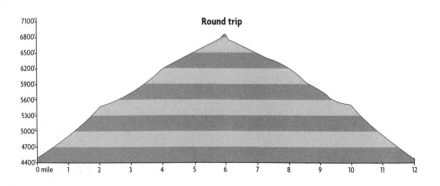

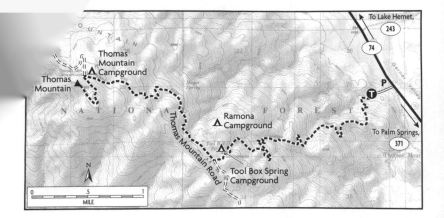

The Ramona Trail is spectacular for several reasons. One, the views of Garner Valley, Desert Divide, and the San Jacintos are phenomenal. Two, there is rarely any traffic on this trail or the road that takes you to the top of Thomas Mountain, so you and your dogs are free to scamper. Three, you travel through four distinct climate zones in 2300 feet of elevation. Four, the trail is evenly graded all the way to the top and shaded from the sun for the last 3 miles of the climb. Five, the trail is the spot of Southern California lore made famous by the late nineteenth-century novel *Ramona*. Helen Hunt Jackson wrote a tragic tale about the half-native/half-Scottish Ramona and her ill-fated Mission Indian lover, Alessandro. Alessandro is murdered after the two are harassed and abused. Jackson wanted her novel to be a staging ground in the struggle for Native American rights. Apparently, there is truth to the story; the Ramona legend remains an enigmatic yet enduring myth for the settlement of Southern California. Many places throughout Southern California bear her name because the book brought many tourists coming to look at the landscape where the Romeo and Juliet of native mythos resided. There are no places of note along the hike that correspond to the novel, but it is an interesting side-story that connects the hiker to the history and literature of the area.

This is a perfect clear-day winter hike; the snow level doesn't get much lower than 6000 feet in these parts, and even though a majority of the hike above that elevation is well-shaded, the snow is often light and the trail is easily followed. The clearest views in Southern California are to be had during the peak of winter, and this climb is a stunner. On top of Thomas Mountain, you'll see for miles and miles, all the way to Mexico. Even in winter, though, it is wise to get an early start. The sun bears down hard on the first 2.5 miles of trail. The ascent is steady and evenly to Tool Box Springs and beyond, but you have to pass th two climate zones before you reach the upper shaded heights of the The lower chaparral and sagebrush scrub give way to upper chapar and yellow pine forest. The sage, manzanita, mountain mahogany, and ribbonwood plant community offers no relief from the sun, but upon reaching the Jeffrey pine forest that adorns the upper reaches of the plateau, you'll enter a woodland wonder above the dryness and heat. This area has some of the cleanest air of all Southern California mountains. It is smack in the middle of the San Jacintos and Santa Rosas, away from Inland Empire smog, buttressed by taller mountains surrounding it; it rises above Garner Valley and Lake Hemet as a sort of island in the middle of this mountain paradise.

Socrates stops on a rock to get a better smell of the mountain air.

you reach Tool Box Springs, which has water flowing year-round ⸲h a pipe and spigot, you'll follow the road to a lovely campground, ⸲h is as good a place as any to turn around. You may also continue ⸲ng Thomas Mountain Road another few miles to the peak. Since this ⸲s about the halfway point, let the water spill into your collapsible dog bowl or container and have them drink to contentedness. They'll be ready for it after the dusty rocky trail and often hot first few miles. Fill them up again on the way out, and that way you will not have to carry much extra water. As stated, the beginning section of the trail is rocky and dusty, but after 2 miles you enter the Jeffrey forest and the trail is dirt- and duff-covered. The roadway is remarkably easy on canine feet, so let the dogs run freely. Just remember, summer weekends at the campgrounds may be busier than other times, so always be respectful and watchful for your dogs around vehicles and other people.

There are trails that traverse the same area as the road, but your best bet is to continue on the road and head up to where a fire lookout once stood. All that remains is the foundation, though campgrounds dot the top of the huge, relatively flat peak area. The road gets infrequent traffic, although mountain bikers are allowed on the trail and, of course, on the road.

You and your canine companions will have a wonderful time on this trail. The clear views are enjoyable on the way in and on the way out. The scented air will remind you of what the mountains are all about. The solitude will allow you and your pets to roam freely. And just perhaps you'll understand what John Muir meant when he said getting out of it was really a way of "going in."

SANTA ROS. MOUNTAINS

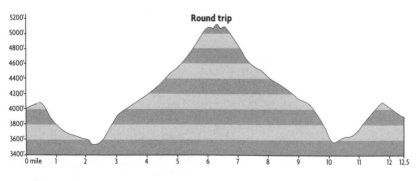

46. Sheep Mountain

Round trip: 12.5 miles
Hiking time: 8.5 hours
High point: 5141 feet
Elevation gain: 2600 feet
Best season: Late fall through late winter, devastatingly hot in summer
Difficulty: Extremely difficult, off-trail desert hiking
Paw comfort: Sand and dirt
Water: Horsethief Creek; Cactus Springs is unreliable and used by
Peninsular bighorn sheep; best to bring your own
Fees and permits: Adventure Pass required
Map: USGS Toro Peak
Contact: San Bernardino National Forest, San Jacinto Ranger District
(909) 382-2921, *www.fs.fed.us/r5/sanbernardino*

Getting there: From Los Angeles take Interstate 10 90 miles east to
Banning. Exit onto Highway 243 to Idyllwild. Follow Highway 243 to

74 and head east for 21 miles. Turn right onto paved Forest Road 7S06. There is a sign for the Ribbonwood Equestrian Park, ⌐awmill Trail, and the Cactus Spring Trail. At the end of the road is ⌐umongous parking lot; usually there are no cars because this is not a ⌐opular area of the forest.

This is a harsh desert trail. The elevation gain and distance are misleading; you and your pets will feel as if you have doubled both mileage and altitude when you return home. Much of the trail is rocky and can be disastrous for your pets unless they are used to hiking 2 to 4 times a week for at least a few hours at a time. There are spiny succulents, yuccas, chollas, and other evil plant life that also conspire against you and your pet. The trail has more ups and downs than a roller coaster and at least part of the way is slogging through semi-soft sand, and another part is off-trail bushwhacking up the side of a sun-scorched desert mountain. If that isn't enough, the return trail seems longer than the trail in, and no matter how paradoxical it seems, this trail is uphill both ways.

With that out of the way, why in the world would anyone want to hike this trail? The answers are quite simple. The stark nature of the Santa Rosa Desert is pure beauty in all of its forms. The air and views are crisp, clean, and unimpeded. Lastly, but of course not least, is solitude; the trail register atop Sheep Mountain has signatures dating back to 1967. As far as mountains go in Southern California, that is a very long time, and the register is by no means full. So, either the difficulty, the off-trail bushwhack, or the barren nature of this trail makes it one of Southern California's best kept secrets. I doubt that mentioning it in this book will make things change any time soon. Make no mistake about it, this is a difficult hike.

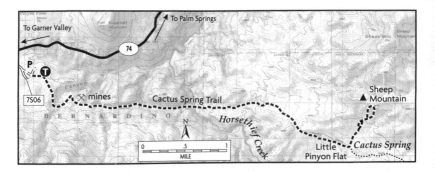

Towering rock formations provide easy landmarks for the off-trail navigation needed to summit solitary Sheep Mountain.

From the parking lot, follow the road through the gate; there are lots of roads around and mine equipment remnants. Follow the map and stay on the road headed east. Soon after you pass the mines, it will turn into the Cactus Spring Trail. Follow that all the way to the spring, then head north off-trail through the main desert wash up to Sheep Mountain. Even though the distance from Cactus Spring to Sheep Mountain is only 1.5 miles, that distance is through rough scrub and brambles. You will be poked, you will stumble as you ascend, and the climb is over hot ground, even in the coldest time of winter. Distances off-trail can be incredibly deceiving, although this is as good a place as any to try it. Good map skills, a compass, and/or a GPS are recommended for

empt beyond Cactus Spring. Supposedly there is an unofficial
that can be followed the entire way to the apex. There are a few
ns and bits of trail near the top, but it is hard to follow any section
or more than a few hundred yards. This trail is just not frequented
enough for an unmaintained trail to remain over time. For those that
are not inclined, Cactus Spring is a good place to stop and enjoy the
surrounding beauty. Even Horsethief Creek can be a nice destination
and turn around point. Monitor your dog on any trip like this and make
sure his health is primary in your concerns.

An added benefit of hiking in a lonely desert environment is that it
makes it easier to train your dogs to stay on the trail. There aren't the
distractions of other people, and the spiky flora makes staying on the
trail much more fun than going off of it.

The scenery on this trail is absolutely fantastic. The tallest summit
areas in Southern California can both be seen from atop the peak and
along the trail. Martinez Mountain looms fantastically to the south
and Toro Peak, the crown jewel of the Santa Rosas, sits above you like
a pine forest island in the sky. Horsethief Creek is idyllic, and along
with the canyon washes provides some of the only shade along the
entire trail. Only a small shoulder of the Salton Sea is visible from the
summit, but the entire range of the Little San Bernardinos and Joshua
Tree National Park can be observed along with the entire expanding
Coachella Valley.

A side note about this trip is the proximity to the elusive and endangered Peninsular bighorn sheep. Obviously the peak is named for the
desert mammals, though their numbers have declined and their habits
have changed drastically. It is doubtful that any sheep come here, at
least not regularly. In 1996 their numbers were estimated to be around
280. These bashful creatures are deathly afraid of domestic dogs and
consider them a predator. Please do not enter any trails in the area if they
are closed because of calving season or other warnings. Do not let your
dogs drink from or get close to natural springs, because the scent they
leave behind can linger and cause the sheep to avoid their usual water
sources. This in turn can lead to death by dehydration for the sheep. A
scared fleeing animal causes it to burn needed energy to evade predators and can also cause the animal harm. These are irreplaceable natural
resources that we all must protect, so please be considerate—their future
may depend upon your interaction with their environment.

47. Toro Peak

Round trip: 3.25 miles
Hiking time: 1.5 hours
High point: 8716 feet
Elevation gain: 1050 feet
Best season: Year-round; entry gate may be closed in winter due to snow or in fire season for safety
Difficulty: Easy, but moderate elevation gain
Paw comfort: Dirt and rock
Water: Stump and Virgin Springs are not on the trail and may not be reliable, so bring your own
Fees and permits: Adventure Pass required
Map: USGS Toro Peak
Contact: San Bernardino National Forest, San Jacinto Ranger District (909) 382-2921, *www.fs.fed.us/r5/sanbernardino*

Getting there: Take Highway 74 east from Hemet for 22 miles. The highway passes through tranquil Garner Valley and into the Santa Rosas on its way to Palm Springs. You'll turn right (south) onto Santa Rosa Road. Follow it for 12.5 miles to the locked gate. Park in the turnout. The road itself is interesting in that it traverses through a variety of ecosystems, from desert to alpine woodlands. This is a bumpy and rutted dirt road, not recommended for low-clearance vehicles. If you are determined, I

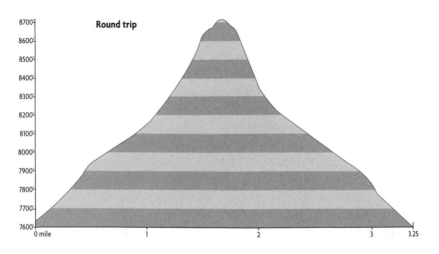

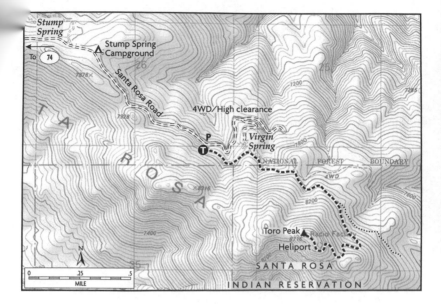

am sure you will make it, but it is best for a four-wheel-drive vehicle or, at the very least, a truck.

Toro Peak and the Santa Rosas may be one of the best-kept secrets in Southern California. A genuine pine forest paradise awaits at the top of the road. This wooded island in the sky is a true treasure above 6800 feet. The ponderosa and Jeffrey pines have grown tall here in this incredibly arid region above the Coachella Valley. This is the highest area of the Santa Rosa Mountains and it gets just enough snow every year to keep it from desertification. However, with bark beetles and the long lasting drought, it might not be enough. This is truly a one-of-a-kind place. Caustic warnings, such as "Rocks don't burn, but trees and man will," have been painted on trees and rocks as you approach this gentle wonderland. It is obvious these are not the usual Smokey Bear warnings from the Forest Service. The soul who painted them was none other than "Desert" Steve Ragsdale, a man who came to these mountains in the 1930s. He built a cabin atop Santa Rosa Peak (the burnt remains are there to this day), helped to build the road into the area, and remained the unofficial protector of these parts until his death in 1970. A short side road leads up to his cabin and should be a must for history buffs and people with children.

The trail to the top of Toro Peak is not a trail at all but a road. The land was leased in the 1970s by the Cahuilla Indians to be used as a mili installation that consists of repeater towers and microwave relays. Eve though it is a great shame that perhaps the best craggy zenith view in all of Southern California has been spoiled by roads and buildings, it still is immensely enjoyable nonetheless. Directions on this hike are simple—follow the road to the top. Only the last half-mile is steep, and by that point you are already there anyway.

Toro Peak was called Wel'a'mo by the Cahuilla and was considered a place of evil spirits. The natives did not go there; perhaps that is why they leased the summit to the U.S. military. Today, the views are still awe inspiring as you overlook the San Jacinto massif, the San Gabriels, the Santa Rosas, the San Bernardinos including San Gorgonio, the Palomars, the Cuyamacas, the Santa Anas, all of Anza Borrego State Park, the Salton Sea, the Coachella Valley, Garner Valley, Joshua Tree National Park, the lower Santa Rosas, and on a clear day the ocean and the southernmost Channel Islands of Santa Catalina and San Clemente. That is quite an impressive list. Virtually all of the major Southern California landmarks can be seen from atop the peak, and although you don't get a 360-degree view due to the installation, you do not have eyes in the back of your head anyway. You can take in 180 degrees with your back toward the buildings and then walk to the other side and take in the other 180 degrees. Dogs love it too. It is an easy, fun outing, with guaranteed small amounts of people. A 3.25-mile walk up a road is not the kind of hike most outdoors type of people go after, so enjoy this one.

Chewee waits for lunch and water on top of Toro Peak.

CLEVELAND NATIONAL FOREST

48. San Juan Loop

Round trip: 2 miles
Hiking time: 1 hour
High point: 2000 feet
Elevation gain: 400 feet
Best season: Year-round, summer is very hot
Difficulty: Easy
Paw comfort: Dirt and rock
Water: San Juan Creek can dry up in summer, so bring your own
Fees and permits: Adventure Pass required
Map: USGS Sitton Peak
Contact: Cleveland National Forest, Trabuco Ranger District
   (951) 736-1811, *www.fs.fed.us/r5/cleveland*

Getting there: Take Highway 74 east for 19.5 miles from Interstate 5 in Orange County, or west from Interstate 15 in Riverside County for 13 miles. Park in the large lot on the north side of the highway. The lot is directly across the road from the legendary Ortega Country Cottage Candy Store. There is ample parking for many cars, and this trail is heavily used by weekenders, hikers, trail runners, and mountain bikers.

The San Juan Loop Trail is a popular destination for many people in both Orange and Riverside Counties. The trailhead is easily the most visible in the Santa Ana Mountains. It is also one of the most frequently used.

Expect at least ten other cars in the parking lot on any given week day. Its proximity to shops and campgrounds makes it a viable out for all types of people. The short length and picturesque setting draw both young and old. The loop begins at the upper end of the parking area and follows the highway for a short distance before turning left into a main drainage of San Juan Creek. There are several large falls and a use trail that dips down to the cascades below. Numerous pools dot the creek bed, some that are even suitable for swimming when the water is flowing and the temperature is hot.

Since this is a popular area, all dogs are required to be on leash. The trail is narrow in spots and since the occasional mountain biker will cross paths with you, control is an absolute necessity. Even a well-heeled dog might have difficulty reacting in close quarters with a bicycle. The trail widens as it drops alongside the creek. Some of the oldest oak trees in Southern California reside in this valley beside the brook. The trail winds back around to the highway and stays in a lovely wooded area that borders the Upper San Juan Campground. At this point the trail becomes wide and shady.

Traffic noise becomes substantially lower as you wrap around the hillside that surrounds the loop. It never truly abates, though, and there isn't much chance you'll feel like you're in the wilderness.

Still, the atmosphere is entirely pleasurable and secluded, especially in consideration of such easy access, popularity, and shortness of the trail. The trail is a perennial favorite of Cub Scout leaders and couples with small children. It is a tranquil way to get away without really getting away. Two miles is attainable for nearly anyone, and at no place along the trail are you more than a quarter-mile from the roadway. The trail itself is a bit rocky in places, and there are some areas to be cautious of. It is actually surprising that people ride their bikes on the loop, but most either shuttle from the Blue Jay Campground, riding down the Chiquito Trail, which intersects at nearly the halfway point, or they climb up the

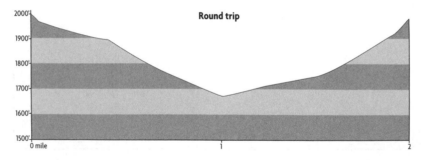

mentioned trail and come back down, making the trail's western
.f the area with the greatest frequency of bikes. Most mountain bikers,
.ke pet owners, are respectful and careful, but you have to always be on
the lookout for those who are not. Your safety and the safety of your pet
may depend on your watchfulness.

As with any lower elevation trail, poison oak and ticks can be present
at any time of the year with winter being the season to be truly mindful. Heavier rainfall, coastal moisture, and mild temperatures combine

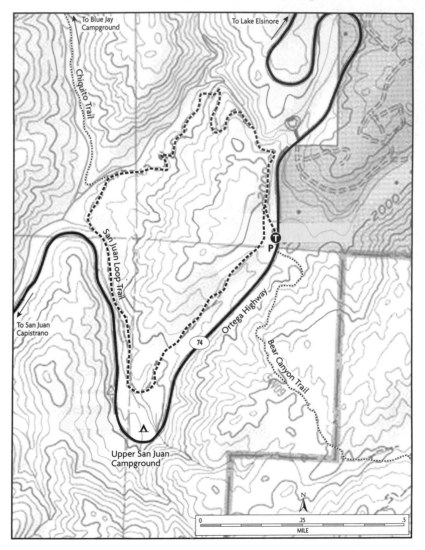

The San Juan Loop winds through a secluded canyon under an arbor of oaks. The width of the path allows for many uses.

to create a perfect habitat for both obnoxious pests. Check yourself and your dogs thoroughly upon exiting. This is an easy beginner hike that can be enjoyable for the most active hiker as well as the couch potato, and that goes for the canine variety as well.

49. Morgan Trail

Round trip: 6 miles
Hiking time: 2.5 hours
High point: 2850 feet
Elevation gain: 350 feet
Best season: Year-round; summer is very hot
Difficulty: Moderate
Paw comfort: Dirt
Water: Morrell Creek dries up in summer, so bring your own
Fees and permits: Adventure Pass required
Map: USGS Sitton Peak
Contact: Cleveland National Forest, Trabuco Ranger District (951) 736-1811, *www.fs.fed.us/r5/cleveland*

Getting there: Take Highway 74 west from Interstate 15 in Lake Elsinore and follow it for 9 miles. Turn left onto South Divide Road. On many maps, the road is still indicated as Killeen Road, but the road signs do not reflect this, although many trail signs and maps still do. Follow the road for 2.5 miles to the signed semicircular turnout for the Morgan Trailhead on the right hand side of the road.

Morgan Trail is one of the best easily reachable escapes in the Santa Ana Mountains. It does not require long distance driving or traveling on a bumpy dirt road. It is off the central beaten path, and most of the people who drive south on South Divide (Killeen) Road are making their way to the Wildomar off-highway vehicle (OHV) area, not to this trailhead. It is used so infrequently, in fact, that only a few names make it into the trailhead register on a monthly basis. While not a secret, this area is more of a clandestine retreat away from the highly traveled San Juan Loop Trail, but only because it is not sitting directly on Highway 74. Just going a little bit out of the way does a lot for solitude in the forest.

The path begins right out of the parking area and descends alongside lovely Morrell Canyon. Sycamores, cottonwoods, alders, black and coast live oaks grow alongside the serene and pastoral riparian setting. A lush richly fed tributary of San Juan Creek flows just below the trail and water should be present in puddles and pools throughout the year. Accessing it through the abundant poison oak that breeds streamside is the only problem. However, just where the trail enters the wilderness is a crossing that always contains water in the wetter seasons of the year. The San Mateo Canyon Wilderness entrance comes exactly 1 mile into the trail. Dogs can remain off leash until this point, but leashes are required in wilderness areas. The mile-long trail works out well enough to have sufficiently burned off ample amounts of your pet's energy. After that, staying leashed won't be too much of a chore for the remaining trek.

Almost immediately upon entering the wilderness, the trail leaves the creek behind and penetrates into a desert sagebrush community. Descending farther into and along a rocky canyon, the trail presents beautiful

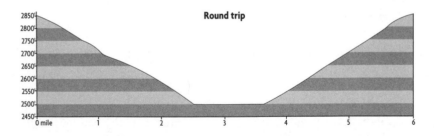

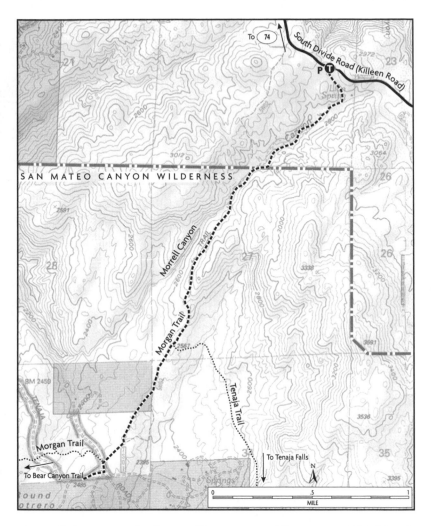

vistas all the way to the Orange County coast. The mountain highlands in front of you provide the backdrop and scenery of isolation and rustic beauty. In the distance you'll notice a few buildings that are still private ranch holdings located on public lands. There are many smaller trails that converge, including one that heads off towards Tenaja Falls. At this point, you have traveled 2 miles and can carry on in any direction you choose. Continuing straight ahead will keep you on the Morgan Trail, which eventually intersects with the Bear Canyon Trail. That trail can be utilized to make this hike a point to point hike with a car shuttle should you so desire.

Chewee and Socs are happy to escape the leash guidelines upon leaving the wilderness area.

Either way you decide to take this hike, the trail is pleasant. There is no real shade after the creek bed, and while it is rocky in certain parts, most of the way is sandy or on firm dirt. This should suit just about any dog's pads just fine. Such infrequent usage on this trail makes it the perfect outing. While this wilderness is still in close proximity to modern life, it retains a feeling of the Wild West. You can almost picture the cozy ranch settlement just over the next ridge, or the salvation that came from finally reaching the ocean. The goal is within grasp and sight. When your thoughts return to the twenty-first century, keep in mind that this is an inverse hike, meaning you'll have to climb back out the entire way. The way in is a gradual descent. The good news is that the same steady grade you walked in on is the same balanced approach you take on the way out.

50. Fishermans Camp

Round trip: 6.5 miles
Hiking time: 3.5 hours
High point: 2000 feet
Elevation gain: 1000 feet
Best season: Late fall through early spring
Difficulty: Moderate
Paw comfort: Dirt
Water: Tenaja Creek
Fees and permits: Adventure Pass required
Map: USGS Sitton Peak; USGS Wildomar
Contact: Cleveland National Forest, Trabuco Ranger District (951)
736-1811, *www.fs.fed.us/r5/cleveland*

Getting there: From Ontario, take Interstate 215 or Interstate 15 about 40 miles south to Murrieta and exit on Clinton Keith Road. Turn right and follow Clinton Keith. It becomes Tenaja Road, although there are no signs to suggest this. From Interstate 215, stay on Clinton Keith/Tenaja Road for 16 miles. Turn right onto Cleveland Forest Road. Follow it for a mile to the large parking area on your left. The trail begins here.

This hike travels through the San Mateo Canyon Wilderness. The wilderness was created in 1984 and covers over 38,000 acres of rolling hills, mountains, steep canyons, grasslands, coastal chaparral, and oak scrub woodland. It is the largest wilderness area in the Cleveland National Forest. The region receives relatively light usage and can be incredibly hot during the summer. There are secluded microclimate areas that receive much cooler air, which can be pleasant even on the hottest of days. In

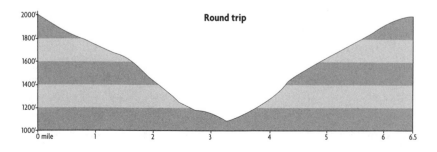

Magpie totes her own gear on all backpacking trips. This one was no exception.

a few areas, some water flows year-round, although in dry years finding it will not be an easy task.

The trail begins at the parking lot and follows an easy footpath down into Tenaja Canyon. Going in is easy as you lose 1200 feet over 3 miles. For the majority of the walk, the trail is evenly graded and steady. The mostly dirt pathway contours along the wall of the canyon, gradually descending through a shady mixed-oak forest and eventually to the canyon bottom itself. Poison oak is very common at this low elevation and is ever-present off the trail. Watch where your pet is sniffing; if you aren't careful, you could end up with the obnoxious oil on yourself. Ticks are yet another thing to watch out for here all year long, especially after rains and during cooler months.

Although you are not likely to see hordes of people along the trail, the area is likely to attract at least one or two groups of people for winter backpacking on the weekends. Fishermans Camp is a nice primitive campsite but definitely a misnomer; it stands to wonder what anyone could fish for in a mostly dry creek bed. San Mateo Creek, which is a couple minutes' walk farther down the trail, usually has a more substantial amount of water in it, but it too hardly seems the Piscean paradise the name brings to mind. If you've brought your pole along, you are most likely going to be disappointed if you've set out to catch anything other than weeds and sticks. The trail to the campsite is easy to follow and you will know the camp when you see it. It is the obvious flatland that sits just above the rocky bed of the creek you have been traversing alongside. It is really the first place you come to that is suitable for camping, and at camp, the trail becomes obscured as it crosses the riverbed. Across the river are trail signs for Tenaja Falls and Wildomar/ Cleveland Forest Road.

If you desire, the trail continues on from Fishermans Camp all the way to Tenaja Falls and beyond. A one-day trip to the falls and back is well over 12 miles, so be prepared for a long all-day outing if that is your agenda. In certain places after Fishermans Camp, finding your way can be difficult, but there have been cairns erected in some areas. Using good trail sense can help too. Always look for the easiest route to take and the openings between trees and brush.

If you do make camp, there are many options to pursue for day hikes. The Bluewater Trail leads northwest out of camp, although it is a little difficult to find and somewhat overgrown. This trail also connects with the San Mateo Canyon Trail. If you decide to use the main trail, the trip to Tenaja Falls is very nice and highly recommended, although when the road is open, the last stretch to the falls themselves can get a lot of traffic and use.

The trip to Fishermans Camp makes for a perfect winter weekend backpacking outing. If you can get to the trailhead a couple of hours ahead of twilight, you can be in camp setting up before the last rays of light settle behind the mountains. This is a fantastic place to spend a winter's night. Taking it easy, all day Saturday can be spent exploring or hiking, and the Sunday walk out consists of a moderate elevation gain with just a 3-mile walk back to the car. The trip can also be turned into a much larger outing with a car shuttle, stretching from the trailhead to Highway 74 as it traverses nearly half of the forest in the Trabuco Ranger District.

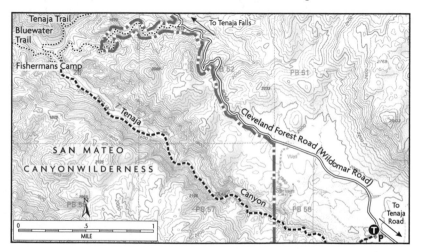

51. Tenaja Falls

Round trip: 1.5 miles
Hiking time: 1 hour
High point: 1600 feet
Elevation gain: 400 feet
Best season: Year-round; hot in summer
Difficulty: Easy
Paw comfort: Dirt
Water: Tenaja Creek
Fees and permits: Adventure Pass required
Map: USGS Sitton Peak
Contact: Cleveland National Forest, Trabuco Ranger District
(951) 736-1811, *www.fs.fed.us/r5/cleveland*

Getting there: From Ontario, take Interstate 215 or Interstate 15 about 40 miles south to Murrieta and exit on Clinton Keith Road. Turn right and follow Clinton Keith. It becomes Tenaja Road although there are no signs to suggest this. From I-215 stay on Clinton Keith/Tenaja Road for 16 miles. Turn right onto Cleveland Forest Road (Wildomar Road). Follow it for nearly 5 miles to the parking area for Tenaja Falls.

This is a very short trip that leads to a popular cascade in southern Riverside County. The longest thing about the excursion is the drive you take to get there. Traveling down Clinton Keith will really give you a feeling of how the other half lives. Private polo grounds notwithstanding, there are some incredible ranches and grand mansions along the way. Some of the homes stretch right up to the border of the forest and beyond, but

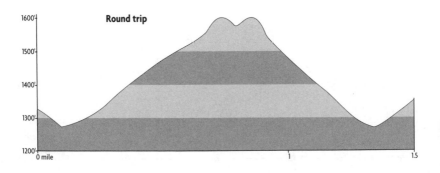

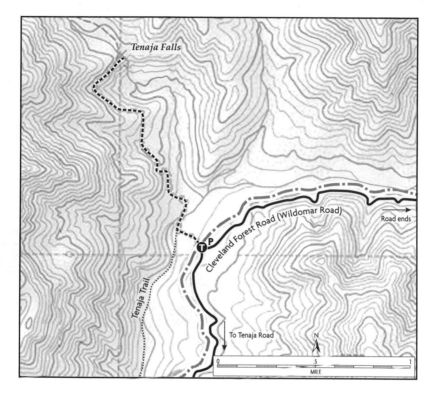

they do not interfere with any of the hikes in the area, especially the falls, which are recessed deep into the canyon.

The falls are reachable by anyone in reasonable shape. There is a slight climb to get there, but nothing that a small child couldn't handle. When added together, the falls drop a total of over 150 feet. If the water is really flowing, such as right after winter rains, Tenaja Falls can be quite a spectacle. In drier years or late in the season, the falls might slow to a trickle, but some water will still be present. No matter what time you visit, there should be pools suitable for recreation if you and your pooch are willing to scramble around some of the drops or down steep hillsides.

From the lot, take the trail nearly 50 yards to the cement bridge where standing water sometimes creates a pond that you must cross to continue on the trail. Poison oak is ubiquitous along waterways in this region, so do not attempt to find your way through the brush—there isn't a passable trail anywhere. If the pool is too deep, just remove your socks and shoes and walk across. The bed is smooth and mostly concrete, but be careful not to step on the enormous tadpoles that frequent the stream.

Tenaja Falls is made up of a number of cascades and pools that collect enough water for swimming.

The trail is an old dirt fire road that has been impassable by vehicles for some time, even before 1984's landmark legislation California Wilderness Act, which enlarged fourteen existing areas and created twenty-five new wilderness designations, along with the expansion of two areas within national parks. That act doubled the land protected as wilderness in California, and is the law that has protected this area for posterity. Since the falls are in the San Mateo Canyon Wilderness, dogs must remain on leashes at all times.

After a short climb up the road, you are rewarded with striking views of the falls from across the valley. The trail circles around and eventually reaches the top of the falls, where you can be content to relax and enjoy the downward view or drop in one of the pools and cool off. This area can be treacherously hot, even in the darkest of winters, and if you've made this hike from an area other than the parking lot, you will want to test the waters. In the winter, ticks are synonymous with low elevations, and especially prevalent in areas where there is plentiful water in close proximity. Do not sit on logs, rocks, or grass, and make certain to check yourself and your pets when you return to the car. Return the way you came or extend your trip by hiking farther in either direction. There are lots of areas to explore with decent trails north and south.

52. Barker Valley

Round trip: 7.5 miles
Hiking time: 4 hours
High point: 5125 feet
Elevation gain: 1000 feet
Best season: Late fall to early spring; road closed when muddy
Difficulty: Moderate
Paw comfort: Dirt, sand, and rock
Water: Bring your own; mostly dry creekbed after early spring
Fees and permits: Adventure Pass required
Map: USGS Palomar Observatory
Contact: Cleveland National Forest, Palomar Ranger District (760)
788-0250, *www.fs.fed.us/r5/cleveland*

Getting there: Take Highway 79 south and east from Temecula for 31 miles. Make a right turn onto Forest Service Road 9S07 (Palomar Divide Truck Trail) a little more than 2 miles past the tiny hamlet of Sunshine Summit. The road is mixed pavement and dirt and should be drivable for cars with moderate clearance, although high-clearance or four-wheel drive is definitely preferable. Drive exactly 7.5 miles to the trailhead. There is parking for two to three vehicles maximum.

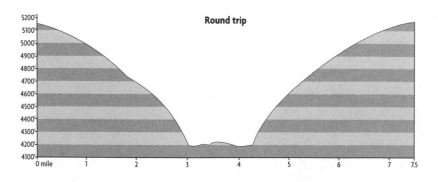

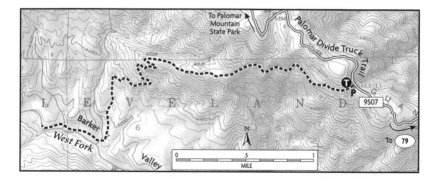

The pine tree goodness of Palomar State Park is almost completely off-limits to dogs. With that in mind, there are other nearby areas to explore that offer variety and beauty without the entrance fees or the crowds. One such outing is the trek to Barker Valley.

The trip to Barker Valley involves an inverse hike, meaning that you lose elevation on the way in, and gain it all back on the way out. Although this may seem like a tiring scheme, it isn't, because the trail is extraordinarily even, losing only 300 feet per mile. This doesn't make the way back home very easy, but it isn't quite debilitating either. However, the inland nature, low elevation, and sun exposure on the trail can make this outing a real scorcher. A lack of water here could be a dangerous proposition, so be sure to bring along extra for you and your dogs. The trail can be preposterously hot, even in winter.

Half of the fun of this trail is driving to the trailhead. The views along the Palomar Divide Truck Road (FS 9S07) border on heavenly. The higher you climb the more there is to see, including a mind-numbing view of Lake Henshaw, glittering like a blue diamond amidst San Diego's rolling hills and mountains. Of course, as you begin the trail, these views are what you are able to marvel at. Once you start descending the views get progressively shallower. This is not necessarily a bad thing though, because you do get closer to the parabolic domes of Palomar Mountain and the oddly flat and manicured Mendenhall Valley, which upon first glance resembles a golf course.

The trail does not need to be traveled in its entirety to be enjoyable. In fact there is a break about 2 miles in where the trail overlooks the entire region. This is a good turnaround point for anyone who does not

Opposite: Smells abound in Barker Valley.

want to take the entire trip. The trail becomes a little steeper after this, and turns into more of a path and less of a fire road. The trail grows a bit rockier at this point, which is also something to watch out for, depending on the strength of your pets and the toughness of their paws. Most of the traveling on this path should be fairly uneventful for your dog. It is primarily an old forest road that has been converted into a trail. The mixture of sand, gravel, dirt, and rock is hardly the kind of thing that will hurt tiny paws, but you should always pay close attention.

Barker Valley is an oaken flatland marked with dry creek beds. There are plenty of campsites, although none are marked on any map. A visitor permit is required for camping outside maintained campsites, and fires are not permitted outside of permanent campgrounds. The solitude in the confines of Barker Valley would make for an excellent one-night outing. There is a spring somewhere in the valley, but it isn't marked either. Plan accordingly and bring loads of water if you are even contemplating pitching a tent.

53. Pacific Crest Trail (PCT) to Eagle Rock

Round trip: 5.5 miles
Hiking time: 2.5 hours
High point: 3520 feet
Elevation gain: 750 feet
Best season: Late fall through early spring
Difficulty: Moderate
Paw comfort: Dirt and rock
Water: Canada Verde flows late depending on rainfall
Map: USGS Warner Springs
Contact: Cleveland National Forest, Palomar Ranger District
(760) 788-0250, *www.fs.fed.us/r5/cleveland*

Getting there: From Temecula take Highway 79 south and east 38 miles to Warner Springs, or from Ramona take Highway 78/79 east and north for 27 miles. Park at the pullout in front of the Warner Springs Fire Department on the south side of the road. There is a gate that marks the entrance to the Pacific Crest Trail (PCT). Cross the wash and head south, opening a couple of gates and stay with the PCT markers. There are many roads and

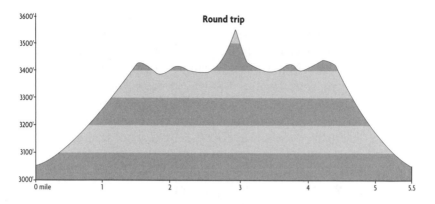

side trails that venture off in other directions. The PCT is clearly marked with plastic and wood posts emblazoned with the upside-down spade emblem of the PCT.

This is a fantastic hike. Your dogs will enjoy the solitude, the scenery, the softness of the trail, the free flowing water, the wildlife, and the variety of terrain. It is doubtful you will see many people other than through-hikers in the early spring and hunters in the winter, and even then your chances are pretty slim of seeing either. This is just not a highly frequented, highly traveled area. Most people shy away from the desert sections of the PCT and head for the high country. This area can be scorching hot at almost any time of the year, but especially so in summer.

The truly amazing thing about this hike is that it traverses so many distinct climate zones. You start out crossing a large desert wash next to the highway. There are some oak trees shading the way at first, along with poison oak in the undergrowth. It is a good idea to not let your dogs run freely on this portion of the trail, as you probably do not have immunity to poison oak. Dogs do not suffer the adverse effects of poison oak, but if the deleterious oil gets on their fur, it will get on your hands and everything your hands touch until it is thoroughly rinsed off. (Some soaps don't remove the oil but only help to spread it around. If you do come in contact, scrub and rinse vigorously.) Cattle also use this ravine, so please be courteous and close all of the gates behind you.

When you pass through the third gate, you start the real section of the trail as it begins to meander through a scrub and cacti desert topography. It is startling how quickly this eco-zone gives way to a lush sylvan creek and oaken woodland. The creek flows well throughout most of the year, and year-round in times of elevated rainfall. If the temperatures are melting thermometers, your dog will have many places to quench his thirst and cool off. Traveling through this area at the right time will yield some wonderful occasions to observe nature's bounty. Wild squash grows in the area along with stunning wildflowers. California quail and various rodents flourish in the area and you almost certainly will spot mule deer and possibly raccoons and skunks should you choose to hike in the evening. The sight of a wooded creek is definitely not what is expected when you begin hiking. From the fire station, it appears the entire trek will wander through the desert, but that is hardly the case. The lush riparian woodland is a pleasant surprise that is more than fitting for an impromptu repast beneath a shady oak tree.

The trail sticks to Cañada Verde for a little over a mile, and then enters an arid hilly chaparral region filled with tall, head-high shrubs. Prickly pear cacti abundantly blossom under foot, so watch those tender paws. The fruit of the prickly pear is edible, but you must know how to pick, cut, and slice it without getting stuck a million times by the seemingly harmless tufts of glochids that symmetrically protrude from the skin. Glochids are tiny hair-like barbed bristles that are hard to see and by sight alone appear to be soft. When brushed by a finger, the glochids will lodge

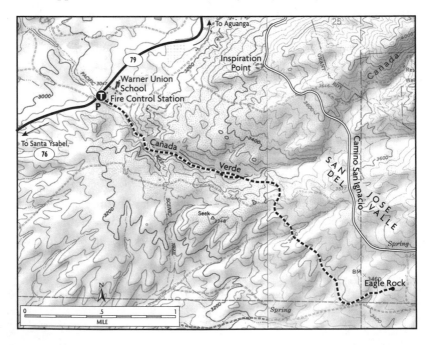

Socs approaches the gigantic and imposing Eagle Rock.

in the skin hundreds at a time. More than one person has described them as surreptitiously evil. Your dogs are incredibly susceptible to being poked and stabbed by spines of any cactus and you will undoubtedly have to remove some from their fur and legs after trekking through this section of the hike. If you notice a limp or a strange gait on your pet, he probably has a spine stuck in a pad. These need to be removed promptly.

Gradually, you exit this eco-zone and enter into rolling semi-arid grassland. The area is reminiscent of the central California coastal region rather than the hot and dry San Diego County backcountry. Lake Henshaw glimmers to the west, resting below the white globe on top of Palomar Mountain, and stone piles mark nearly every nearby hill and those off in the distance. Eagle Rock is clearly discernible from afar and so is the trail, although the actual shape is not as clearly apparent. The neatest thing about Eagle Rock is that as you approach, you see the backside of the eagle. You have to walk around it to get the true pose. It is quite amazing how much this huge rock formation looks like an eagle in three dimensions. The backside even resembles the back of an eagle. I would be surprised if the Native Americans in the area did not have a legend for this spot, and if the ground itself was not hallowed and sacred.

The trip is a good one, all on solid trail. There is a bit of up and down, and the way can get devastatingly hot in summer. The only bummer is that when you get close to Eagle Rock, you realize you are nowhere near alone. A road that passes through Warner Springs, Camino San Ignacio, runs no more than a few hundred feet from where you stand. Not very many cars travel along its pavement, but when the first hum of an engine interrupts your solitude, don't be surprised. An old service or farm road cuts a path almost directly to the fantastic formation. For being so close to a road, this is still an extraordinary hike. It is amazing that society has not crept in upon the finely formed natural statuary. There is no trash, no graffiti, and no riff-raff. In short, it is a great place to hike if the weather is cool.

GREATER SAN DIEGO AREA

54. San Elijo Lagoon

Round trip: 2 to 3 miles
Hiking time: 1 to 2 hours
High point: 50 feet
Elevation gain: 50 feet
Best season: Year-round
Difficulty: Easy
Paw comfort: Dirt and packed sand
Water: Bring your own
Map: USGS Encinitas
Contact: San Elijo Lagoon Conservancy (760) 436-3944, *www*
.sanelijo.org, or San Elijo Ecological Reserve (858) 467-4201,
www.dfg.ca.gov

Getting there: From Interstate 5 (San Diego Freeway) in Solana Beach,
exit onto Manchester and turn left. Both the north and south exits face
southward, so you'll be heading east either way. Drive a short distance
down the road and you will see a kiosk, trailhead, and roadside parking
on your right-hand side. Park off the road as well as you can, and close
the gate behind you.

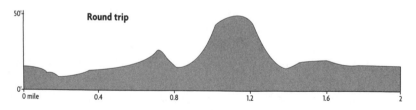

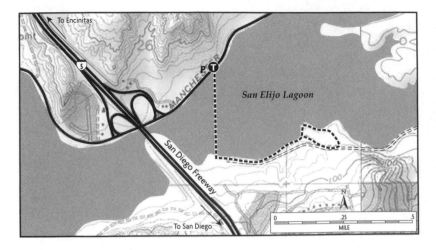

San Elijo Lagoon feels a little more remote than its neighbor to the north, Batiquitos Lagoon. The path meanders very close to the actual lagoon and skirts along the sometimes muddy edge. It is difficult to feel like you are away from the city, but you can almost get a sense of solitude here. You wander among well-trodden paths that showcase the variety of wetland plants and birds, and if you take the time to imagine, you can picture yourself in a bygone era. Don't close your eyes, though; the hum of Interstate 5 is constant and will immediately snap you out of your daydream. This, however, is life in Southern California. Unfortunately, you're not likely to find a solitary stretch of beach or oceanside lagoon that doesn't have a freeway running right by it south of Santa Barbara County, or at least not one where dogs are allowed. This is as close as it gets in San Diego County to water wildlands. The sound of the freeway is not so bad; this is a beautiful area, and the opportunity to observe migrating birds up close is well worth the short trip.

San Elijo is a coastal estuary reserve that covers roughly 900 acres of varied habitats. Within the reserve boundaries there are six distinct plant communities: salt marsh, freshwater marsh, coastal strand, coastal scrub, riparian scrub, and chaparral. There are separate basins that are divided by the freeways that crisscross the estuary. The water is very shallow in each, but this allows for a fantastic habitat for migrating and nesting birds.

You enter the lagoon across a gangplank and causeway that provides incredible access for bird lovers and photographers. If you have your 35mm camera along and a tripod, you can set up shop right on the bridge and shoot away all day long. Your dog might get a little bored with that, but still, it is a tempting option. There are lots of waterfowl that use the lagoon as a temporary shelter and some that make it a permanent home. Even someone with no experience can enjoy the avian varieties found here.

The lagoon offers a few options for hiking. There are trails that continue on for the entire distance of the lagoon, and it really depends on how much time you want to spend exploring and bird watching. The property has over 5 miles of hiking that stretch from the Pacific Ocean

Mallard ducks patrol the friendly waters of San Elijo Lagoon.

to Rancho Santa Fe. San Elijo is a wonderful place to relax and take it easy. At a few of the overlooks perched upon a mesa there are benches for sitting and enjoying the atmosphere. There truly is ample ambiance here; sunsets can be magical, especially in winter. Here you can also spot majestic egrets and brown pelicans as they spread their glorious wings and hover above the water. Time seems to stop and hold you captive to the magic of the wetlands. It is a magnificent area to bring children. A lot of people do visit this area, and with the wildlife, it is a requirement that all domestic animals remain leashed.

55. North Beach—Del Mar Dog Beach

Round trip: 0.5 mile
Hiking time: 0.5 hour
High point: 25 feet
Elevation gain: 20 feet
Best season: Year-round, but dogs allowed off-leash September through June only
Difficulty: Easy
Paw comfort: Sand and surf
Water: Bring your own
Map: USGS Del Mar
Contact: City of Del Mar (858) 755-1556, *www.delmar.ca.us /business/GeneralInformation/FAQ/BeachesParks.htm*

Getting there: From San Diego take Interstate 5 north just past the town of Del Mar. Exit Via De La Valle, and turn left. Turn left again at the ocean, onto Old Highway 101/Camino Del Mar. Follow it to the roadside parking just a few hundred feet in front of you. Pay your oodles of money at the vending machine that takes bills up to twenties should you desire

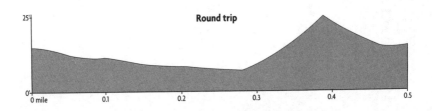

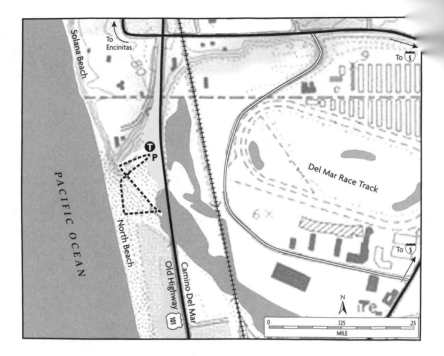

an all-day outing. Place your ticket on your dash and head down to the beach. The meters cost $2 an hour, and ticketing is aggressive.

This is not so much a hike as just one of those rare Southern California beaches that allows dogs. For the most part, on beaches south of San Luis Obispo County, dogs are *canina non-grata*, and attempting to bring even a leashed pooch onto a beach is to subject yourself to quite a large fine. It is truly a shame that "man's best friend" has so little ocean foam in which to roam. Here is one of the last vestigial holdouts of a bygone era when just about anything was allowed on the beach.

For anyone who has ever seen a dog that is truly at home at the beach, it is a joy beyond compare. Dogs will frolic and play, they will jump and run with flag-like ears pinned backward by the forward force of their undeniable trajectories. Even a dog that does not like the water can feel right at home running along the sand. The sheer lack of reservation your pet unleashes when set free to tramp along the beach is poetry in dog form. Words do little justice to the ecstatic energy that can even inspire an old dog into sprinting along with other dogs in the cold wet sand. There must be no feeling quite on earth like it. I've seen dogs sprint down the

Del Mar's North Beach provides a friendly haven where dogs can find new canine companions while running in the surf and sand.

beach only to sprint right back up it, and then do it again. Certainly, if you want your companion to get some exercise and he is friendly, take him to a dog beach. There is no lack of like-minded dogs that want to party in the surf.

This would not be the place to come to if you are looking for exercise. The beach is only about a quarter of a mile long and once you've walked up and down it, you've pretty much seen it all. There are volleyball nets and usually a pickup game or two, just not for the dogs. The bluffs overhead have a hikeable section, but unfortunately are off limits for dogs. The fine is reputedly somewhere in the neighborhood of $300. If you feel an itch for more exercise and your dogs have exhausted some of their unlimited beach energy, feel free to travel a little farther up the coast and hit one of the two spectacular lagoons that are also nestled just off the San Diego Freeway.

56. Iron Mountain

Round trip: 5.75 miles
Hiking time: 2.5 hours
High point: 2696 feet
Elevation gain: 1100 feet
Best season: Year-round, very hot in summer
Difficulty: Moderate
Paw comfort: Sand and dirt, some rocks
Water: An unnamed spring collects in a pool just off the trail to the left a little past 1.5 miles, just before beginning the switchbacks; bring your own
Map: USGS San Vicente Reservoir
Contact: City of Poway (858) 688-4723, *www.ci.poway.ca.us*

Getting there: From Interstate 15 just north of Miramar Air Base, take Highway 56 east through the town of Poway. Highway 56 ends in 8.5 miles at Highway 67. Turn south on Highway 67 and park on the east side of the road. The only safe parking is on the dirt strip, not in the bike lane. The city has plans to build a large parking area in the near future. The trail begins under the canopy of planted oak trees.

San Diego is one of the fittest counties in the nation. People hike, bike, run and exercise everywhere, and this is a decent-size peak with incredible clear-day views closely located to a major urban area. The trail is easily accessible, can be utilized by everyone, and almost anyone with a little effort can attain the summit. This is an extremely well-traveled trail; it

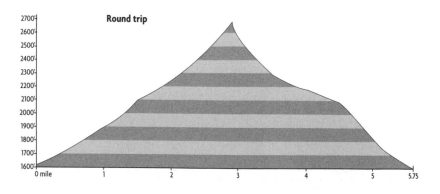

is easily navigated and perfectly signed. The trail is a mixture of dirt and rock, but it shouldn't be too hard on the paws unless your pet is very sedentary. If your pup is not used to exercise, this trail might be just the right distance to really tear up his pads and put him out of commission for a few days. Make certain your dog is conditioned before undertaking any hike over 3 miles in length and with any rockiness in the trail description. This one may be the right size for you to start with, but not your dog, although you could opt for the shorter trip to the Ramona overlook on the same trail.

The city of Poway maintains this trail and it requires dogs to be leashed, although you will probably see numerous examples of dogs being off-leash. Do the right thing and follow regulations. There are so many people on this trail that it would be ridiculous to have to keep unleashing your dog, only to have to leash up again and again. There are plenty of areas for your dog to roam off-leash; this is just not one of them. The trail can at times seem more like a freeway than a hiking trail, but the people are friendly and almost everyone says hello. They are even very kind to dogs.

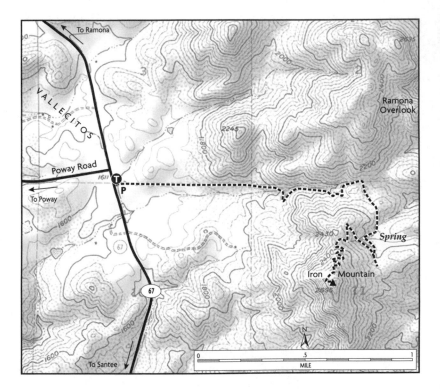

The city of Poway does an excellent job of marking and maintaining its trails.

Hikers without dogs often stop to pet and admire them.

While the elevation gain on this hike is not extreme, it is more than enough to get your heart pumping, and some of the sections, even early on, are incredibly steep. Wear shoes with good traction, because the way up and down can be slippery on the rocky dirt. In the last three-quarters of a mile, you gain over 600 feet of elevation, which is pretty steep uphill climbing. That is the type of gain that compares with the toughest of hikes around the state, albeit for much greater sustained distances.

The Cedar Fire burned this entire area in 2003, but you wouldn't know it from certain sections of the trail. The underbrush has all grown back, and much of the flora returned with the deluge of rainwater in the

.004–2005 season. You can still make out plants that were burnt, but the area has bounced back surprisingly well. Don't expect much in the way of shade. Even before the fire, this area was a desert, and nothing has changed that, even with the record amount of rainfall. Attempting this hike on a hot midsummer afternoon would be the dumbest mistake a person could make. This sun-exposed mountain can be blistering even in wintertime, so when you go, get an early start. Go on an overcast day, or bring your tanning oil, because you can plan on getting scorched by the sun. The city of Poway stresses the importance of bringing enough water and the severe danger of heat exhaustion for both you and your pet. Use caution and common sense on this trail.

The top of the peak affords magnificent views in all directions. The Pacific Ocean glitters to the west in magnificent glory, Lake San Vincente sits to the south, and if you bring a good map, you'll be able to recognize all the mountain landmarks around you, including peaks in Mexico, and many from the city as well. This is perhaps the most magnificent place in San Diego County on a clear day.

57. Cedar Creek Falls

Round trip: 5.25 miles
Hiking time: 2.5 hours
High point: 1950 feet
Elevation gain: 1100 feet
Best season: Year-round; very hot in summer
Difficulty: Moderate
Paw comfort: Dirt
Water: The road in and out is dry and hot, but there is ample water in the creek and the pools that collect behind and below the falls
Fees and permits: Adventure Pass required
Map: USGS Tule Springs
Contact: Cleveland National Forest, Descanso Ranger District (619) 445-6235, *www.fs.fed.us/r5/cleveland*

Getting there: From Ramona, take Highway 78/79 east 20 miles to Julian. Turn south (right) onto Pine Hills Road and follow it for a little more than 1.5 miles. Veer right onto Eagle Peak Road, and follow it to its completion a little more than 10 miles later. The road is partly paved

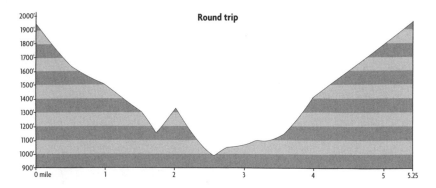

and partly dirt, but is passable for all types of cars and trucks. Park at the locked gate, and head down the road behind the gate. Cleveland National Forest officials do not endorse this trail. In fact, they discourage use due to numerous rescues, accidents, and deaths that occur every year. PLEASE BE CAREFUL! If you have any doubt at all about your physical abilities, best to find another trail.

If your dogs like the water, they will love this area. While this is not a hidden hike, it certainly is a gem of San Diego County, even though at times it seems like everyone in San Diego is at the main swimming hole. The water here flows year-round, despite its low elevation, and while the best time of year to visit is during the spring, autumn can be quite lovely as well, often with thinner crowds. The base of the falls sits close to 1000 feet above sea level, and the temperatures here can sizzle, especially in the mid-day summer sun. It's not a good idea to take a mid-day hike here when it is hot, but if you are beneath the falls during the hottest time of day, you'll know exactly why this place is a treasure. The falls drop over 90 feet into the pool at the bottom, and in high rain years the cascade resembles a more northern locale rather than arid San Diego County.

This "trail" is really an old road, and you will follow it down the whole way, unless you choose to go to the more secluded top of the falls. I'd recommend the top, because there is a pool right before the main falls that is deep and clear enough to be rather enjoyable and not many people venture there, instead opting for the party-like atmosphere in the big pool under the falls, which has its benefits as well. To find your way to the top pools, you have to leave the main road after 1.4 miles. The trail forks to the left and there are signs warning you of the danger of the water, the falls, and diving. Another sign tells you that this trail is not

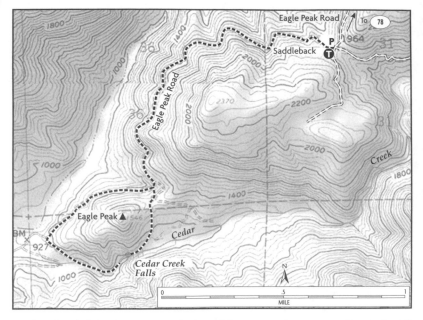

maintained. It isn't pretty or designed for as much usage as it gets, but it is legal, and it is easy enough to get down to the creek. Follow the creek to its conclusion and find the wading pool at the very end right next to the falls. Do use caution; many people have fallen to their deaths here. The rock is slick, so stay back from all edges.

Remember, the trip in is 1.4 miles and an 1100-foot elevation loss, which means the road out is a desiccated 1.4 miles up and an elevation gain of 1100 feet. You must take that into account and bring plenty of water. This area can be incredibly hot even in "cool" weather, and people fall and need to be rescued every year on this trail. The danger of heat exhaustion and stroke are very real. It is easy to underestimate the strenuous nature of the trip out because the descent is very easy. Coupled with extreme heat, the trail is ripe for disaster for those who aren't careful. Again, use good judgment.

The falls and the area surrounding them have been very dangerous in the past and the sheriff's office maintains that there is at least one death per year either en route to the falls, drowning in the lower pool, or from ridiculously stupid diving stunts. Although most of these deaths are alcohol-related, some are accidental. There are many hazards: it is very hot here, enough to cause extreme dehydration when people do not bring enough water, especially for the trip out; rattlesnakes abound in temperatures and locales such as this; and the area is also prime mountain lion country, judging by the amount of animals that drink from the pool and the tracks often found here. Of course, diving into the pool from anywhere is not advised.

With all of that said, the Forest Service has not banned any activity at the falls, nor blocked access to the trail, but it does caution its users to use prudence when partaking in activities in the Cedar Creek region. There are signs everywhere warning people of the dangers, but if you are vigilant and take precautions, this place is no more dangerous than your own backyard. Use common sense and this place can be an enjoyable outing for the entire family. At times, the place is very family-oriented, and then there are other instances where the place feels like a giant frat party. You never know what atmosphere it will be, but it is guaranteed that there will be people, especially on summer weekends.

To get to the lower pools, you can work your way down the steep northern cliffside to the pool, and remember that you will have to work your way out that direction as well, or you can follow the road to the no trespassing signs. The entire area below 1000 feet is controlled by the water district that operates El Capitan Reservoir below the falls. It is illegal

Chewee and Socs cool off in Cedar Creek, just above the falls.

to trespass on their property; instead follow the use trail that remains just above the property line and follows along the hillside around to the swimming hole.

The lower swimming hole was partially filled in due to the Cedar Fire of 2003, which started very close to this location (hence the name). The entire area along the hike was burned, but the flora has recovered well. The pool is only ten feet deep in places, and it is not advisable for diving of any sort. The heavy rains of 2004 washed some of the silt away, but not nearly enough to return the swimming hole to its former glory. Still, this is a can't-miss hike with a wonderful destination.

58. Pioneer Mail Trail

Round trip: 1.75 miles
Hiking time: 1 hour
High point: 5500 feet
Elevation gain: 250 feet
Best season: Year-round, very hot in summer
Difficulty: Easy
Paw comfort: Dirt and rock
Water: Bring your own
Fees and permits: Adventure Pass required
Map: USGS Monument Peak
Contact: Cleveland National Forest, Descanso Ranger District
    (619) 445-6235, *www.fs.fed.us/r5/cleveland*

Getting there: From Julian take Highway 79 south for 6 miles, then veer left onto Sunrise Highway. Follow Sunrise Highway for nearly 8.5 miles, and make the left turn into the picnic grounds. Park all the way at the

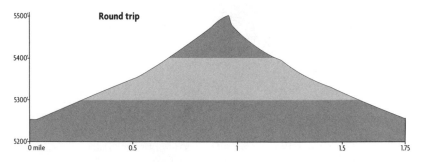

end by the trail sign and head up the old use road. Don't be confused by the two trailheads. The southbound Pacific Crest Trail (PCT) is also located here and leads down through the picnic area.

This is an incredible trail for stunning total field of vision desert-spanning views. The entire Anza Borrego Desert State Park lies 3000 feet beneath you. It is the kind of view you can only get from the clear crisp dehydrated desert air, and it is a vista that you will never forget. The mountains seem to float in all directions, and you teeter on the edge of a precipitous canyon that offers up one of the best "looking into the abyss" feelings that Southern California has to offer. To say the absolute least, the views are nothing short of superb. Getting a picture of your dog poised above the slope with high desert peaks in the background is priceless, and the best reason to come here is for the visual display. The spectacle stretches all the way to San Jacinto and San Gorgonio in the north and south into Mexico.

The trail itself is nothing really special, simply a roadway complete with concrete barriers in places to protect the cars that once trod upon it from careening over the edge into the brink of nothingness. Your path roughly follows the contours of Sunrise Highway, but thankfully you are spared the vehicle noise due to some incredibly large rock formations that lie between the trail and the thoroughfare. The road is mostly a sand and gravel mixture and should not pose any sort of problem for your dog. There is no way to get lost, due to the shortness of the trip and the broadness of the path. It narrows at the top after you meet up once again with the street, and you can clamber atop some rocks, technically known as Garnet Mountain (not to be confused with nearby Garnett Peak). From there, the trip is unceremoniously ended by an Anza Borrego State Park sign that directs you to follow all park regulations, although it does not tell you exactly what those regulations might be. Regrettably, dogs are not allowed in most state parks, and Anza Borrego is no exception to this rule, so instead of being able to continue this spectacular trek along the northbound PCT, you must return the way you came, completing nearly 2 miles in total distance.

That alone does not have to be a bad thing. It just makes this a perfect trek for doggies that are out of shape and need an introductory hike. Or, if you are fit and your pets can amble for mile upon mile, then think of this as a sunrise/early morning hike that serves to begin the day for further exploration into the area. It could also function as a small hike

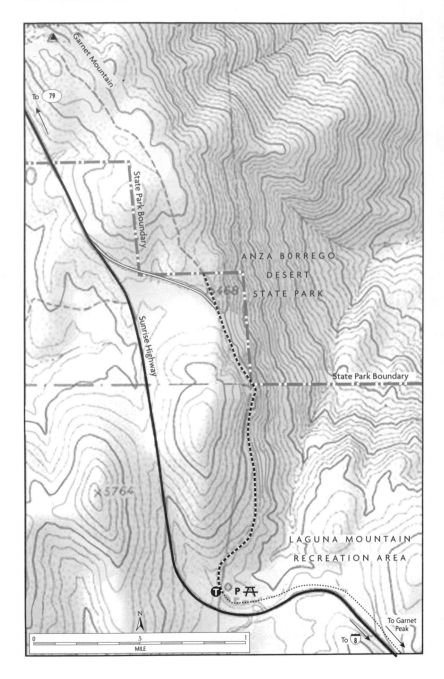

Garnet Mountain

To 79

State Park Boundary

Sunrise Highway

ANZA BORREGO
DESERT
STATE PARK

468

State Park Boundary

×5764

LAGUNA MOUNTAIN
RECREATION AREA

T P ⛺

N

To Garnet
Peak

To 8

0   .5   1
MILE

The windswept edge of the Laguna Mountain Recreation Area meets the stark Anza Borrego Desert on the vista-filled Pioneer Mail Trail.

when time does not permit a larger one. Once you visit this place and the surrounding area, from the deserts to the pine-filled forests, you will want to return. The region creates a magical aura, and the austere splendor is a powerful sorcerer that will enchant visitors with a spell that may very well last a lifetime.

The sun begins its diurnal course far to the east above the Arizona-bordering Chocolate Mountains, but the view at dawn in wintertime can be a multihued technicolor extravaganza. On days where oranges and purples are mixed with stratospheric clouds, you can't imagine a better place to enjoy the majesty of nature that signifies the beginning of every day. Why not use this as a jump-off to other trails in the region, such as Garnett Peak or any of the other wonderful trails in Laguna Mountain Recreation Area? There are other choices, but unfortunately, enormous Rancho Cuyamaca State Park to the west is mostly off-limits for doggies, except for one road that takes you and your leashed canine to the top of Cuyamaca Peak. Instead your best bet is the recreation area, which this hike borders.

If there is a downside to this diminutive adventure, it is the fact that this hike has been easily accessible to everyone for a while, which means that some of the rocks display the sloppy artwork of some of the less enlightened members of our species, and in places there are shards of broken glass that future archaeologists might interpret as part of a ceremony, where imbibing of spirits allowed these specimens to channel their creativity onto the living rock. In the modern world, we know better, but please do not let this detract from your outing. When you view the overlook that serves as this wonder of the world, your back is always to the spray paint side, and in truth there isn't very much of it, but there is enough to mention.

59. Laguna Mountain Recreation Area—Sunset Trail

Round trip: 3.25 miles
Hiking time: 2 hours
High point: 5600 feet
Elevation gain: 350 feet
Best season: Year-round
Difficulty: Easy
Paw comfort: Dirt and duff
Water: Water-of-the-Woods and Big Laguna Lake always have water in wet years, but both may be dry by summer's end and into fall
Fees and permits: Adventure Pass required
Map: USGS Monument Peak
Contact: Cleveland National Forest, Descanso Ranger District (619) 445-6235, *www.fs.fed.us/r5/cleveland*

Getting there: From San Diego, take Interstate 8 east to Sunrise Highway, where the only direction you can go is north. Drive for around 5.5 miles until you see large pullouts on both sides of the roadway halfway between mile markers 19 and 19.5. The trailhead begins on the north side

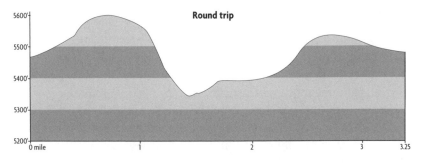

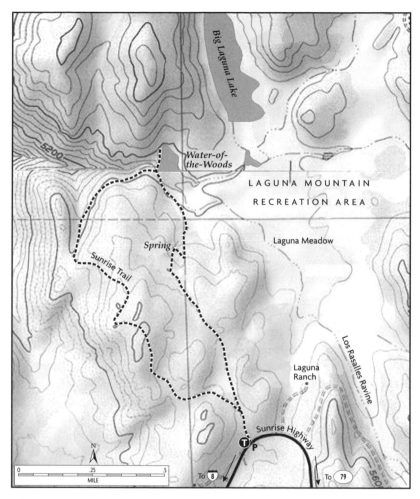

of the highway, and is not clearly marked from the road; however, after a hundred feet of walking northward, you will come to a plastic marker that indicates the Sunset Trail. Take the left fork and follow the fence along the signed trail. The right fork is shorter and cuts a direct path to Water-of-the-Woods, but it is not a marked trail, and instead makes for a perfect return loop.

The Laguna Mountains are not so secret, but they are far enough away from San Diego that they miss the big crowd turnout of places like Mission Hills Regional Park or Iron Mountain in Poway. This area is also not Cuyamaca State Park, because dogs are allowed on more than just one road, and off-leash if under voice command. Big Laguna is a dream come true for hikers with dogs in San Diego County. The landscape is rugged and beautiful, and reminiscent of "big sky country" in Montana or the Rocky Mountains rather than the usual scenery of Southern California. It is filled with large basins and meadows that are guarded by giant pine trees that tower into the skyline. In short, Laguna Mountain is an area that it is hard not to fall in love with. The Sunset Trail is a perfect introduction to this fantastic region, and a great place to get your dogs acquainted with its beauty. As a bonus, it is a hikers-only trail, so there are no bikers or horse droppings.

The trail is pleasantly wooded, shady, and a bit dusty. The path is primarily dirt, although it is rocky in places. However, this is a beginning hike that almost any dog should be able to accomplish, even if they are used to lying on the sofa all day long every day of their lives. The elevation gain is minimal, but there are a couple of short steep sections. Gnats and mosquitoes can be a problem for humans on the trail, so bring along some deet-based insect repellant just to be sure.

The climax of the hike comes at Water-of-the-Woods, a quaint little lake that sits in the middle of a large basin that functions as a blooming green meadow in the spring or after a rainfall. The basin is called Laguna Meadow and it holds three separate bodies of water including Water-of-the-Woods. The entire park surrounds the meadow, and Sunrise Highway snakes around it far enough away to make this region peaceful and entirely free of noise from cars or other such distractions.

The hike is named for the views it attains rather quickly from the parking area. From atop an unmarked spot three-quarters of a mile into the hike, there is a view that rivals any in Southern California, especially during a multi-hued sunset. You overlook Crouch Valley, Noble Canyon, the Cuyamacas, and the entire mountainous region of lower San Diego County. It truly is a remarkable view, for a spot that is simple enough to reach for everyone, even small children. In fact, the loop itself is also a perfect introductory hike for children, although the distance might gather some complaints from children who are less hardy than the most adventurous of sorts. Return the way you came or continue on the use trail that follows along the south side of the lake. It is unmarked, although it appears to be popularly traveled. This trail meets up at the fork near

Opposite: Dogs are free to roam off-leash in the Laguna Mountain Recreation Area.

the beginning of the trail.

Hunting, equestrian, and mountain biking are allowed in the park, but you will not see bikes or horses on this particular trail because of the hikers-only determination. This is an area that is growing in popularity due to the Cedar Fire of 2003, when nearby Cuyamaca Rancho State Park was completely obliterated by the fire. Many frequent visitors to that area are finding their way into Laguna, which remained relatively untouched by the conflagration. The fire did burn into the northern reaches of the recreation area, which shares a border with the state park, but those areas are quickly recovering and represent only a small portion of the entire region. Visitors are flocking back to Cuyamaca as well, but most state parks are not very dog friendly.

If you are so inclined, you can continue on to Big Laguna and Little Laguna Lakes, thereby making the trek an all-day outing; just be sure to return the way you came or follow the use trail mentioned earlier. The Sunset Trail continues all the way around to a junction with the Big Laguna Trail and farther on connects with the Noble Canyon Trail; however, these trails do not loop back to the parking area, so you will have to either leave a car shuttle or backtrack. Also, Noble Canyon and Big Laguna are popular with mountain bikers and both trails allow equestrian users.

60. Cowles Mountain

Round trip: 5 miles
Hiking time: 2 hours
High point: 1592 feet
Elevation gain: 1150 feet
Best season: Year-round
Difficulty: Moderate
Paw comfort: Dirt and rock
Water: Bring your own; stream at beginning of hike
Map: USGS La Mesa
Contact: Mission Trails Regional Park (619) 668-3281, *www.mtrp.org*

Getting there: From Interstate 15, take Highway 52 east for 5 miles and exit on Mission Gorge Road. Turn right onto Mission Gorge, and make a left onto Mesa Road. Follow it to the gate and park. Walk up the road and at the second trailhead, make a right and cross the creek. The Mesa

Trail is signed relatively well for the remainder of the hike. It intersects with the Big Rock Trail and ascends the summit of Cowles Mountain. Another option is to follow the dirt portion of Mesa Road. The dirt road continues on to the top and is only slightly longer than the trail. It should be noted that mountain bikers do use the road, and the trail itself is slightly more scenic.

Cowles Mountain is the highest point within the city limits of San Diego. It is named after George Cowles, an early ranch pioneer in Southern California. The surname is pronounced coals, even though the spelling suggests otherwise. The mountain almost lost its historical moniker, but the good folks at Mission Trails Regional Park were able to preserve the name and this wonderful urban recreational area for posterity. This region was slated for development in the early 1970s, and a mix of visionary developers, elected officials, and community leaders helped to get the area turned into a regional park. More recently, a few bond measures have resulted in the current boundaries of the park property as it now stands, and new trails are currently in the works.

As this is San Diego, the people here are fit, perhaps the fittest in the nation. There are many trails, and all are used to varying degrees. The trip from Mesa Road to Cowles Mountain is one of the less-utilized areas, perhaps due to its distance, and the fact that there are two shorter ways to reach the same summit. The shortest route is by far the most popular, but it is also the steepest, and trail runners perform a daily ant-like procession to the top. Ascending from Mesa Road affords you more openness and less occupied trail space. Still, you will see people, just

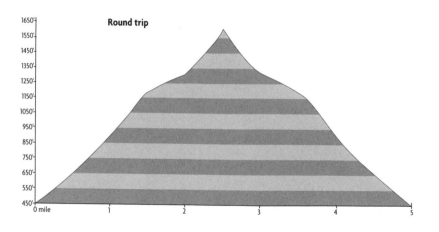

much fewer and farther in between. Your pets do need to be leashed—it is a requirement within the park and you can be cited for not following the strict guidelines.

Mission Trails is an urban park; you will not be able to escape the hum of automobiles along the freeways that surround it, nor will you have open-ended vistas that extend beyond housing development tracts and buildings. However, the scenery and the park itself are pleasant and enjoyable. While the city aura is palpable, it is not domineering or ruinous. The open spaces of the park are a welcome relief that offer recreation for thousands of people. It would be wonderful if all urban area planners had the foresight to include wild natural spaces within the confines of their cities. The views do open wide and extend to the Pacific Ocean and beyond on clear days. Since this is the highest point in San Diego, locals will have no trouble at all identifying nearby landmarks, freeways, and favorite spots.

The trek to the top of Cowles Mountain has been and remains a local favorite. San Diegans have journeyed upward to relax and take in the wonderful sights for almost a century. The mountain can be seen from anywhere in San Diego; the students from nearby San Diego State Uni-

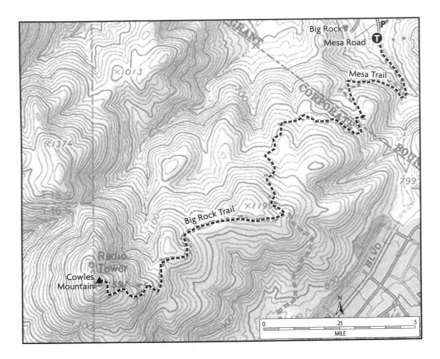

Always check kiosks for dangers and posted regulations before entering any hiking area.

versity used to paint a giant S on the peak to mark their territory. That tradition no longer takes place; still, many students use this mountain as a personal gym. You can't beat free admission and being so close to home. If you are not from San Diego, Mission Trails Regional Park is still worth a trip. It is a great place to take a quick getaway and not have to worry about hours of driving or safety. Many solo females use the trail system because so many people are present. There is a good mix of safety, exercise, and a down-home sort of feel to this place. Enjoy it and return the way you came, or loop down to Big Rock and walk up the road a few hundred feet back to your car upon exiting.

Your dog should have no trouble within the confines of this park. The ground is not rocky and the trails are short enough, even for beginners.

61. Fiesta Island

Round trip: 3 to 5 miles
Hiking time: 2 to 3 hours
High point: 10 feet
Elevation gain: 10 feet
Best season: Year-round
Difficulty: Easy
Paw comfort: Sand
Water: Bring your own
Map: USGS La Jolla
Contact: City of San Diego (619) 525-8219, *www.sandiego.gov*

Getting there: Fiesta Island sits right at the junction of Interstates 5 and 8 at the heart of transportation in San Diego. It is located right next to Sea World in Mission Bay. From Interstate 5 north, exit Sea World Drive; make a left heading towards the beach and amusement park. Across the freeway, make the first right onto East Mission Bay Drive. There is a sign for Fiesta Island; turn left onto Fiesta Drive. Once you cross the water, you can park anywhere on the right side of the one-way road.

While this is not technically a "hike," to leave this area out of a book on hiking with dogs in Southern California would be a complete shame. To put it bluntly, this is dog paradise. The entire island (except for the private children's camp) is open to unleashed dogs. Dogs can trample through the waters of Mission Bay, they can run on the sandy beaches, and they can climb the dunes on the inner part of the island. They can wander through the coastal grasses and other wetland plant life that grows wildly in the interior. There are more than enough smells to keep your dog active, engaged, and happy for a lifetime of enjoyment. Your dog would live here if you let him.

The island is open to all types of recreation. Kayakers drive their cars right up to the shore and paddle the waters; cyclists rapidly pedal the

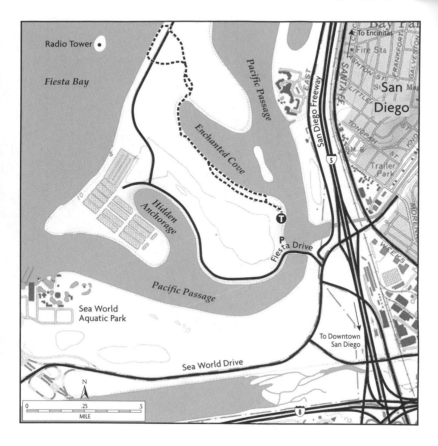

Radio Tower
Fiesta Bay
Pacific Passage
Enchanted Cove
Hidden Anchorage
Pacific Passage
Sea World Aquatic Park
Fiesta Drive
To Downtown San Diego
Sea World Drive
San Diego Freeway
Santa Fe
To Encinitas
Fire Sta
San Diego
Trailer Park
Bay Trail
N
0   .25   .5
MILE

one-way road for the 4 miles of pavement that encircle most of the island. There is even an area for waterskiing, which does not appear to be used very often. However, mostly this area is just for dogs. It is evident when walking along the beaches. There are dogs everywhere, and you will come across people from all walks of life exercising with their dogs. Despite all the dogs, the interior section of the island is so large you might not even see other dogs during your wanderings.

The best part about Fiesta Island is that you can vary your hike by spending time in the lonely interior, walking along paths, creating your own, or following the roads. Then, you can exit the gates on the road or climb a sand spit and head toward the water. Your dogs will love the variety of this place. The island is also a temporary retirement home for tennis balls. Once your dog finds them, they immediately return back to the world of the living. You can kick and throw the balls and

The entirety of Fiesta Island is a haven for canines. Dogs are free to roam off-leash anywhere.

run your dog until he dreams of Fiesta Island at night. For pet owners, the great thing about Fiesta Island is that it is free. Obviously, it is not a choice beach for sunbathers or bodysurfers; a bay/lagoon does not offer the types of recreation that the usual beachcomber looks for in outdoor activity, but your pet doesn't know the difference. This beach suits your dog better than most even though there are no waves to frolic in. The car noise from West Mission Bay Drive and Interstates 5 and 8 is only a minor annoyance to humans; your pet will not mind at all.

Fiesta Island does have one caveat. There are limitless amounts of dog poop in certain areas of the inner island, mostly just over the sand spit hills from the water access areas. It appears that unscrupulous dog owners take their pets just out of bounds, so to speak, so they do not have to clean up after their pets. Do not be an irresponsible pet owner and always clean up after Fido. In the first place it is disgusting and unsanitary, and more importantly, it is one of the reasons dogs are often excluded from places where they should be allowed. Even though you will probably find only dog owners in the middle section of the island, it is still gross and creates a problem for all of us. Be responsible in the care of your pet; he cannot clean up after himself, or he would.

Another great thing about this island is that it lets you choose the distance and time you spend. There are no peaks to be summited, no trail overlooks, no hidden lakes to find, just some sand, room to run, free parking, and all the time you wish to spend. Your dog already wants to spend more time at this place, even if he has never been there.

62. Cabrillo Tide Pools

Round trip: 0.5 mile
Hiking time: Less than 1 hour
High point: 60 feet
Elevation gain: 20 feet
Best season: Year-round
Difficulty: Easy
Paw comfort: Sand
Water: Bring your own
Fees and permits: National parks pass or $5 entrance fee
Map: USGS Point Loma
Contact: Cabrillo National Monument (619) 557-5450, *www.nps* *.gov/cabr*

Getting there: Take Interstate 8 west to its completion and veer left onto Nimitz Boulevard. Take the overpass a little over half a mile down the road to your right to get onto Catalina Boulevard. Catalina becomes Cabrillo Memorial Drive when you enter the military zone. It is signed for Cabrillo National Monument. Follow Catalina for 5 miles, all the way to the entrance kiosk for the monument. Pay the $5 entrance fee or show your national parks pass, and head down the signed road to the right for the tide pools.

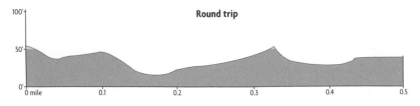

Cabrillo Tide Pools is the only area in Cabrillo National Monument where your dog is allowed. If you visit the other areas of the monument, your dog has to stay in the car. This is usual policy at many national and state parks. Even though the only "trail" in the monument is a road with a stunning view of San Diego Bay, no dogs are allowed. The consolation for this is that dogs are permitted to walk on leash to the tide pools. You may get strange looks and even verbal jostles from some people along the way, because you clearly pass a sign when you enter the monument that says "All pets must remain in vehicles." Just kindly point them to the visitor brochure that shows where dogs are allowed in the monument.

The walk is very short, less than a quarter-mile to the tide pools from the parking area, but it is enough to stretch your legs, and get your faithful companion out among the surging water, ocean wildlife, and amazing bluff-side scenery. Bringing children along to this magical spot will also enhance the experience for everyone involved. The views along the trail are spectacular. Waves frequently batter the unprotected coast where Point Loma juts out into the Pacific Ocean. The eroded sandstone layers protrude at intriguing angles and your leashed dogs can walk around on them and then take a trip down to the ocean.

Always be certain to clean up after your pooch because it is definitely

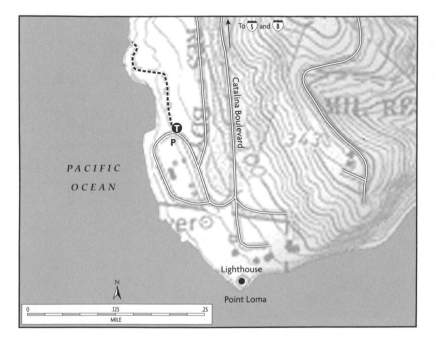

Chewee and Socs explore the rocks along the short Bayside Trail in Cabrillo National Monument.

a privilege to be able to bring dogs into a national monument like this, and even though your hirsute companion cannot gambol freely in the surf, there is plenty here to explore when the tide is out. Have fun and enjoy the time spent in this beautiful place. When the tide is in, there is less to explore, but the scenery is still just as stunning. The variety of wildlife in the tide pools is amazing, and your dog may have fun sniffing at different creatures. Just make sure he keeps his sensitive snout away from any frisky crabs.

APPENDIX: CONTACTS AND ADDITIONAL RESOURCES

Books

McKinney, John. *Day Hikers Guide to Southern California*. Santa Barbara, California: Olympus Press, 1998.

McKinney, John. *Walking the California Coast: One Hundred Adventures Along the West Coast*. New York, New York: HarperCollins, 1994.

Robinson, John W. *San Bernardino Mountain Trails: 100 Hikes in Southern California*. Berkeley, California: Wilderness Press, 2003.

Robinson, John W. *Trails of the Angeles: 100 Hikes in the San Gabriels*. Berkeley, California: Wilderness Press, 2002.

Schad, Jerry. *101 Hikes in Southern California: Exploring Mountains, Seashore, and Desert*. Berkeley, California: Wilderness Press, 2005.

Stienstra, Tom, and Ann Marie Brown. *California Hiking*. Emeryville, California: Foghorn Press, 2003.

Contacts

Angeles National Forest
Supervisor's Office
701 N. Santa Anita Avenue
Arcadia, CA 91006
(626) 574-5200
www.fs.fed.us/r5/angeles

Chilao Visitor Center
Angeles Crest Highway
 (Highway 2)
La Cañada, CA 91011
(626) 796-5541

Grassy Hollow Visitor Center
Angeles Crest Highway
 (Highway 2)
Wrightwood, CA 92397
(626) 821-6737

Mount Baldy Visitor Center
P.O. Box 592
Mt. Baldy, CA 91759
(909) 982-2829

Cabrillo National Monument
1800 Cabrillo Memorial Drive
San Diego, CA 92106
Headquarters: (619) 557-5450
Visitor Information: (619)
 222-8211
www.nps.gov/cabr

City of Del Mar
1050 Camino del Mar
Del Mar, CA 92014
(858) 755-9313
*www.delmar.ca.us/business
 /GeneralInformation/FAQ/
 BeachesParks.htm*

City of Poway Public Works
13325 Civic Center Drive
Poway, CA 92074
(858) 679-5423
www.ci.poway.ca.us

City of San Diego
202 C Street
San Diego, CA 92101
(619) 525-8219
www.sandiego.gov

Cleveland National Forest
Supervisor's Office
10845 Rancho Bernardo Road,
Suite 200
San Diego, CA 92127
(858) 673-6180
www.fs.fed.us/r5/cleveland

Descanso Ranger District
3348 Alpine Boulevard
Alpine, CA 91901
(619) 445-6235

Palomar Ranger District
1634 Black Canyon Road
Ramona, CA 92065
(760) 788-0250

Trabuco Ranger District
1147 East Sixth Street
Corona, CA 92879
(951) 736-1811

Devils Punchbowl Natural Area
28000 Devils Punchbowl Road
Pearblossom, CA 93553
(661) 944-2743
www.devils-punchbowl.com

Griffith Park
4730 Crystal Springs Drive
Los Angeles, CA 90027
(323) 664-6903
www.laparks.org/dos/parks
/griffithPK

Lake Perris State Recreation Area
17801 Lake Perris Drive
Perris, California 92571
(951) 657-0676
www.parks.ca.gov

La Purísima Mission SHP
2295 Purísima Road
Lompoc, CA 93436
(805) 733-3713
www.parks.ca.gov

Los Padres National Forest
Forest Headquarters
6755 Hollister Avenue, Suite 150
Goleta, CA 93117
(805) 968-6640
http://www.fs.fed.us/r5/lospadres

Santa Barbara Ranger District
3505 Paradise Road
Santa Barbara, CA 93105
(805) 967-3481

Ojai Ranger District
1190 East Ojai Avenue
Ojai, CA 93023
(805) 646-4348

Mission Trails Regional Park
One Father Junipero Serra Trail
San Diego, CA 92119
(619) 668-3281
www.mtrp.org

Nojoqui Falls County Park
Park Administration
300 North Goodwin Road
Santa Maria, CA 93455
(805) 934-6123
www.sbparks.org

Point Sal State Beach
La Purísima Mission SHP
2295 Purísima Road
Lompoc, CA 93436
(805) 733-3713
www.parks.ca.gov

Preservation Society of
Huntington Dog Beach
PMB 342 7071 Warner Avenue,
Suite F
Huntington Beach, CA 92647
(714) 841-8644
www.dogbeach.org

Refugio State Beach
10 Refugio Beach Road
Goleta, CA 93117
(805) 968-1033
www.parks.ca.gov

San Bernardino National Forest
Supervisor's Office
1824 South Commercenter Circle
San Bernardino, CA 92408
(909) 382-2600
www.fs.fed.us/r5/sanbernardino

Big Bear Discovery Center
41397 North Shore Drive,
Highway 38
Fawnskin, CA 92333
(909) 382-2790

Lytle Creek Ranger Station
1209 Lytle Creek Road
Lytle Creek, CA 92358
(909) 382-2850

Mill Creek Ranger Station
34701 Mill Creek Road
Mentone, CA 92359
(909) 382-2881

San Jacinto Ranger District
54270 Pinecrest
Idyllwild, CA 92549
(909) 382-2921

Skyforest Ranger Station
28104 Highway 18
Skyforest, CA 92385
(909) 382-2782

San Elijo Lagoon Conservancy
PO Box 230634
Encinitas, CA 92023
(760) 436-3944
www.sanelijo.org

San Elijo Ecological Reserve
Lands and Facilities Branch
1812 9th Street
Sacramento, CA 95814
(858) 467-4201
www.dfg.ca.gov

**Santa Monica Mountains
National Recreation Area**
401 West Hillcrest Drive
Thousand Oaks, CA 91360
(805) 370-2301
www.nps.gov/samo

**University of California at
Santa Barbara**
Office of Campus Planning and
Design
University of California
Santa Barbara, CA 93106
(805) 893-3971
http://facilities.ucsb.edu/

Vasquez Rocks Natural Area Park
10700 West Escondido Canyon
Road
Agua Dulce, CA 91350
(661) 268-0840
http://parks.co.la.ca.us

Online Sources of Dog Hiking Gear
www.altrec.com
www.granitegear.com
www.planetdog.com
www.rei.com
www.ruffwear.com

Hiking and Conservation Organizations
American Hiking Society
1422 Fenwick Lane
Silver Spring, MD 20910
(800) 972-8608
www.americanhiking.org

Greenpeace USA
702 H Street Northwest, Suite 300
Washington, DC 20001
(202) 462-1177
www.greenpeace.org/usa

National Parks Conservation
Association
1300 19th Street Northwest,
Suite 300
Washington, DC 20036
(800) 628-7275
www.npca.org

National Wildlife Federation
11100 Wildlife Center Drive
Reston, VA 20190
(800) 822-9919
www.nwf.org

Sierra Club
85 Second Street, 2nd Floor
San Francisco, CA 94105
(415) 977-5500
www.sierraclub.org

The Wilderness Society
1615 M Street Northwest
Washington, DC 20036
(800) 843-9453
www.wilderness.org

Useful Websites

www.caldog.org
CalDOG is a nonprofit organization that lobbies for recreational access to public lands for people with dogs.

www.caldogtravel.com/index.htm
This site contains information about the book *The Dog Lover's Companion to California.*

www.dogfriendly.com
Publishers of pet travel guides

www.ilovethisplace.com/dogfun/ca
The dog fun directory for California.

www.scdoc.org
The Southern California Dog Obedience Council

INDEX

ABOUT THE AUTHOR

Allen Riedel is an English teacher at Lakeside Middle School in the Val Verde Unified School District. He received his bachelor's degree in English with honors from the University of California at Santa Barbara, and holds a masters degree in education from Chapman University. Allen is the top reporter for *www.localhikes.com* and authors a freelance monthly hiking column for the Inland Empire newspaper *The Press-Enterprise*. In his spare time, he loves to travel, hike, camp, take photographs, and play bass guitar. Allen lives in Moreno Valley with his wife, Ta'Shara, and twin daughters, Sierra and Makaila. The boys in the family are Chewbacca ("Chewee") and Socrates ("Socs"); both were rescued through the Los Angeles County Board of Supervisors Pet Adoption Program, which is coordinated through the Los Angeles County Department of Animal Care and Control. Chewee is a Jack Russell terrier/chihuahua mix, and Socs is a schnauzer/terrier mix. Both dogs love hiking in the local mountains, especially off-leash.

Allen and his daughter Sierra enjoy an outing in Joshua Tree National Park (where, unfortunately, no dogs are allowed).

THE MOUNTAINEERS, founded in 1906, is a nonprofit outdoor activity and conservation club, whose mission is "to explore, study, preserve, and enjoy the natural beauty of the outdoors. . . ." Based in Seattle, Washington, the club is now the third-largest such organization in the United States, with 15,000 members and five branches throughout Washington State.

The Mountaineers sponsors both classes and year-round outdoor activities in the Pacific Northwest, which include hiking, mountain climbing, ski-touring, snowshoeing, bicycling, camping, kayaking and canoeing, nature study, sailing, and adventure travel. The club's conservation division supports environmental causes through educational activities, sponsoring legislation, and presenting informational programs. All club activities are led by skilled, experienced volunteers, who are dedicated to promoting safe and responsible enjoyment and preservation of the outdoors.

If you would like to participate in these organized outdoor activities or the club's programs, consider a membership in The Mountaineers. For information and an application, write or call The Mountaineers, Club Headquarters, 300 Third Avenue West, Seattle, WA 98119; 206-284-6310.

The Mountaineers Books, an active, nonprofit publishing program of the club, produces guidebooks, instructional texts, historical works, natural history guides, and works on environmental conservation. All books produced by The Mountaineers Books fulfill the club's mission.

Send or call for our catalog of more than 500 outdoor titles:

The Mountaineers Books
1001 SW Klickitat Way, Suite 201
Seattle, WA 98134
800-553-4453
mbooks@mountaineersbooks.org
www.mountaineersbooks.org

OTHER TITLES YOU MIGHT ENJOY FROM
THE MOUNTAINEERS BOOKS

100 Hikes in Yosemite National Park
Mark Soares
Gorgeous full-color guidebook to the park and
surrounding area

Best Short Hikes in California's
South Sierra
Terry Whitehall, Paul Richins
The best day hikes in the region

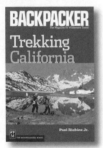

Trekking California
Paul Richins
The best multi-day treks in the state

Mount Whitney: The Complete
Trailhead-to-Summit Hiking Guide
Paul Richins
The definitive guide to the Lower
48's highest mountain summit

Conditioning for Outdoor Fitness:
Functional Exercise & Nutrition
for Every Body, 2nd Ed.
David Musnick, M.D., Mark Pierce A.T.C.
Exercises to get you fit for specific outdoor activities

Digital Photography Outdoors:
A Field Guide for Adventure and
Travel Photographers
James Martin
Special digital techniques for outdoor
adventure shooting